Teaching and Researchin

This third edition of *Teaching and Researching Writing* continues to build upon the previous editions' work of providing educators and practitioners in applied linguistics with a clearly written and complete guide to writing research and teaching. The text explores both theoretical and conceptual questions, grapples with key issues in the field today, and demonstrates the dynamic relationship between research and teaching methods and practice. Reorganized to incorporate discussions of technology, identity and error correction, this edition contains new chapters that address the innovative directions the field has taken since the previous edition's publication. Boxes throughout such as "Concepts" and "Quotes" highlight key ideas and figures in the field, thereby reinforcing readers' understanding of the topics. In addition, the updated glossary and resource sections allow readers to further investigate areas of interest. The third edition of *Teaching and Researching Writing* is the ideal resource for language teachers, practitioners and researchers to better understand and apply writing research theories, methods and practices.

Ken Hyland is Chair Professor of Applied Linguistics and Director of the Centre for Applied English Studies at the University of Hong Kong.

Applied Linguistics in Action
Series Editor: Christopher N. Candlin

Applied Linguistics in Action is a series which focuses on the issues and challenges to teachers and researchers in a range of fields in Applied Linguistics and provides readers and users with the tools they need to carry out their own practice-based research.

Teaching and Researching Lexicography
R.R.K. Hartmann

Teaching and Researching Computer-Assisted Language Learning, 2nd Edition
Ken Beatty

Teaching and Researching Motivation, 2nd Edition
Zoltán Dörnyei and Ema Ushioda

Teaching and Researching Speaking, 2nd Edition
Rebecca Hughes

Teaching and Researching Language Learning Strategies
Rebecca L. Oxford

Teaching and Researching Autonomy in Language Learning, 2nd Edition
Phil Benson

Teaching and Researching Reading, 2nd Edition
William Peter Grabe and Fredricka L. Stoller

Teaching and Researching Language and Culture, 2nd Edition
Joan Kelly Hall

Teaching and Researching Translation, 2nd Edition
Basil A. Hatim

Teaching and Researching Listening, 3rd Edition
Michael Rost

Teaching and Researching Writing, 3rd Edition
Ken Hyland

Teaching and Researching Writing

Third Edition

Ken Hyland

Routledge
Taylor & Francis Group

NEW YORK AND LONDON

Third edition published 2016
by Routledge
711 Third Avenue, New York, NY 10017

and by Routledge
2 Park Square, Milton Park, Abingdon, Oxon, OX14 4RN

Routledge is an imprint of the Taylor & Francis Group, an informa business

First edition published 2002 by Pearson Education Limited

Second edition published 2009 by Pearson Education Limited

Library of Congress Cataloging-in-Publication Data
Hyland, Ken.
  Teaching and researching writing / Ken Hyland. — Third Edition.
    pages cm. — (Applied Linguistics in Action)
  Includes bibliographical references and index.
 1. Written communication—Study and teaching. 2. Written
communication—Research. I. Title.
  P211.H95 2016
  808'.04207—dc23
  2015023176

ISBN: 978-1-138-85945-6 (hbk)
ISBN: 978-1-138-85946-3 (pbk)
ISBN: 978-1-315-71720-3 (ebk)

Typeset in Times New Roman
by Apex CoVantage, LLC

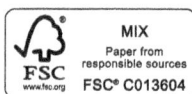

MIX
Paper from
responsible sources
FSC
www.fsc.org   FSC® C013604

Printed and bound in Great Britain by
CPI Group (UK) Ltd, Croydon, CR0 4YY

Contents

Series Editor Preface

Applied Linguistics in Action, as its name suggests, is a series which focuses on the issues and challenges to teachers and researchers in a range of fields in Applied Linguistics and provides readers and users with the tools they need to carry out their own practice-related research.

The books in the series provide the reader with clear, up-to-date, accessible and authoritative accounts of their chosen field within applied linguistics. Starting from a map of the landscape of the field, each book provides information on its main ideas and concepts, competing issues and unsolved questions. From there, readers can explore a range of practical applications of research into those issues and questions, and then take up the challenge of undertaking their own research, guided by the detailed and explicit research guides provided. Finally, each book has a section which provides a rich array of resources, information sources and further reading, as well as a key to the principal concepts of the field.

Questions the books in this innovative series ask are those familiar to all teachers and researchers, whether very experienced, or new to the field of applied linguistics:

- What does research tell us, what doesn't it tell us and what should it tell us about the field? How is the field mapped and landscaped? What is its geography?
- How has research been applied and what interesting research possibilities does practice raise? What are the issues we need to explore and explain?
- What are the key researchable topics that practitioners can undertake? How can the research be turned into practical action?
- Where are the important resources that teachers and researchers need? Who has the information? How can it be accessed?

Each book in the series has been carefully designed to be as accessible as possible, with built-in features to enable readers to find what they want quickly and to home in on the key issues and themes that concern them. The structure is to move from practice to theory and back to practice in a cycle of development of understanding of the field in question.

Each of the authors of books in the series is an acknowledged authority, able to bring broad knowledge and experience to engage teachers and researchers in following up their own ideas, working with them to build further on *their* own experience.

The first editions of books in this series have attracted widespread praise for their authorship, their design, and their content, and they have been widely used to support practice and research. The success of the series, and the realisation that it needs to stay relevant in a world where new research is being conducted and published at a rapid rate, have prompted the commissioning of this third edition. This new edition has been thoroughly updated, with accounts of research that has appeared since the previous edition and with the addition of other relevant material. We trust that students, teachers and researchers will continue to discover inspiration in these pages to underpin their own investigations.

Chris Candlin
David Hall

Preface

The original *Teaching and Researching Writing* first appeared early in 2002 in Longman's 'Applied Linguistics in Action' Series edited by Chris Candlin and David Hall. It was my third book—my first specifically written for teachers and students—and I was quite pleased with it. I never thought, however, that it would still be selling over a decade later, with a second publisher and in a third edition, but I am delighted that Routledge has offered me a chance to update and revise it.

I noted in my preface to the second edition that it can be harder to rewrite than to write: there are things that need expanding, changing and deleting as the field moves on, but one is constrained by the frame of the original and what people seemed to like about it. In general terms, the broad scope of what we know about writing and how we might best teach it remains, but the field has also changed. Analysts have continued to extend the field into the study of new electronic genres and specialised areas of use while writing has continued to establish itself as a key metric in the life chances of millions of people around the world: a measure of educational success, academic competence, professional advancement and institutional recognition. Teachers, too, have cast their net wider in their search for more effective teaching practices, turning to a range of electronic, online and social media resources as well as making greater use of learner corpora and student assembled D-I-Y corpora. Writing has also consolidated its importance in how the social sciences understand the world, playing a more central part in contemporary questions of politics, gender, personal relationships, power, identity and culture.

Essentially though, and despite the fact that they increasingly interact in very different ways, we are still concerned with writers, with readers and with texts, and it is these components of writing which remain the core of the book.

Those familiar with earlier editions of the book will recognise that I have retained many of the features which make this series distinctive. So readers will find the concept and quote boxes still figure prominently, that the resource section and the glossary are still here, and that I have tried to preserve a style which presents the topic in an accessible way. I hope that together these features will mean that students, teachers and those who come to the topic without a specialised knowledge of writing research won't be too daunted. All chapters, however, have been extensively rewritten and updated to include new thinking on old topics and to take account of novel directions which have emerged in writing studies.

I have also taken advantage of Routledge's more generous word allowance and the opportunity to restructure the book. So while the third edition has the original four sections of the first two, I have swapped Sections II and III to put *Researching* before *Teaching* to better illustrate how the former informs the latter. I have also added new chapters in each section and new topics in each chapter. In Section I, for instance, there are now discussions of technology, identity, plagiarism, error correction, automated marking and the dominance of English which were not covered before. The case studies illustrating research have been extensively updated to include diary blogs, keystroke logging and synthesis research, and the chapters on materials and teaching practices now include sections on specific EAP courses, corpora-assisted learning and wordlist software. The intention behind the book, however, remains the same: to provide a clear and critical introduction to the field of writing research and teaching.

Writing remains, of course, a central topic in Applied Linguistics and continues to be an area of lively intellectual research and debate in a range of disciplines. Its complex, multifaceted nature constantly evades adequate description and explanation, and many forms of enquiry have been summoned to help clarify both how writing works and how it should best be taught. One factor which both drives this interest and complicates its study is the overarching significance writing has in our lives, not only in our professional and social activities, but in determining our life chances. Writing is central to our personal experience and social identities, and we are often evaluated by our control of it. The various purposes of writing, its myriad contexts of use and the diverse backgrounds and needs of those wishing to learn it, all push the study of writing into wider frameworks of analysis and understanding.

This book seeks to identify and survey these frameworks, setting out the dominant paradigms, exploring their key concepts, elaborating some applications of writing research, raising some important researchable issues, and providing a compendium of resources on writing. The three chapters in Section I offer a conceptual overview of the area and raise some of the key issues and questions currently occupying the field. Section II focuses on the main ways of approaching writing research, including the design of studies, commonly used methodologies and frequently explored topics, together with examples of these different approaches taken from the literature with a summary and brief critical evaluation. Section III provides a brief review of how the main theoretical understandings of writing translate into classroom practices, outlining the general orientations to teaching they involve and drawing on examples of classroom syllabi, materials and practices from around the world. Finally, Section IV is a compendium of resources, indicating the major areas of writing research and practice and providing information on the key sources and contacts.

Throughout the book, I hope the reader can see what the main understandings of writing are and how these relate to research and teaching, and also see the strong cycle of practice–theory–practice inherent in the field of writing. I also hope that the book will encourage readers to engage with the topics discussed and perhaps be encouraged to explore some of the issues the book raises.

Acknowledgements

I want to use these acknowledgements to remember and thank the two original editors of the series in which this book appears, Chris Candlin and David Hall, both of whom sadly passed away recently. David died in early February, 2014, and Chris on 9 May, 2015, just as I was completing this edition. Both showed amazing spirit and courage throughout the course of their illnesses, and both will long be remembered for their many contributions to the development of Applied Linguistics. David will be remembered as a very active member, Head of Department and Associate Dean at Macquarie University, and Chris for his tremendous vision and energy, at Lancaster, City University of Hong Kong and Macquarie, and as a leading figure in our discipline who enriched the academic lives of so many. Both were passionate about their work and their students and had many friends in Applied Linguistics. More immediately, the books in this series owe a great deal to the encouragement and good advice they provided for the authors. It was a privilege to know them.

I would also like to acknowledge colleagues and friends who have shared their research and materials with me. Here I would particularly like to thank John Swales and Chris Feak for extracts from their writing guides for graduate students; Derek Wallace and Janet Holst of the Victoria University of Wellington for the materials and comments on *Writ 101*; Beverly Derewianka and Sally Humphrey for their insider thoughts on the new Australian National English curriculum; Stephen Hill for his Foundation Degree materials; and Jane Stokes and Laura Wakeland of the Centre for Applied English Studies (CAES) at Hong Kong University for their English for Clinical Pharmacy materials. More formally, I would like to thank the following for allowing me to use their copyright material.

Laurence Anthony for permission to reprint screenshots of his *AntConc* programme on pages 201–204.

Dee Gardner and Mark Davies for permission to reprint screenshots of their 'Word and Phrase' site and the Top 50 words in the Academic Vocabulary List on pages 208–211.

Carol Rutz and Carleton College for permission to reprint 'requirements for the portfolio' and 'the scoring form' from the Carleton Writing Program webpage on portfolios in part 9.6.

Arthur McNeill of the Center for Language Education at Hong Kong University of Science and Technology for permission to reproduce screenshots from *My Words* software ('Check My Words' and 'Mark My Words') in Part 9.5.

University of Michigan Press for permission to reprint p. 19, Task 8 from *Abstracts and the Writing of Abstracts* by Christine B. Feak and John W. Swales (Ann Arbor: The University of Michigan Press, 2009) and p. 13, Task 5 from *Creating Contexts: Writing across Genres* by Christine B. Feak and John W. Swales (Ann Arbor: The University of Michigan Press, 2011) in Part 9.1.

Derek Wallace of the Victoria University of Wellington for permission to reprint pages from *Writ 101: Becoming an Effective Writer* in Part 8.1.

Pearson Education Limited for permission to reprint the Table of audience awareness from page 32 of Process Writing by White, R. and Arndt, V. (1991) *Process writing*. Harlow, UK: Longman on page 160.

Academic Books for permission to reprint two figures: A writing frame for planning a discussion (p. 126) and A writing frame for first draft of a discussion (pp. 128–9) from Wray, D., & Lewis, M. (1997). *Extending literacy: children reading and writing non-fiction*. London: Routledge, in Part 9.4

The State of South Australia to quote from pages 16 and 18 of the DECD 'Professional Learning Module: Genres in Primary School'; the first text box titled 'Key ideas in this module' (page 2 of the DECD 'Professional Learning Module: Genres in Primary School'); the first text box covering 'purpose/social function; variations within the genres; structural features; language features' (page 14 of the DECD 'Professional Learning Module: Genres in Primary School'); and the table titled 'Typical Genres in Education Contexts and Their Social Purposes' (page 101 of the 'Department of Education and Children's Services (DECS) (2004): SACSA Companion Document Series R-10 English Teaching Resource'). These are reproduced in section 8.2 on pages 174–180.

Section I
Understanding Writing

1   An Overview of Writing

This chapter will . . .

- offer a guiding summary of the main approaches to understanding writing;
- explore research into main dimensions of writing: the code, the encoder and the decoder;
- examine the principal ideas, key figures, significant findings and major weaknesses of each view.

In this chapter I want to provide an overview of the different ways of understanding writing. Rather than a comprehensive treatment of what we know, I intend this to be more a map of the territory which picks out the main landmarks and offers a direction of travel. To do this, I discuss three broad approaches to researching and teaching writing, focusing in turn on theories that are mainly concerned with texts, with writers and with readers. The classification implies no rigid divisions, but I hope it highlights something of what we know about writing and what each approach offers to our understanding of this complex area. The implications of these views for classroom practice are discussed in Section III of this book.

Concept 1.1   Approaches to Writing

- The first approach focuses on the products of writing by examining *texts*, either through their formal surface elements, the vocabulary and grammar, or their discourse structure.
- The second approach, divided into Expressivist, Cognitivist and Situated strands, focuses on the *writer* and describes writing in terms of the processes used to create texts.
- The third approach emphasises the role that *readers* play in writing, adding an interactional dimension by elaborating how writers engage with an audience in creating texts.

1.1   Text-Oriented Understandings

The study of the tangible, analysable aspects of writing has a long history and perhaps informs most research into writing around the world today. By looking at surface forms, these approaches share an interest in the linguistic or rhetorical resources available to writers for producing texts, and so reduce the complexities of communication to words on a page or screen. Text-focused theories come in many guises, but I will describe the two main ones here.

1.1.1   Texts as Objects

The dominant model of writing for many years saw it as a textual product, a coherent arrangement of elements structured according to a system of rules. Writing was an outcome, a finished product that could be studied for what it told us about language, rather than about meaning-making.

Concept 1.2   Texts as Objects

Based on ideas inherited from structuralism and implicit in the Transformational Grammar of Noam Chomsky, a basic premise of this approach is that texts are autonomous objects which can be analysed and described independently of particular contexts, writers or readers. Texts have a structure, they are orderly arrangements of words, clauses and sentences, and by following grammatical rules writers can encode a full semantic representation of their intended meanings.

The idea that texts can function independently of a context carries important ideological implications, and one of the most serious is the mechanistic view that human communication works by transferring ideas from one mind to another via language (Shannon and Weaver, 1963). Writing is disembodied. It is removed from any context and from the personal experiences of writers and readers, because meanings can be fully encoded in texts and recovered by anyone with the right decoding skills. Meaning lies in the words, not in the minds of text users, and writers are passive in following the rules of grammar.

Such a focus on form has led to considerable research into the regularities we find in texts. In recent years, for example, computer analyses of large corpora have been used to identify how features such as evaluative adjectives like *nice, good, great* (De Cock, 2011) are typically used, and to determine the significance of regular high-frequency bundles such as *at the same time as* and *on the other hand* (Hyland, 2008a) in creating texts. An orientation to formal features of texts has also underpinned a great deal of research into students' writing development. From this perspective, writing improvement can be measured by counting increases in features such as relative clauses, modality and passives through successive pieces of writing. White (2007), for instance, sought to assess language improvement in student writing by measuring increases in the number of morphemes, words and clauses in student essays. Alternatively, learner corpora can be studied to see the effect of L1 (first language, with L2 referring to second language) transfer (e.g. Nesselhauf, 2005).

From a perspective that regards texts as autonomous objects, then, learners' compositions are seen as *langue*—that is, a demonstration of the writer's knowledge of forms and his or her awareness of the system of rules to create texts. Good writing is accurate and conveys the writer's meaning explicitly. But the claim that good writing is fully explicit and needs no context for its sense draws on the old-fashioned *conduit metaphor*: that we transfer ideas from one mind to another through language. In this view a text has a single watertight sense, as meanings can be written down and understood by others in exactly the way they were intended. There can be no conflicts of interpretations, no reader positions, no different understandings, because we all see things in the same way. Meanings correspond with words, and writing is transparent in reflecting meanings rather than constructing them.

Quote 1.1   On 'Explicitness'

A text is explicit not because it says everything all by itself but rather because it strikes a careful balance between what needs to be said and what may be assumed. The writer's problem is not just being explicit; the writer's problem is knowing what to be explicit about.

Nystrand, Doyle and Himley (1986: 81)

However, focusing exclusively on formal features of texts as a measure of writing competence ignores how texts are the writer's response to a particular communicative setting. Written texts cannot be autonomous precisely because they respond to a particular situation, including a relationship between the writer and reader, and display that situation in their pages.

Quote 1.2   Brandt on Autonomous Texts

Identifying the mode of a text or enumerating its T-unit length or the density and range of its cohesive devices may lend insights into the structure of written texts, however, it can describe only one or another static outcome of the writer's dynamic and complex effort to make meaning. Yet the finished text need not be abandoned in our pursuit to understand the composing act—not, that is, if we shift our focus from the formal features of an isolated text toward the whole text as an instance of language functioning in a context of human activity.

Brandt (1986: 93)

Modern perspectives, however, point out that this fails to take account of the beliefs and knowledge writers assume readers will draw on in reading their texts. Even legal contracts, which are the most explicit of genres, are open to multiple interpretations and endless disputes by lawyers. Similarly, the apparently unambiguous and impersonal surface of academic articles draw on readers' presumed background knowledge. Through technical jargon, references to other research and assumed familiarity with particular ways of constructing arguments, writers work to establish a coherent context which will persuade a particular community of readers (e.g. Bazerman, 1988; Hyland, 2004a). In sum, inferences are always involved in recovering meanings: no text can be both coherent and context-free.

1.1.2 Texts as Discourse

While an autonomous model views texts as forms which can be analysed independently of any real-life uses, another way of seeing writing as a material thing looks beyond surface structures to see texts as *discourse*—the way we use language to communicate, to achieve purposes in particular situations. Here the writer is seen as having certain goals and intentions, and the ways we write are resources to accomplish these. So instead of forms being disembodied, independent of contexts, a discourse approach sees them as located in social actions. Teachers following this line therefore aim to identify the ways that texts actually work as communication by linking language forms to purposes and contexts.

Concept 1.3   Discourse

Discourse refers to language in action, and to the purposes and functions linguistic forms serve in communication. Here the linguistic patterns of texts point to contexts beyond the page, implying a range of social constraints and choices which operate on writers in any context. The writer has certain goals and intentions, certain relationships to his or her readers, and certain information to convey, and the forms of a text are resources used to accomplish these. These factors draw the analyst into a wider perspective which locates texts in a world of communicative purposes and social action, identifying the ways that texts actually work as communication.

A variety of approaches has considered texts as discourse, but all have tried to discover how writers organise language to produce coherent, purposeful prose. An early contribution was the 'functional sentence perspective' of the Prague School, which sought to describe how we structure text to represent our assumptions about what is known (*given*) or *new* to the reader (e.g. Firbas,

1986). This was taken up and elaborated in the work of Halliday (e.g. Halliday and Matthiessen, 2013) in the concept of *theme—rheme* structure. Roughly, theme is what the writer is talking about and rheme is what he or she is saying about it: the part of the message that the writer considers important. Theme and rheme help writers organise clauses into information units that push the communication forward through a text and make it easy for readers to follow. This is because we expect old information to come first as a context for new, but breaking this pattern can be confusing. In example (1) below, the writer establishes a pattern in which the rheme of the first sentence becomes the themes of the next three, clearly signposting the progression. The theme of the final sentence, however, breaks the sequence, surprising the reader and disturbing processability:

(1) *Non-verbal communication* is traditionally divided into paralanguage, proxemics, body language and haptics. *Paralanguage* refers to the non-verbal vocal signs that accompany speech. *Proxemics* concerns physical distance and orientation. *Body language* describes expression, posture and gesture. The study of touch is called *haptics*.

A different strand of research has tried to identify how writers organise units of texts to help the reader see how the purpose of the message is unfolding by examining what pieces of text are trying to do and how they fit into a larger structure. Winter (1977) and Hoey (1983), for example, distinguish several typical text patterns which they label *problem-solution, hypothetical-real* and *general-particular*. They show that even with no explicit signaling, readers are able to draw on their knowledge of recognisable text patterns to infer the connections between clauses, sentences or groups of sentences. For example, we all have a strong expectation of how a story will proceed; we anticipate a problem–solution pattern where, following a context introducing the participants and situation (Cinderella is a downtrodden girl bullied by her sisters), we anticipate a problem will arise for the participants to solve (she can't go to the dance), then we look for a response to the problem (the fairy godmother works some magic) and finally an evaluation whether the response worked (she goes to the party and marries the prince). This problem–solution pattern is found in other genres too, such as the conference abstract in Concept 1.4.

Concept 1.4   Problem–Solution Pattern

1. *Situation*: We now accept that grammar is not restricted to writing but is present in speech.
2. *Problem*: This can lead to assumptions that there is one kind of grammar for writing and one for speech.

3. *Response*: A large-scale corpus survey of English has been undertaken.
4. *Evaluation of response*: Results show the same system is valid for both writing and speech.

(Example based on a conference abstract.)

These kinds of descriptions lead us to the idea that we must draw on some notion of shared assumptions to account for what we recognise as connected text. That is to say, part of what makes writing coherent lies in the readers' background knowledge and interpretive abilities rather than in the text. One model of how this is done suggests that readers call on their conventionalised knowledge to impose a coherent frame on a message. They interpret discourse by analogy with their earlier experiences, which are organised in their heads as *scripts* or *schemata* (e.g. Schank and Abelson, 1977). Thus, we carry around stereotypical understandings which we use as 'scaffolding' to interpret the texts we encounter every day, allowing us to read texts as diverse as detective thrillers and postcards.

A second approach, based on philosophical pragmatics rather than cognitive psychology, proposes that writers try to create texts which are as relevant to readers as possible, and that readers anticipate this when trying to recover meaning. This approach originates with Grice's (1975) principles of conversational inference, which explain successful communication in terms of interactants' mutual assumptions of rationality and cooperation. Building on this idea, Sperber and Wilson (1986) argue that readers construct meanings by comparing the information they find in a text with what they already know about the context to establish meanings that are relevant. In other words, when we read, we assume that the writer is being cooperative by thinking of what it is we need to fully understand what is going on, and so we look for ways of interpreting what we read as relevant to the ongoing discourse in some way.

In these theories, interpretation depends on the ability of readers to supply needed assumptions from memory, but the construction of meaning from texts is a rhetorical and not just a cognitive process, as suggested by Kramsch (1997) in Quote 1.3.

Quote 1.3 A Rhetorical Approach to Text Interpretation

1. Texts both refer to a reality beyond themselves and a relationship to their readers.
2. The meaning of texts is inseparable from surrounding texts, whether footnotes, diagrams or conversations. Intertextuality refers to the extent our texts echo other texts.

3. Texts attempt to position readers in specific ways by evoking assumed shared schemata.
4. Schemata are created by relating one text or fact to another through logical links.
5. Schemata reflect the ways of thinking of particular communities or cultures.
6. Schemata are co-constructed by the writer in dialogue with others.
7. Schemata are rhetorical constructions, representing the choices from other potential meanings.

Kramsch (1997: 51–2)

The idea that forms express functions and that they vary according to context is a central notion of discourse analysis and underpins the key notion of *genre*.

Concept 1.5   Genre

*Genre*s are abstract, socially recognised ways of using language. It is a term for grouping texts together, representing how writers typically use language to respond to recurring situations. Every genre has a number of features which make it different to other genres: each has a specific purpose, an overall structure, specific linguistic features, and is shared by members of a culture. For many people it is an intuitively attractive concept which helps to organise the common-sense labels we use to categorise texts and the situations in which they occur.

The concept of genre is based on the idea that members of a community usually have little difficulty in recognising similarities in the texts they use frequently and are able to draw on these repeated experiences with such texts to read, understand and perhaps write them relatively easily. This is, in part, because writing is a practice based on expectations: the reader's chances of interpreting the writer's meanings and purpose are increased if the writer takes the trouble to anticipate what the reader might be expecting based on previous texts the reader has read of the same kind. We know immediately, for example, whether a text is a recipe, a joke or a love letter, and we can respond to it and write a similar one if we need to. We all have a repertoire of these responses we can call on to communicate in familiar situations, and we learn new ones, perhaps lesson plans and student reports, as we need them.

Genres encourage us to look for organisational patterns, such as the problem—solution structure we mentioned above. These patterns show how texts are designed to achieve a social purpose, and we find them in even apparently very personal kinds of writing, such as the acknowledgements in the opening pages of a student dissertation. The acknowledgments in 240 dissertations written by Hong Kong Ph.D. and M.A. students, for example, showed a three-move structure consisting of a main Thanking Move sandwiched between optional Reflecting and Announcing Moves (Hyland, 2004b).

As shown in Concept 1.6, the writer typically begins with a brief introspection on his or her research experience, and this is followed by the main Thanking Move, where credit is given to individuals and institutions for help with the dissertation, and this can consist of up to four steps. The first step is a sentence introducing those to be thanked, followed by thanks for academic help. This was the only step that occurred in every single text, and supervisors were always mentioned and always before anyone else. Next there is thanks for providing resources such as clerical, technical and financial help, and then thanks for moral support from family and friends for encouragement, friendship, etc. The final Announcing Move is rare, but here writers take responsibility and ownership of the thesis to claim it is theirs and not that of those they have thanked.

Concept 1.6   Dissertation Acknowledgements

Move	Example
1 Reflecting Move	The most rewarding achievement in my life, as I approach middle age, is the completion of my doctoral dissertation.
2 Thanking Move	
2.1 Presenting participants	During the time of writing I received support and help from many people.
2.2 Thanks for academic help	I am profoundly indebted to my supervisor, Dr. Robert Chau who assisted me in each step to complete the thesis.
2.3 Thanks for resources	I am grateful to The Epsom Foundation whose research travel grant made the field work possible and to the library staff who tracked down elusive texts for me.
2.4 Thanks for moral support	Finally, thanks go to my wife who has been an important source of emotional support.
3 Announcing Move	However, despite all this help, I am the only person responsible for errors in the thesis.

The analysis showed this structure was common in almost all the acknowl-edgements, and that where steps occurred, they did so in this sequence. It also showed that, of the many ways of expressing thanks (*I am grateful to, I appre-ciate, I want to thank*, etc.) the noun *thanks* was used in over half of all cases, and this was modified by only three adjectives: *special, sincere* and *deep*, with *special* comprising over two-thirds of all cases. Writers also always stated the reason for thanking the person, as in these examples:

(2) First of all, special thanks to my supervisor, Dr. Franco Lin, for his consis-tent and never-failing encouragement, support and help.

> My special gratitude goes to my family who made it possible for me to embark on writing a Ph.D. thesis at all.

> I should also thank my wife, Su Meng, who spent days and nights alone with our daughter taking care of all the tasks that should have been shared with me.

This suggests that writers weren't only addressing the people they acknowl-edged, who knew the help they had given, but a wider audience which included examiners. In this way they were able to represent themselves as good research-ers and real human beings deserving of the degree. Examining specific genres by studying patterns and recurring features, therefore, tells us a lot about what writers are trying to achieve and the language they are using to do it.

We cannot, however, assume that a particular text will always rigidly observe a given genre structure. Often analyses show that moves overlap or occur out of sequence, and there is frequently less uniformity than might be expected. This is partly because writers make different choices from optional elements and partly because local communities may have specific uses that override common structures. Moreover, the same genre can look very different in different communities or when written in different lan-guages, while a report in one discipline may differ considerably from that in another.

There is also the danger that our genre descriptions might oversimplify a more complex reality, particularly if we ignore that writers may have indirect purposes, or 'private intentions', in addition to 'socially-recognised' ones (Bha-tia (2004). Analysts also need to be cautious about imposing their intuitions on the structure of the text, which often leads them to support their analyses both through the linguistic features which writers' moves routinely contain and the comments of text users (Crookes, 1986). Analysts have therefore attempted to show how texts, or parts of texts, are typically characterised by particular clus-ters of features. Thus research shows the importance of hedging in academic texts and how the presence of lexical bundles like *as a result of, it should be noted that* and *as can be seen* help identify a text as belonging to an academic genre, while *with regard to, in pursuance of* and *in accordance with* are likely to mark out a legal text (Hyland, 2008a).

Other genre variations are the result of interdiscursivity (or the use of conventions from other genres), particularly the increasing intrusion of promotional elements into genres often considered non-promotional (such as job announcements which advertise the hiring company) and the growing 'synthetic personalisation' of formal public genres (such as letters from companies which seem to be from close friends) (Fairclough, 1995). Mixing genres in this way blurs clear distinctions, sometimes to the extent that new genres become recognised in a community (e.g. *infotainment, advertorial* and *docudrama*). Ultimately, however, genres are the ways that we engage in, and make sense of, our social worlds, and our competence to use them does not lie in our ability to identify monolithic uses of language, but to modify our choices according to the contexts in which we write.

1.2   Writer-Oriented Understandings

The second broad approach takes the writer, rather than the text, as the point of departure. The theories in this section ask what it is that good writers do when composing, and they seek to help learners acquire these skills. Here I want to sketch the main contours of three positions which together have contributed to the hugely influential process writing movement:

- The first position focuses on the personal creativity of the individual writer.
- The second position focuses on the cognitive processes of writing.
- The third position focuses on the writer's immediate context.

1.2.1   *Writing as Personal Expression*

Concept 1.7   Expressivist View of Writing

Originating with the work of Elbow (1998), Murray (1985) and others, this view encourages writers to find their own voices to produce writing that is fresh and spontaneous. There is an underlying assumption that thinking precedes writing, and that the free expression of ideas can encourage self-discovery and cognitive maturation. Writing development and personal development are seen as symbiotically interwoven to the extent that "good therapy and composition aim at clear thinking, effective relating, and satisfying self-expression" (Moffett, 1982: 235).

The Expressivist view strongly resists a narrow definition of writing based on notions of correct grammar and usage. Instead, it sees writing as a creative act of discovery in which the process is as important as the product to the writer. Writing is learnt, not taught, and the teacher's role is to be non-directive and facilitating, providing writers with the space to make their own meanings through an encouraging, positive and cooperative environment with minimal interference. Because writing is a developmental process, teachers are encouraged not to impose their views, give models or suggest responses to topics beforehand. On the contrary, they are urged to stimulate the writer's thinking through pre-writing tasks, such as journal-writing and analogies (Elbow, 1998), and to respond to the ideas that the writer produces. This, then, is writing as self-discovery.

Quote 1.4 **Rohman on 'Good Writing'**

'Good writing' is that discovered combination of words which allows a person the integrity to dominate his subject with a pattern both fresh and original. 'Bad writing', then, is an echo of someone else's combination which we have merely taken over for the occasion of our writing . . . 'Good writing' must be the discovery by a responsible person of his uniqueness within his subject.

Rohman (1965: 107–8)

Unfortunately, as North (1987) points out, this approach offers no clear theoretical principles from which to evaluate 'good writing' nor does it furnish advice that can help accomplish it. This is because good writing, for Expressivists, does not reflect the application of rules but that of the writer's free imagination.

The Expressivist manifesto, as Faigley (1986) observes, is essentially a romantic one. It promotes vague goals of 'self-actualisation' and even vaguer definitions of good writing which depend on subjective, hazy and culturally variable concepts such as *originality, integrity* and *spontaneity*. This, then, is the extreme learner-centred stance. The writer is the centre of attention, and his or her creative expression is the principal goal. Unfortunately, the basic assumption that all writers have similar innate intellectual and creative potential and simply require the right conditions to express this now seems rather naïve. Essentially the approach is seriously under-theorised and leans heavily on an asocial view of the writer, operating in a context where there are no cultural differences in the value of 'self-expression', no variations in personal inhibition, few distinctions in the writing processes of mature and novice writers, and no social consequences of writing.

While Expressivism has helped to move writing teaching and research away from a restricted attention to form, it ignores communication in the real-world contexts where writing matters. But despite its limitations, the Expressivist approach is still influential in many U.S. first-language classrooms, underpins courses in creative writing, and has helped inspire research to support a cognitive view of writing.

1.2.2   *Writing as a Cognitive Process*

Interest in writers' composing processes has been extended beyond notions of creativity and self-expression to focus on the cognitive aspects of writing. This is a very different view of process, as it draws on the techniques and theories of cognitive psychology and not literary creativity. Essentially it sees writing as a problem-solving activity: how writers approach a writing task as a problem and bring intellectual resources to solving it. This view of writing has developed a range of sophisticated investigative methods, generated an enormous body of research and was, until recently, the dominant approach to teaching writing.

Concept 1.8   The Writing Process

At the heart of this model is the view that writing is a 'non-linear, exploratory and generative process whereby writers discover and reformulate their ideas as they attempt to approximate meaning' (Zamel, 1983: 165). Following Emig's (1983) description of composing as 'recursive' rather than as an uninterrupted, *Pre-writing->Writing->Post-writing* activity, a great deal of research has revealed the complexity of planning and editing activities, the influence of different writing tasks and the value of examining what writers do through a series of writing drafts. Case studies and think-aloud protocols, rather than just texts themselves, have been widely used as research methods to get at these processes.

Historically, Flower and Hayes' (1981) model was decisive. It suggested that the process of writing is influenced by the task and the writer's long-term memory. Its main features are that:

- Writers have goals.
- Writers plan extensively.
- Planning involves defining a rhetorical problem, placing it in a context, then exploring its parts, arriving at solutions and finally translating ideas onto the page.
- All work can be reviewed, evaluated and revised even before any text has been produced.
- Planning, drafting, revising and editing are recursive, interactive and potentially simultaneous.
- Plans and text are constantly evaluated in a feedback loop.
- The whole process is overseen by an executive control called a monitor.

This, then, is a computer model typical of theorising in cognitive psychology and Artificial Intelligence, giving priority to mechanisms such as *memory, Central Processing Unit, problem-solving programmes* and *flow-charts*.

Faigley (1986) points out that the Flower and Hayes model helped to promote a 'science-consciousness' among writing teachers which promised a 'deep-structure' theory of how writing could be taught. The beauty of the model is its simplicity, as the wide range of mental activities which can occur during composing can be explained by a fairly small number of sub-processes. The model also purports to account for individual differences in writing strategies, so immature writers can be represented as using a composing model that is a reduced version of that used by experts and so guided towards greater competence by instruction in expert strategies.

The process approach to teaching writing was also assisted by the increasing availability and affordability of personal computers in the early 1980s. Word processing was not just a new form of typing but a different way of manipulating texts, making it easier to re-draft, revise and edit. Teachers were quick to see the pedagogical possibilities of this, and specialist programmes emerged such as Daedalus (www.daedalus.com) which contained modules to support the stages of the writing process: questions for generating material, multi-screens for editing, and connectivity for peer review and discussion. In discussing this approach to teaching, Bloch (2008: 52) observed: 'The ease with which one could make changes or incorporate new ideas made it clear how all of these aspects of the writing process were now integrated'.

The impact on research and teaching has been enormous, and we now know much more about composing processes. Process approaches also extended research techniques beyond experimental methods and text analyses to the qualitative methods of the social sciences, often seeking to describe writing from an *emic* perspective by taking account of the views of writers and readers themselves. In particular, these studies have made considerable use of writers' verbal reports while composing (e.g. Manchon, Murphy and de Larios, 2005), keystroke logging of writers (van Waes, Leijten and van Weijen, 2009), task observation (e.g. Bosher, 1998) and retrospective interviews (e.g. Ferris, Liu, Sinha and Senna, 2013). Often research is longitudinal, following a few students over an extended period of their writing development (F. Hyland, 1998) and uses multiple techniques which may include recall protocols and product analyses of several drafts.

Overall, however, the extension of this research into studies of L2 writers has been disappointing. Many teachers will find little that is surprising in the findings of process writing studies summarised in Concept 1.9, and the research generally supports our intuitions about the practices of skilled and unskilled writers. Even less encouraging for teachers is the fact that different studies often produce contradictory findings, often because they are limited to small samples of writers in a particular context and so lack generalisability to wider populations of writers. Moreover, despite the massive output of this research, serious doubts have been raised about the methods used to get at the cognitive processes of writing.

Concept 1.9   Process Findings of L2 Writing

Silva (1993) summarises the main results of research into composing practices as:

- General composing process patterns seem to be similar in L1 and L2.
- Skilled writers compose differently from novices.
- Skilled writers use more effective planning and revising strategies.
- Skilled writers revise more at the global level while L2 writers focus revisions at word and sentence levels.
- L1 strategies may or may not be transferred to L2 contexts.
- L2 writers tend to plan less than L1 writers.
- L2 writers have more difficulty setting goals and generating material.
- L2 writers revise more but reflect less on their writing.

One serious problem is that these results often rely on concurrent *think aloud protocols*, a method where researchers ask writers to report their thoughts and actions while involved in a writing task. Thus, Li (2006) and Leighton and Gierl (2007), for example, argue that protocols provide a detailed record of what a writer attends to when he or she is writing, but they have been criticised as offering an incomplete picture of the complex cognitive activities involved, many of which are unconscious and not available to verbal description. In addition, asking subjects to simultaneously write and verbalise what they are doing slows down task performance by overloading short-term memory due to 'a crowding of the cognitive workbench' (Afflerbach and Johnson, 1984: 311). Worse, the act of reporting itself may merely be a story that participants construct to explain, rather than reflect, what they do, potentially distorting the thought processes being reported on.

Reservations have also been expressed about the status of the writing models themselves. Scardamalia and Bereiter (1986), for example, argue that such models do not represent fully worked-out theories and fail to either explain or generate writing behaviour. The models do not tell us *why* writers make certain choices and therefore cannot help us to advise students on their writing practices. In fact, Flower and Hayes' original model was too imprecise to predict the behaviour of real writers or to carry the weight of the research claims based on it, and they have subsequently emphasised the importance of appropriate goal-setting and rhetorical strategies far more (Flower et al., 1990). But such refinements cannot obscure the weaknesses of a model which seeks to describe cognitive processes common to all writers, both novice and expert, and all learners in between these poles.

Bereiter and Scardamalia (1987) suggest that because skilled and novice practices differ so radically, two models account for the research findings better than one (see Concept 1.10).

Concept 1.10   Knowledge-Telling and Knowledge-Transforming

A knowledge-telling model addresses the fact that novice writers plan less often than experts, revise less often and less extensively, and are primarily concerned with generating content from their internal resources. Their main goal is simply to tell what they can remember based on the assignment, the topic, or the genre.

A knowledge-transforming model suggests how skilled writers use the writing task to analyse problems and set goals. These writers are able to reflect on the complexities of the task and resolve problems of content, form, audience, style, organisation, and so on within a content space and a rhetorical space, so that there is continuous interaction between developing knowledge and text. Knowledge transforming thus involves actively reworking thoughts so that in the process not only text, but also ideas, may be changed (Bereiter and Scardamalia, 1987).

Bereiter and Scardamalia's model certainly adds psychological insight to writing activity and helps explain the difficulties often experienced by unskilled writers because of the complexity of the writing task and their lack of topic knowledge. It also helps account for reflective thought in writing, and therefore suggests that students should participate in a variety of challenging writing tasks and genres to develop their skills. It also draws attention to the importance of feedback and revision in the process of developing both content and expression. It remains unclear, however, how writers actually make the cognitive transition to a *knowledge-transforming* model, nor is it spelt out what occurs in the intervening stages and whether the process is the same for all learners. Many students, for example, continue to have considerable difficulty with their writing despite intensive teaching in expert strategies.

Concept 1.11   Main Pros and Cons of Process Approaches

Pros

- major impact on the theory and methodology of teaching writing to L1 and L2 students
- a useful corrective to preoccupations with 'product' and student accuracy
- important in raising teachers' awareness of what writing involves—contributing to a professionalisation of writing teaching
- gives greater respect for individual differences among student writers
- raises many new research questions which remain to be answered

---

Cons

- overemphasises psychological factors in writing
- focuses on the writer as a solitary individual and fails to recognise social aspects of writing
- based on individualistic ideologies which may hamper the development of English as a Second Language (ESL) students
- ignores important influences of context, especially differences of class, gender and ethnicity
- downplays the varied conventions of professional and academic communities
- uncertain whether this approach greatly improves student writing

The impact of process ideas on writing instruction has been enormous, in both L1 and L2 classrooms, with the adoption of a range of brainstorming, pre-writing, drafting and feedback practices (see part 7.2). But while there is a great deal of case-study and anecdotal support for this model, there is actually little hard evidence that process-writing techniques lead to significantly better writing. Writers, situations and tasks differ, and no single description can capture all writing contexts or be applied universally with the same results.

In sum, the process-writing perspective allows us to understand writing in a way that was not possible when it was seen only as a finished product. It does, however, overemphasise psychological factors and fails to consider the forces outside the individual which help guide problem-definition, frame solutions and ultimately shape writing.

1.2.3   *Writing as a Situated Act*

A third writer-oriented perspective goes some way to addressing the criticisms levelled at cognitive modeling by giving greater emphasis to the actual *performance* of writing.

Concept 1.12   Writing as a Situated Act

Writing is a social act that occurs within particular situations. It is therefore influenced both by the personal attitudes and prior experiences that the writer brings to writing and the impact of the specific political and institutional contexts in which it takes place. By using detailed observations of acts of writing, participant interviews, analyses of surrounding practices and other techniques, researchers have developed interesting accounts of local writing contexts. These descriptions give significant attention to the experiences of writers and to their understandings of the demands of the immediate context as they write.

Less a single theory than several lines of enquiry, this research incorporates the writer's prior experiences and the impact of the immediate, local context on writing, and it has had an important influence on both the ways we see writing and how it might be studied. This perspective takes us beyond the possible workings of writers' minds and into the physical and experiential contexts in which writing occurs to describe how 'context cues cognition' (Flower, 1989). Of crucial importance is the emphasis placed on a notion of context as the 'situation of expression' (Nystrand, 1987). Flower (1989: 288) elaborates this as the effects of prior knowledge, assumptions and expectations, together with features of the writing environment, which selectively tap knowledge and trigger specific processes. The goal is to describe the influence of this context on the ways writers represent their purposes and so studies seek to analyse, often in considerable detail, how writing is constituted as a feature of local situations.

Quote 1.5 **Prior on Situated Writing**

Actually writing happens in moments that are richly equipped with tools (material and semiotic) and populated with others (past, present and future). When seen as situated activity, writing does not stand alone as the discrete act of a writer, but emerges as a confluence of many streams of activity: reading, talking, observing, acting, making, thinking and feeling as well as transcribing words on paper.

Prior (1998: xi)

To accomplish such exhaustive or 'thick' descriptions (Geertz, 1973) of writing contexts, researchers have relied heavily on *ethnographic* methods. The term 'ethnographic' remains somewhat fuzzy and contested, but it essentially refers to research which is highly situated and minutely detailed, attempting to give an holistic explanation of behaviour using a variety of methods and drawing on the understandings of insiders themselves to minimise the assumptions brought to the event by the researcher (Watson-Gegeo, 1988; Ramanathan and Atkinson, 1999b). Applying this method to an understanding of how and why people write involves detailed observations of the setting, such as a classroom, and the writing that occurs within it over a period of time, without interfering with either the writers or the writing context.

Concept 1.13 **Ethnographic Research**

Ethnography is a type of research which attempts to make sense of events in terms of the meanings people bring to them. The key features include studying people's behaviour in everyday rather than experimental settings and gathering data from a range of sources, mainly observation and

> relatively informal interviews, that are not based on pre-set categories or hypotheses but which arise out of an interest in an issue. Research is typically small in scale, focused on a single setting or group and involves prolonged engagement by the researcher.

In addition to close examination of interactions, data are also typically collected through interviews with participants about their writing and relevant biographical issues, together with analyses of diaries and other written texts (e.g. Jarratt, Losh and Puente, 2006). Course books, handouts, course outlines and so on are also often studied, as is student writing itself and teachers' responses to this. Sometimes the researcher participates in the class and follows students around to observe their daily activities and gain insights into the contexts and practices which might illuminate the writing process (Weissberg, 2006; Starfield, 2015).

Ethnography, however, is not a term that everyone feels comfortable with. Its origins in anthropology carry connotations of the researcher's total immersion in another culture rather than simply an attitude towards research. Because of this, John Swales' (1998) coining of the term *textography* in his case studies of particular writing contexts and discipline-specific texts in a university building has offered a more manageable way of exploring the richness of writing contexts while avoiding a full cultural description (see also Starfield, Paltridge and Ravelli, 2014).

Quote 1.6   Swales on Textography

As textographer of the second floor I have tried to do justice to a number of themes that have emerged over a three-year involvement with its practices, rhythms, texts and personalities. One is a sense of locale, a sense of autonomous *place* . . . Juxtaposed to that, I have tried to capture a feeling of the academic personalities, and especially the scriptural personalities, of those I have chosen for inclusion . . . And juxtaposed to the partial accounts of careers that a textography engenders, the use of close, but nontechnical, analysis of particular stretches of text, illuminated on occasion by text-based interview data, shows how the language of normal science can . . . reveal the individual humanities of the authors.

Swales (1998: 141–2)

The features of local setting that have particularly interested 'situated' researchers have been the roles individual writers perform and how writers' interactions with local participants feed into the writing task, especially in collaborative contexts. Contexts are sites for interactions where relationships, and the conventions which organise them, can both assist and constrain writing.

The social routines surrounding acts of writing have therefore been studied in detail (e.g. Storch, 2005) and attention given to certain tangible features of the local environment which have meaning for writers. Thus, Chin (1994) has shown how students on a journalism course saw the use of physical space in their department as barriers which excluded them and restricted access to the material resources they needed for writing. Similarly, Canagarajah (1996) has revealed how the absence of resources like libraries and computers can serve to exclude Third World scholars from publishing their writing.

There is little doubt that this research has produced rich, detailed descriptions of particular contexts of writing, expanding greatly our understanding of the personal, social and institutional factors which can impinge on writing. One problem, of course, is that while these methods might illuminate what goes on in a particular act of writing, they cannot describe everything in either the writer's consciousness or the context which might influence composition, so we can never be certain that all critical factors have been accounted for. More importantly, this approach runs the risk of emphasising writers' perceptions and the possible impact of the local situation to the detriment of the rhetorical problems to which writing responds. In other words, by focusing on the context of production, we might be neglecting the effects of the wider social and institutional orders of discourse which influence writers' intentions and plans for writing.

One potential impact of such wider social worlds is the experiences writers might bring to the classroom as a consequence of prior negative evaluation of their writing. Social inequalities of power, educational and home backgrounds, and so on can result in what has been called *writing apprehension* (Faigley, Daly and Witte, 1981) where individuals experience high degrees of anxiety when asked to write. This apprehensiveness about oneself as a writer, one's writing situation, or one's writing task can seriously disrupt the writing process and educational success. The term is used to describe writers who are intellectually capable of the task at hand, but who nevertheless have difficulty with it (e.g. McLeod, 1987), feeling their writing isn't sufficiently creative, interesting, sophisticated or well expressed. This can result in students avoiding courses or careers which involve writing, low self-esteem and confidence, or the production of poor texts.

Overall, then, a focus on writers lacks a developed theory of the ways experience is constituted and interpreted in *social communities* and underplays the workings of wider factors. As a result, it fails to move beyond the local context to take full account of how an evolving text might be a writer's response to a reader's expectations. This neglect of the social dimension of writing has eventually led research away from internally directed process models to more socially situated approaches.

1.3 Reader-Oriented Understandings

A final broad approach expands the notion of *context* beyond features of the composing situation to the purposes, goals and uses that the completed text may eventually fulfill. The perspectives discussed in this section share the view that writers select their words to engage with others and to present their ideas in ways that make the most sense to their readers. This involves what Halliday and Mathieson (2013) refer to as the *interpersonal function* of language, and it is encoded in every sentence we write. Our ability as writers to draw readers in, influence or persuade them depends on our ability to make language choices which are not only grammatical, but which are set out in ways familiar to readers and which show we are taking their processing needs, background understandings and possible objections into account. Thus, writing is an interactive, as well as cognitive, activity which employs accepted resources for the purpose of sharing meanings in that context. I will discuss this social view under three headings:

* writing as social interaction
* writing as social construction
* writing as power and ideology

1.3.1   Writing as Social Interaction

"Writing, when properly managed, is but a different name for conversation". This was written some 250 years ago by Laurence Stern in *The Life and Opinions of Tristram Shandy, Gentleman* (1883). The idea that writing is an interaction between writers and readers moves away from our stereotype of an isolated writer hunched over a keyboard to explain composing decisions in terms of the writer's projection of the interests, understandings and needs of a potential audience. This view was elaborated by Martin Nystrand, who argued that the success of any text is the writer's ability to satisfy the rhetorical demands of readers, which means embedding our writing in a non-local discourse world.

Quote 1.7   **Nystrand on Writing as Social Interaction**

The process of writing is a matter of elaborating text in accord with what the writer can reasonably assume that the reader knows and expects, and the process of reading is a matter of predicting text in accord with what the reader assumes about the writer's purpose. More fundamentally, each presupposes the sense-making capabilities of the other. As a result, written communication is predicated on what the writer/reader each assumes the other will do/has done.

Nystrand (1989: 75)

In a social interactive model, meaning is created via 'a unique configuration and interaction of what both reader and writer bring to the text' (Nystrand, Greene and Wiemelt, 1993: 299). A discourse is shaped by writers attempting to balance their purposes with the expectations of readers through a process of negotiation. For Nystrand, a text has 'semantic potential', or a variety of possible meanings, all but a few of which are closed down by a combination of the writer's intention, the reader's cognition and the language of the text itself. In other words, meaning is not transmitted from mind to mind as in the model of autonomous texts, nor does it reside in the writer's mind as in process models. Instead, it is created between the participants themselves.

Hoey (2001) suggests that these writer–reader interactions essential to achieving coherence and understanding are like dancers following each other's steps, each building sense from a text by anticipating what the other is likely to do. Skilled writers are able to create a mutual frame of reference and anticipate when their purposes will be retrieved by their audiences, providing greater elaboration where they expect that there may be misunderstanding. The drafting process thus becomes a way of responding to an inner dialogue with readers, part of how the writer monitors the evolving text for potential trouble-spots. Writing, then, is not an act of an isolated individual but a joint endeavour between writers and readers, co-constructed through the active understanding of rhetorical situations and the likely responses of readers.

Audience can be a difficult concept for writers. Clearly, a writer who understands something of the needs and interests of his or her audience possesses important rhetorical knowledge about appropriate genre, content, stance and style. The ability to analyse an audience, however, obviously becomes more problematic the larger and less immediately familiar the audience gets. It becomes even more complex where texts are addressed to several audiences simultaneously. As I write this book, for example, I am picturing you, the reader, as someone with more than a passing interest in writing, but I cannot predict your cultural background, your knowledge of the subject, or what you want from this book. Perhaps you are a teacher, a student, a trainer; maybe someone supervising a thesis or a casual browser scanning a few free pages on Amazon. In other words, I am aware that my book could be read by specialists, novices, practitioners and lay people, and while I try to make the subject as explicit as I can, I know that not all readers will recover every intended meaning.

The notion of audience is a contentious area of debate in literary studies (e.g. Lecercle, 2000), has been much discussed in rhetoric (Park, 1982), and has become more complex in the era of electronic writing (e.g. Pecorari, 2016). Audience is, in fact, rarely a concrete reality, particularly in academic and professional contexts, and must be seen as something imagined by the writer and created in the linguistic choices he or she makes while writing.

Concept 1.14   Audience

Two main models of audience have traditionally been influential in writing theory. Ede and Lunsford (1984) refer to these as ***audience addressed***, the actual or intended readers who exist independently of the text, and ***audience invoked***, a created fiction of the writer rhetorically implied in the text and which can be persuaded to respond to it in certain ways. Park's more sophisticated conception focuses less on people and more on the writer's awareness of the external circumstances which define a rhetorical context and requires the text to have certain characteristics in response. Audience therefore exists in the writer's mind and shapes a text as 'a complex set of conventions, estimations, implied responses and attitudes' (Park, 1982: 251).

A key idea here is that texts display how authors understand an audience because they exploit readers' abilities to recognise *intertextuality* between texts. The notion of *intertextuality* originates in Bakhtin's (1986) view that language is dialogic: a conversation between writer and reader in an ongoing activity. Writing builds on and anticipates other texts because when we write, we respond to what others have said and how they have said it. In this way the choices a writer makes about a new text are influenced by an awareness of what earlier, similar texts were like, so that genres can be seen as parts of repeated and typified social situations rather than particular forms. The text, then, is the place where readers and writers meet to jointly create meanings.

Concept 1.15   Intertextuality

Intertextuality is a relationship between a given text and one or more earlier texts which have influenced it. Because texts are not produced in a social vacuum, intertextuality is a feature of all texts, but it varies in terms of how directly visible the influences of the earlier texts are. Fairclough (1992) distinguishes between ***manifest intertextuality***, or ways of incorporating or responding to other texts through quotation, paraphrase, irony and so on, and ***interdiscursivity***, which is the writer's use of sets of conventions drawn from a recognisable genre. This connects text-users into a network of prior texts and so provides a system of options for making meanings which can be recognised by other texts-users.

1.3.2   *Writing as Social Construction*

The idea of *interdiscursivity* encourages us to step back and see interaction as a collection of rhetorical choices rather than as specific encounters with real readers. Here the writer is neither a *creator* working through a set of cognitive processes nor an *interactant* engaging with a reader, but a member of a *community*. The communicating dyad is replaced by the discourses of socially and rhetorically constituted groups of readers and writers.

Concept 1.16 Social Construction

Social construction is based on the idea that the ways we think, and the categories and concepts we use to understand the world, are 'all language constructs generated by knowledge communities and used by them to maintain coherence' (Bruffee, 1986: 777). The everyday interactions that occur between people produce the world that we take for granted. Language is not just a means of self-expression, it is how we construct and sustain reality, and we do this as members of communities, using the language of those communities. The features of a text are therefore influenced by the community for which it was written and so best understood, and taught, through the specific genres of communities.

Originating in sociology and post-modern philosophy, this approach takes the view that what we know and do is relative to a collectively organised conceptual schema. Writing is a social act, and to understand it fully we must go beyond the decisions of individual writers to explore the regular features of texts as the preferences of particular communities. A text carries certain meanings and gains its communicative force only by displaying the patterns and conventions of the community for which it is written. Essays produced by biology students, for example, draw on very different forms of argument, interpersonal conventions and ways of presenting facts and theories than those written by business students. So, whereas interactionists work from individuals to groups, constructionists proceed from social group to individuals: writing is a form of cultural practice tied to forms of social organisation.

Another way of putting this is that writers always have to demonstrate their credibility and that their text has something worthwhile to say by positioning themselves and their ideas in relation to other ideas and texts in their communities. The notion of a *discourse community* draws attention to the idea that we do not use language to communicate with the world at large but with other members of our social groups, each with its own norms, categorisations, sets of conventions and ways of doing things (Bartholomae, 1986). The value of the term lies in the fact that it offers a way of bringing writers, readers and texts together into a common rhetorical space, foregrounding the conceptual frames that individuals use to organise their experience and get things done using language.

More than this, however, through notions of community we can see writing as a means by which organisations actually constitute themselves, and how individuals signal their memberships in them. By engaging with others through writing, we enter into a culture of shared beliefs concerning what is worth discussing and how things should be discussed. Our language choices allow us to align ourselves with, challenge or extend what has been said before, and at the same time to confirm our membership. Community is a means of accounting for how communication succeeds through the individual's projection of a shared context, whether this is a group of stamp collectors or high court judges. Communities help us to see that valued ways of writing are not just conventional templates or regularities of style, but they activate specific recognizable and routine responses to recurring tasks.

Concept 1.17   Discourse Community

The term 'discourse community' is one of the most indeterminate in the writing literature. It is possible to see discourse communities as real, relatively stable groups whose members subscribe, at least to some extent, to a consensus on certain ways of doing things and using language. On the other hand, 'community' can be regarded as a more metaphorical term for collecting together certain practices and attitudes. Overall, the expectations, practices and norms of communities have an effect on writing and knowledge in these communities—at the same time, it is the routine practices and conventions they use which turns groups into communities.

In a real sense, it is through these repeated practices that we 'construct' the institutions we participate in. Texts are created in terms of how their authors understand reality and, in turn, these understandings are influenced by their membership in social groups. But there is considerable disagreement about what a discourse community is. Swales (1990), for instance, sets out criteria for using language to achieve collective goals or purposes, while other writers have suggested a weaker connection (e.g. Barton, 2007).

Quote 1.8   Barton on Discourse Community

A discourse community is a group of people who have texts and practices in common, whether it is a group of academics, or the readers of teenage magazines. In fact, discourse community can refer to the people the text is aimed at; it can be the people who read a text; or it can refer to the people who participate in a set of discourse practices both by reading and writing.

(Barton, 2007: 75–6)

As Bazerman (1994: 128) notes, 'most definitions of discourse community get ragged around the edges rapidly'. To see discourse communities as determinate and codifiable runs the risk of framing them as closed, self-sufficient and predictable arenas of shared and agreed-upon values and conventions. On the other hand, reducing them to mere collections of competing voices reduces the idea's explanatory authority. Clearly we have to avoid the strong structuralist position of a single deterministic consensus which separates a community from its moments of creation in writing, but at the same time we need to acknowledge the obvious effects of groups on the ways individual communicative practices are realised.

The fuzziness of the term means that it is often unclear where to locate a discourse community. Can it, for example, refer to all academics, or is it those in a university, a discipline, or just a specialism? We also have to account for the ways these groupings come into being, how people can join or leave, how they exercise power and accommodate differences and conflict, and how they develop and change. Clearly the term is only useful if it is seen as connected to real individuals and the cultural frames that carry meaning for them. As a result, some writers have sought to 'localise' the concept into '*place discourse communities*' (Swales, 1998) or '*communities of practice*' (Lave and Wenger, 1991), defining a community in terms of the literacy practices and relations which emerge in some mutual endeavour over time.

Despite the term's imprecision, there is a core meaning of like-mindedness or *membership*, and this concept has proved central to research on writing. It has contributed to how we understand writing in engineering (Pogner, 2003), the law (Bhatia, Candlin and Engberg, 2008), health care (Little, Jordens and Sayers, 2003), and technology (Killingsworth and Gilbertson, 1992). Constructionism has been most influential, however, in describing academic writing. This approach tells us that essays, reports, memos, dissertations and so on are not the same in all courses and disciplines, and that the ability to produce them does not involve generic writing skills. Only when we use a language to create genres in specific contexts does our competence in writing cease to be a display of control of a linguistic code and take on significance as discourse. Expert writers are obviously better able than novices to imagine how readers will respond to a text because they are familiar with the ways experience is typically constructed in their communities.

1.3.3   *Writing as Power and Ideology*

A third reader-oriented view of writing also emphasises the importance of social context on writing but stresses that the key dimension of context is the relations of power that exist in it and the ideologies that maintain these relations. The importance of power as a force which mediates discourse and social groups has been most extensively explored by researchers working in *Critical Discourse Analysis* (CDA). CDA views language as a form of social practice and attempts "to unpack the ideological underpinnings of discourse that have become so naturalized over time that we begin to treat them as common, acceptable and natural features of discourse" (Teo, 2000). In other words, CDA links language to the activities which surround it, focusing on how social relations, identity, knowledge and power are constructed through written and spoken texts in communities, schools and classrooms. Discourse is thus a mediator of social life: simultaneously both constructing social and political reality, and conditioned by it.

> ### █Quote 1.9█ Fairclough on Critical Discourse Analysis
>
> By 'critical' discourse analysis I mean analysis which aims to systematically explore often opaque relationships of causality and determination between (a) discursive practices, events and texts, and (b) wider social and cultural structures, relations and processes; to investigate how such practices, events and texts arise out of and are ideologically shaped by relations of power and struggles over power; and to explore how the opacity of these relationships between discourse and society is itself a factor securing power and hegemony.
>
> Fairclough (1992: 135)

A central aspect of this view is that the interests, values and power relations in any institutional and sociohistorical context are found in the ways that people use language.

Concept 1.18   Principles of Critical Discourse Analysis (CDA)

- CDA addresses social problems and not simply language use by itself.
- Power relations are discursive.
- Discourse constitutes society and culture, and every instance of language use contributes to reproducing or changing them.
- Discourse does ideological work, representing and constructing society in particular ways.
- Discourse is historical, and must be related to other discourses.
- The link between texts and society is mediated by 'orders of discourse'.
- Discourse analysis is interpretive and explanatory, requiring systematic methods.
- Discourse is a form of social action, and CDA is a socially committed paradigm.

(Wodak, 1996: 17–20)

The notion of *ideology* is important because it is concerned with how individuals experience the world and how these experiences are, in turn, reproduced through their writing. Fairclough (borrowing from Foucault) uses the term '*orders of discourse*' to refer to the relatively stable configurations of discourse practices found in particular domains or institutions. These are frames for interaction such as patient case-notes, lab reports, newspaper editorials, student records, academic articles and so on, which have prestige value in different institutions and which are rhetorically shaped by its dominant groups. They provide writers with templates for appropriate ways of writing, which means that any act of writing, or of teaching writing, is embedded in ideological assumptions.

But while these frameworks help enforce the authority of particular forms of discourse in any community, they do not exclude possibilities for change. This is because when we write, we not only take up socially ratified social roles and relationships, but also draw on our personal and social experiences which cross-cut what we write. We are not just English teachers, for example, but we belong to certain age groups, genders, ethnicities, social classes and so on.

Of importance in this perspective is the view that writing is both texts *and* contexts: the work of both individuals and institutions. This requires us to consider not only texts but also their relationship to the wider social environment and the part they play for individuals within specific situations. CDA is, therefore, analysis with attitude. It proclaims an interest and sets an agenda, as Fairclough and Wodak (1997: 259) make clear: 'What is distinctive about CDA is both that it intervenes on the side of the dominated and oppressed groups and against dominating groups, and that it openly declares the emancipatory interests that motivate it'.

While CDA does not subscribe to any single method, Fairclough (2003) and Wodak (Wodak and Chilton , 2007) draw on *systemic functional linguistics* (SFL). This is because the model sees language as systems of linguistic features offering choices to users, but these choices are considerably circumscribed in situations of unequal power. Young and Harrison (2004: 1) claim that SFL and CDA share three main features:

1.   a view of language as a social construct, or how society fashions language;
2.   a dialectical view in which "particular discursive events influence the contexts in which they occur and the contexts are, in turn, influenced by these discursive events";
3.   a view which emphasises cultural and historical aspects of meaning.

SFL thus offers CDA a sophisticated way of analysing the relations between language and social contexts, making it possible to ground concerns of power and ideology in the details of discourse.

In practice, CDA typically examines features of writing such as:

•   vocabulary—particularly how metaphor and connotative meanings encode ideologies
•   transitivity—which can show who is presented as having agency and who is acted upon

- nominalisation and passivisation—how processes and actors can be repackaged as nouns or agency otherwise obscured
- mood and modality—which indicate relationships such as roles, attitudes, commitments and obligations
- theme—how the first element of a clause can be used to foreground particular aspects of information or presuppose reader beliefs
- text structure—how text episodes are marked
- intertextuality and interdiscursivity—the effects of other texts and styles on texts—leading to *hybridisation*, such as where commercial discourses influence texts in other areas

Unfortunately, much CDA analysis has relied exclusively on the researcher's interpretations of texts, cherry-picking both the texts it studies and the features it chooses to discuss. This has the effect of simply confirming the analyst's prejudices while reducing pragmatics to semantics in assuming just one possible reading of the text (Widdowson, 2000). Moreover, as Blommaert (2005) observes, this privileging of the analyst's viewpoint is often reinforced by appeal to an explanatory level of social theory which lies above any analysis of the text itself. In other words, there is little dialogue with real readers, and interpretation becomes a black box rather than a product of analysis. The plausibility of any interpretation of a text, however, depends on our willingness to accept it, and this is best achieved by getting the views of the text producers and readers. So, although it might be acknowledged that no analysis can be neutral, and that a clear political agenda helps to redress the invisible ideological assumptions in much writing research, we need to go beyond good intentions. It is essential that any theory of writing is thoroughly grounded in the contextual understandings of the users that give it significance.

1.4   Conclusion

In this overview I have been concerned not only to cover the major frameworks used to look at writing, but also to question the widely held views that writing is either simply words on a page or an activity of solitary individuals. Rather, modern conceptions see writing as a social practice, embedded in the cultural and institutional contexts in which it is produced and the particular uses that are made of it. When we pick up a pen or sit at a word-processor, we adopt and reproduce certain roles, identities and relationships to engage in particular socially approved ways of communicating: to write an essay, make an insurance claim, or complain about a supermarket delivery. So while every act of writing is in a sense both personal and individual, it is also interactional and social, expressing a culturally recognised purpose, reflecting a particular kind of relationship and acknowledging an engagement in a given community. Chapter 2 looks more closely at some of the issues that this raises.

Further Reading

Casanave, C. (2004) *Controversies in second language writing*. Ann Arbor, MI: University of Michigan Press.

A book addressing some key issues for teachers of second language writers.

Fairclough, N. (2004) *Analyzing discourse*. London: Routledge.

A mix of introductory SFL and social theory—a good primer for CDA in the social sciences.

Hyland, K. (2005) *Metadiscourse.* London: Continuum.

A framework for studying how writing works as interaction

Kroll, B. (ed) (2002) *Exploring the dynamics of second language writing*. Cambridge: Cambridge University Press.

An accessible introduction to second-language writing research and teaching.

Silva, T. and Matsuda, P. (eds) (2001) *Landmark essays on ESL writing*. Mahwah, NJ: Lawrence Earlbaum Associates.

Just what the title says.

2 Key Issues in Writing

This chapter will . . .

- address some key topics in current understandings of writing and writing research, namely *context, literacy, technology, social media, identity* and *dominance*, the last concerning the global spread of English to many domains of writing;
- examine what these topics tell us about writing and elaborate the questions that they raise about the analysis and use of written texts;
- discuss the main views currently held on these topics and point to some of the important thinkers, theories and studies in these areas.

2.1 Writing and Context

The ways we understand writing have developed through increasingly sophisticated understandings of context. We recognise that meaning is not something that resides in the words we write and send to someone else, but is created in the interaction between a writer and reader as they make sense of these words in different ways, each trying to guess the intentions of the other. As a result, analysts and teachers now try to take account of the personal, institutional and social factors which influence acts of writing.

Traditionally, context was largely seen as a collection of 'objective' variables such as class, gender or race, but now tends to be viewed as what the participants see as relevantly impinging on a communicative situation. So, the references to shared understandings in an email to a friend, for example, might be opaque to an outsider unable to read between the lines and recover these meanings.

> **Quote 2.1 Van Dijk on Context**
>
> It is not the social situation that influences (or is influenced by) discourse, but the way the participants **define** such a situation. Contexts thus are not some kind of 'objective' condition or direct cause, but rather (inter) subjective constructs designed and ongoingly updated in interaction by

participants as members of groups and communities. If they were, all people in the same social situation would speak in the same way. Contexts are participant constructs.

van Dijk (2008: viii)

So instead of seeing context as a cluster of static variables that surround language use, we have to see it as socially constituted, interactively sustained and time bound (Duranti and Goodwin, 1992). It has to be admitted, however, that context is rarely analysed in its own right and is usually taken for granted or defined rather impressionistically. After all, given all the situations in which we can read or write, context might intuitively include everything. Cutting (2002: 3) suggests that there are three main aspects of this interpretive context:

- the *situational context*: what people "know about what they can see around them"
- the *background knowledge context*: what people know about the world, what they know about aspects of life, and what they know about each other
- the *co-textual context*: what people "know about what they have been saying"

These aspects of interpretation have come to be rolled into the idea of *community*. As discussed in Chapter 1, this is something of a troubled concept and produces difficulties in defining what a community is and where its borders are, but it offers a principled way of understanding how meaning is produced *in interaction*. This means that all uses of written language can be seen as located in particular times and places: in the home, school, workplace or university, and in particular communities who recognise particular combinations of genres, interpretive shortcuts and communicative conventions.

An alternative approach is to look for contexts in texts themselves and see how the properties of a social situation are systematically encoded in linguistic choices. The most developed approach to discovering the ways contexts leave their traces (or are expressed) in patterns of language use is SFL. In this theory of language, Halliday developed an analysis of context based on the idea that any text is the result of the writer's language choices in a particular *context of situation* (Malinowski, 1949). That is, language varies according to the situation in which it is used, so we can look at a text and make guesses about the situation or, as writers, make linguistic choices based on that situation. How formal or polite do we need to be? How assertive or concessive? What information do we need to include and what can we safely assume? The context of situation, or register, is the immediate situation in which language is used, and this language varies according to *field, tenor* and *mode* (Halliday and Mathieson, 2013).

Concept 2.1   Halliday's Dimensions of Context

- *field*: refers to what is happening, or what the text is about (the topic together with the socially expected forms and patterns typically used to express it)
- *tenor*: refers to who is taking part, the roles and relationships of participants (their status and power, for instance, which influences involvement, formality and politeness)
- *mode*: refers to the way the language is being used and what the participants are expecting it to do for them (whether spoken or written, instructive or persuasive, etc.)

These three elements make it possible for the speaker/writer to orient to the situation and select the appropriate language needed. Register is therefore an attempt to characterise configurations of writing (or speech) which limit the choices a writer will make in a situation. So, some registers contain fairly predictable features which allow us to identify a connection between text and context. Legal documents and computer manuals, for example, are likely to be highly formulaic in the conventions of lexis and grammar they contain, while more open registers, such as editorials and personal emails, contain a less restricted range of meanings and forms.

This immediate *context of situation* operates within a more abstract context Halliday calls the *context of culture*. This refers to the ways social structures, hierarchies and institutional ideologies influence the language used in particular circumstances. Russell's (1997) investigation into a university cell biology course, for example, shows that students' writing in the course was situated both in the micro-level context (e.g. the professor's research lab, the course, the university administration, and related disciplines) as well as in the macro-level social and political structures (e.g. drug companies, families, government research agencies).

So, the influence of the context of culture on language use is more diffuse and indirect, operating at a more abstract level than contexts of situations. It is expressed in, or 'through', more specific contexts of situation, so that we describe social situations as part of a broader culture. What is not clear, however, is how this broader culture actually impinges on our local experiences. How language users understand these constraints in their everyday acts of writing and speaking remains an open question, but the ways the global relates to the local in actual acts of writing have been picked up by writers in CDA who see *discourse* as the link between the two (Fairclough, 1992).

This is because it is in discourse where approved institutional practices such as university assignments, seminars, essays and so on (what Fairclough calls '*orders of discourse*') operate to maintain existing relations of power and authority. In education, for example, these discourses regulate what is worth knowing and who can know it, thus confirming status of those who have the knowledge and the power to exercise it. So by teaching students socially autho-rised ways of communicating, such as the conventions of academic essays, we are simultaneously promoting the values of powerful social groups by rein-forcing particular social roles and relationships between writers and readers.

These various perspectives allude to the richness and complexity of context in writing and the necessity for a more comprehensive approach to its study.

2.2   Literacy and Expertise

Writing, together with reading, is an act of literacy: how we actually use lan-guage in our everyday lives. Modern conceptions of literacy encourage us to see writing as a social practice rather than as an abstract skill separable from people and the places where they use texts. As Scribner and Cole (1981: 236) put it: 'literacy is not simply knowing how to read and write a particular script but applying this knowledge for specific purposes in specific contexts of use'. Literacy helps us to understand how people make sense of their lives through their routine practices of writing and reading.

Traditional views regard literacy as a learnt ability which facilitates logi-cal thinking, access to information, and participation in the roles of modern society. This perspective is psychological and textual, something which can be measured and assessed. Literacy is seen as a set of discrete, value-free technical skills which include decoding and encoding meanings, manipulating writing tools, perceiving shape–sound correspondences, etc., which are learnt through formal education. Writing is seen as personal empowerment, but it is also defined in terms of its opposite: the personal stigma attached to illiteracy. You either have it or you don't. 'Literacy' is therefore a loaded term, a deficit label which carries with it the social power to define, categorise and ultimately exclude people from many aspects of life.

A contrasting position is taken by those who advocate a *social literacies* view (note the plural form). Here writing (and reading) are means of connect-ing people with each other in ways that carry particular social meanings, so writing varies with context and cannot be distilled down to a set of cognitive or technical abilities. The idea of 'functional literacy', the ability of individuals to fit in and succeed within their societies by using writing and reading skills for particular purposes, is married to the notion of 'critical literacy', the refusal to take such purposes for granted. This approach sees literacy as a relative term, so there is no single literacy but a wide variety of different 'practices' relevant to and appropriate for particular times, places, participants and purposes. The competencies required to participate in a betting syndicate or a political party involve particular configurations of genres and language forms. Moreover, these practices are not something that we simply pick up and put down, but are integral to our individual identities, social relationships and community mem-berships (Street, 1995; Barton, Ivanic, Appleby, Hodge and Tusting, 2007; Street and Lefstein, 2008).

Concept 2.2   A Social View of Literacy

1. Literacy is a social activity and is best described in terms of people's literacy practices.
2. People have different literacies which are associated with different domains of life.
3. People's literacy practices are situated in broader social relations, making it necessary to describe the settings of literacy events.
4. Literacy practices are patterned by social institutions and power relationships, and some literacies are more dominant, visible and influential than others.
5. Literacy is based on a system of symbols as a way of representing the world to others and to ourselves.
6. Our attitudes and values with respect to literacy guide our actions to communication.
7. Our life histories contain many literacy events from which we learn and which contribute to the present.
8. A literacy event also has a social history which helps create current practices.

Barton (2007: 34–5)

Barton and Hamilton (1998: 6) define literacy *practices* as 'the general cultural ways of utilising written language which people draw on in their lives'. It therefore stresses the centrality of context, as discussed in part 2.1, and suggests how the activities of reading and writing are related to the social structures in which they are embedded and which they help shape. But while these practices are 'what people do with literacy', they are rather abstract as they refer to not only reading and writing but also the values, feelings and cultural conceptions that give meaning to these uses (Street, 1995: 2). In other words, they include shared understandings, ideologies and social identities as well as the social rules that regulate the access and distribution of texts. More concretely, these practices cluster into what Heath (1983) calls 'literacy events'.

Quote 2.2   Literacy Events

Literacy events are observable episodes where literacy has a role. Usually there is a written text, or texts, central to the activity and there may be talk around the text. Events are observable episodes which arise from practices or are shaped by them. The notion of events stresses the situated nature of literacies, that it always exists in a social context.

Barton and Hamilton (1998: 7)

How texts are produced and used in different events is a key aspect of studying literacy. The assumption that writing is always associated with particular domains of cultural activity means we need to study literacy in a new way, using detailed ethnographic accounts of how writing is put to use by real people in their schools, homes, neighbourhoods and workplaces.

Quote 2.3   **Baynham on Researching Literacy**

Investigating literacy as practice involves investigating literacy as 'concrete human activity', not just what people do with literacy, but also what they make of what they do, the values they place on it and the ideologies that surround it.

Baynham (1995: 1)

Some studies have focused on the situated nature of routine literacy events, such as letter-writing, and the cultural beliefs and values attached to this in different times and places (e.g. Barton and Hall, 1999). More often, however, research has sought to describe literacy practices as events in people's everyday lives. Thus, Jones (2000) describes the practices of agriculture officials translating bureaucratic English into vernacular Welsh when interacting with farmers at a Welsh cattle auction. More recently, Barton et al. (2007) explored the complex relationships between learning and adults' lives through a series of case studies of individuals at various learning sites, such as a drug support centre, a homeless shelter, and a domestic violence refuge. Studies such as these show that writing is located in the interactions between people, and that texts are inextricable from the local and institutional contexts in which they are created and interpreted.

When we look beyond words to the social aspects of the activity in which they are embedded, we find that writing is typically secondary to some other purpose. Writing a letter may be a means of keeping in touch with a distant friend, for example, while completing a form can be incidental to applying for a loan. Social literacy research also shows us how far talk is often closely related to texts in such settings. This is illustrated in multilingual communities where relatives, friends or professional 'literacy-brokers' often help people cope with the demands of bureaucratic literacy. Shuman (1993), for instance, describes how Puerto Rican teenage girls in the United States often take responsibility for translating government forms in English into spoken Spanish for their parents. In British Gujarati homes, it may be the mother who takes on the main literacy role when writing to family members in India, translating verbal messages into Gujarati for her non-Gujarati speaking children (Barton and Hamilton, 1998: 183).

These studies not only reveal something of the many varied ways that people use texts in their everyday lives, but also how literacy may reflect unequal social relationships of generation or gender within the home or community. In turn, this points to the unequal access people have to particular texts and discourses in society. Socially powerful institutions, such as education, the law, the academy and other professions, tend to support dominant literacy practices, while vernacular and home literacies are less visible and less valued.

Concept 2.3   Literacy and Power

Not all literacy practices are equal. The state has enormous power to define literacy, label illiterates, regulate entry into particular groups, and restrict access to knowledge. The question of access to, and production of, valued texts is central to the notions of power and control in modern society. The meanings of dominant literacy practices are constructed in contexts which have considerable power in our society, such as education and law. These controlling institutions erect and support particular prestigious practices and then maintain social inequalities through exclusion from them. Other, more everyday acts of writing, in contrast, are less supported and are less influential.

The fact that the conventions of particular literacies become endowed with authority and prestige means that they serve as effective mechanisms for legitimising particular views of the world. Once again, this leads us back to the position that language is not simply a neutral carrier of ideas, but is fundamental to constructing our relationships with others and for understanding our experience of the world. As such, language is central to how we negotiate and change our understanding of our societies and ourselves.

By looking at different literacy events, it becomes clear that there is not one single literacy but different *literacies*. That is, there are different configurations of practices which are recognizable, named and associated with different aspects of cultural life, such as *academic literacy*, *legal literacy* and *workplace literacy*. The increased literacy demands of the modern world mean that people must constantly move beyond the familiarity of their vernacular practices to engage with those of dominant institutions. One example is access to higher education. In acquiring disciplinary knowledge and skills, students simultaneously encounter a new and dominant literacy with its own norms, jargon, sets of conventions and modes of expression which constitute a separate culture (Bartholomae, 1986).

Quote 2.4   Bartholomae on Academic Literacy

Every time a student sits down to write for us, he has to invent the university for the occasion—invent the university, that is, or a branch of it, like History or Anthropology or Economics or English. He has to learn to speak our language, to speak as we do, to try on the peculiar ways of knowing, selecting, evaluating, reporting, concluding, and arguing that defines the discourse of our community.

Bartholomae (1986: 4)

Because academic ability is frequently evaluated in terms of competence in a specialist written register, students often find their own vernacular writing practices regarded as failed attempts to approximate these standard forms. But institutional views of literacy disguise variability and misrepresent academic literacy as a self-evident way of participating in academic communities. This, in turn, encourages the idea that there is one general 'academic English' and one set of strategies for approaching reading and writing tasks that can be applied across disciplines and courses. All this means, of course, that writing instruction often becomes an exercise in 'fixing up' language problems. English for Academic Purposes (EAP) is largely a response to this, finding ways to undermine a 'single literacy' view and to replace 'remedial' views of teaching with approaches that address students' own writing practices.

This view of literacy, then, has implications for notions of expertise and writing competence. We can no longer regard a 'good writer' as someone who has control over the mechanics of grammar, syntax and punctuation, as in the autonomous view of writing. Nor is it someone who is able to mimic expert composing and 'knowledge-transforming' practices by reworking his or her ideas during writing, as in process models. Instead, modern conceptions of literacy define an expert writer as 'one who has attained the local knowledge that enables her to write as a member of a discourse community' (Carter, 1990: 226).

Concept 2.4   The Nature of Expertise

Research in educational psychology sees the shift from novice to expert as a gradual acquisition of experiences which provide templates for competent behaviour in particular situations. Novices develop more sophisticated schemata or procedural knowledge as they gradually learn how to work in a specific domain. The novice begins with general strategies, and while the need for these diminishes as he or she gains familiarity with a situation, they are not entirely eliminated. Expertise is therefore a continuum rather than an end state, as general knowledge is increasingly applied in a specific context. When applied to writing, Carter (1990) characterises the development of expertise through five stages of increasingly more context-specific strategies, culminating in fluid, unreflective practice. Experts react intuitively to familiar situations, not relying on rules or strategies but simply doing what works based on the understanding that comes from experience.

Writing competence is now signaled as a marker of expertise in a wide range of professional activities where it refers to the writer's orientations to specific features of the institution. Candlin (1999) identifies a number of macro features which characterise expertise, including the ability to tailor both information and interpersonal aspects of messages to recipient needs and knowledge, and micro-discursive acts such as negotiating, formulating and mediating. This is not to say that there are no transferable strategies, as both general and local knowledge seem necessary to account for writing expertise. However, the more learners become familiar with the genres and expectations of their target communities, the greater the accumulated store of experiences they can draw on to meet those expectations. These local competencies remain to be explored and specified for many domains.

2.3   Writing and Technology

To be a literate person today means having control over a range of print and electronic media. Many of the latter have had a major impact on the ways we write, the genres we create, the authorial identities we assume, the forms of our finished products, and the ways we engage with readers. Some of the most significant of these are listed in Concept 2.5.

Concept 2.5   Effects of Electronic Technologies on Writing

- change creating, editing, proofreading and formatting processes
- combine written texts with visual and audio media more easily
- encourage non-linear writing and reading processes through hypertext links
- challenge traditional notions of authorship, authority and intellectual property
- allow writers access to more information and to connect that information in new ways
- change the relationships between writers and readers as readers can often 'write back'
- expand the range of genres and opportunities to reach wider audiences
- blur traditional oral and written channel distinctions
- introduce possibilities for constructing and projecting new social identities
- facilitate entry to new on-line discourse communities
- increase the marginalisation of writers who are isolated from new writing technologies
- offer writing teachers new challenges and opportunities for classroom practice

---

Perhaps the most immediately obvious, and by now very familiar, feature of computer-based writing is the way that electronic text facilitates composing, dramatically changing our writing habits. Commonplace word-processing features which allow us to cut and paste, delete and copy, check spelling and grammar, import images and change every aspect of formatting mean that our texts are now longer, prettier and more heavily revised.

Equally significant changes result from the way electronic media allow us to integrate images with other modes of meaning relatively easily. Electronic technologies, in fact, are accelerating a growing preference for image over text in many domains so that the ability to both understand and even produce multimodal texts is increasingly a requirement of literacy practices in scientific, educational, business, media and other settings. Writing now means 'assembling text and images' in new visual designs, and writers often need to understand the specific ways of configuring the world which different modes offer. For Kress (2003), different modes have different affordances, or potentials and limitations for meaning.

Quote 2.5 **Kress on 'Affordances'**

The two modes of writing and of image are each governed by distinct logics, and have distinctly different affordances. The organization of writing is governed by the logic of time, and by the logic of sequence of its elements in time, in temporally governed arrangements. The organization of the image, by contrast, is governed by the logic of space, and by the logic of simultaneity of its visual/depicted elements in spatially organized arrangements. To say this simply: in speaking I have to say one thing after another . . . meaning is attached to 'being first' and to 'being last', and so on. In a visual representation the placement of elements in the space of representation—the page, the canvas, the screen, the wall—will similarly have meaning. Placing something centrally means that other things will be marginal. Placing something at the top means that something else will likely be below. Both these places can be used to make meaning: being central can mean being the 'centre', in whatever way; being above can mean being superior, and being below can mean 'inferior'.

Kress (2003: 2)

Images therefore have a structure similar to writing and can be analysed as a visual grammar (e.g. Kress and van Leeuwen, 2006). For example, 'given' and 'new' information are often represented spatially, so that advertisements will tend to situate visual elements of what is known on the left, usually a problem, and what is new on the right, the solution. Think of teeth whitening or weight loss ads, for example. Clearly, contemporary electronic texts such as web pages and CD ROM screens are more often like images in their organisation and ask the reader to perform different semiotic work, offering different entry points to the 'page' and different reading paths from the order of words in a sentence, therefore providing opportunities for readers to design the order of the text for themselves. As a result, Kress and Van Leeuwen (2006) draw attention to consequent shifts in authority, in changes in the ways we read, and shifts in forms of engagement with the world.

Given cultural differences in visual design, the use of multimedia in writing classrooms is therefore not just an aid for improving student writing, but for teaching new forms of writing which involve both how texts and images are arranged on a screen and how links are made to others.

This linking is *hypertext*: the glue that holds the Internet together, where active connections are provided to different parts of the current text and beyond it. This allows writers to provide links to digitised graphics, video, sounds, animation and other prose sources, enabling readers to construct different pathways through the text that reflect their own interests and decisions. This web of interconnected textual elements has important implications, as it transforms the familiar writing space of print and gives the reader greater freedom in how he or she can approach the text. A major effect of hypertext, then, is to actualise intertextuality, transforming the potential connections between texts into real ones by allowing readers immediate access to associated texts. While much of the promise of hypertext has been subverted by the aggressive commercialism of the Internet, it nevertheless offers great advantages to writers who want to express their arguments in more reflexive and relativistic ways by exploiting the explicit presence of other voices and interpretations.

Perhaps more radically, the shift from print to screen undermines the immutability of an author's text. The ease with which we can collect large numbers of texts and paste them together in ways their writers never conceived of means that original writing is no longer inviolate and that plagiarism becomes harder to police. Any text becomes a temporary structure in a fluid maze of other texts from other times and contexts. In addition, it becomes harder to identify when a piece of writing is actually finished, since not only can readers alter it, but it is constantly changing before it reaches the reader. This is most obvious in the architecture of wikis which not only allow individuals to post ideas but others to modify them (most famously in the online encyclopedia *Wikipedia* that anyone can edit). But virtually all electronic texts exist in multiple versions which the author may not always succeed in controlling. Electronic writing, in other words, heralds not only the death of the author but the death of the canon.

Quote 2.6   Douglas on Hypertext Argument

The beauty of hypertext is . . . that it propels us from the straightened 'either/or' world that print has come to represent and into a universe where the 'and/and/and' is always possible. It is an environment more conducive

> to relativistic philosophy and analysis, where no single account is privi-
> leged over any others, yet, because it is written in code, writers can ensure
> that readers traverse some bits of the argumentative landscape more eas-
> ily and more frequently than others, or that readers are left to make their
> own connections between one bit of text and another.
>
> Douglas (1998: 155)

Clearly there are new literacy skills involved here. The ability to read and write hypertext texts is not merely an extension of those required for linear texts but draws on very different competencies. This gains additional impor-tance as there are no established gatekeepers to screen what is published, so the ability to critically evaluate websites can require crucial composing and read-ing skills. Teachers often find a massive range of variation in both the quality and genres students cite in their academic term papers (Stapleton, 2003), for example, and are increasingly finding they must introduce these competencies into their writing classes.

But while technological innovations present challenges to writers, they also open up new identities, genres and communities to them. The emergence and huge popularity of blogs, chatrooms and listservs, for example, produce a sense of immediacy and speed of transmission which radically alters textual practices by encouraging a simulated conversational style in writing. Additionally, the ability of writers to link blogs together on a single page, to create blogrolls (lists of blogs alongside the main text), and to create specific wikis and listerv groups all offer opportunities to build new communities around writing and texts.

Much has also been made of the absence of physical co-presence in computer-mediated communication (CMC) as this has had a tremendous impact on the ways writers see themselves and interact with others online (Beatty, 2010). Bloch (2008), for instance, recalls a *New Yorker* cartoon of a dog sitting in front of a computer saying 'on the internet, nobody knows you are a dog'. Indeed, an online poll by *Read Write Web* in 2007[1] found that 55% of respon-dents admitted to routinely fashioning fictional personalities. Turkle (1995) argues that the Internet allows people to 'try out' different aspects of their identity, and while this can range from the playful to the scary, it may actually benefit reticent or self-conscious language users who may be more inclined to express themselves online (Bloch and Crosby, 2006).

2.4   Writing and Identity

Recent research has emphasised the close connections between writing and an author's identity. In its broadest sense, *identity* refers to 'the ways that people display who they are to each other' (Benwell and Stokoe, 2006: 6): a social performance achieved by drawing on appropriate linguistic resources. Identity is therefore seen as constructed by both the texts we engage in and the linguistic choices we make, thus moving identity from the private to the public sphere, and from hidden processes of cognition to its social and dynamic construction in discourse. In other words, this view questions whether there is an absolute, unchanging self lurking behind discourse and suggests that identity is a *performance*. We perform *identity work* by constructing ourselves as credible members of a particular social group, so that identity is something we *do*, not something we *have*. Almost everything we say or write, in fact, says something about us and the kind of relationship we want to establish with others.

As Bloemmaert (2005) observes, however, our identities are only successful to the extent that they are recognised by others, and this means employing, appropriating and transforming existing discourses that we encounter (Bakhtin, 1986). Clearly, writers do not create a representation of themselves from an infinite range of possibilities, but make choices from culturally available resources. The ways we perform an identity therefore involve interactions between the conventional practices of the literacy event and the values, beliefs and prior cultural experiences of the participants.

Concept 2.6   Writing and Identity

Current notions of identity see it as a plural concept, socially defined and negotiated through the choices writers make in their discourses. These choices are partly constrained by the dominant ideologies of privileged literacies in particular communities, and partly open to writers' interpretations as a result of their personal and sociocultural experiences. Identity thus refers to the various 'selves' writers employ in different contexts, the processes of their connection to particular communities, and their responses to the power relations institutionally inscribed in them.

Identity therefore needs to be distinguished from the notion of *voice* in the Expressivist literature. Voice is a complex idea with various meanings and connotations, but it essentially refers to the writer's distinctive signature, the individual stamp that he or she leaves on a text (Elbow, 1994). Writing teachers value this assertion of personal authority and often exhort student writers to 'discover their own unique voice' and achieve self-expression in their writing. In other words, this view sees identity as the manifestation of a private self, a highly individualistic concept deeply rooted in mainstream western culture and often antithetical to the communicative norms of ESL students from more collectivist cultures (Ramanathan and Atkinson, 1999a).

In contrast, instead of looking for textual evidence of the writer's private self, identity is located in the public, institutionally defined roles people create in writing as community members, including 'their representation of audience, subject matter, and other elements of context' (Cherry, 1988: 269). This social view sees identity as rhetorical traces of *membership*: the commitment to particular ways of seeing the world and representing it to others as an insider. In our public lives, we play out professional roles and claim professional identities, writing as store-keepers, company executives or cognitive psychologists, using the discourses of our trade. Identity here then concerns how writing takes on the discursive and epistemological features of a particular culture: how writers project an insider ethos and signal their right to be heard as competent members of a group.

Concept 2.7   On Membership

Membership refers to a writer's ability to recognise, replicate and, within limits, innovate a community's organisational structures, current inter-ests, and rhetorical practices. It involves following certain conventions of impression management to project an insider status, the shared aware-ness of these conventions providing the defining feature of a community. We claim the competence to address colleagues by drawing on intertex-tual knowledge which includes typical ways of selecting and exploiting topics, referring to shared knowledge, interacting with our content and readers, and using specialised terminology. So, writing as an accountant, a magnetic physicist or a production supervisor means positioning your-self within the apparently natural borders of your community through control of its legitimate forms of discourse.

In any context, then, one discourse is likely to be dominant and hence more visible, so that writers often consciously or unconsciously take up the identity options this privileged discourse makes available (Wertsch, 1991). Scollon and Scollon (1981) use the term 'essayist literacy' to refer to the specific literacy prac-tices which are privileged in higher education. Students are typically required to adopt a style of writing at university which involves anonymising themselves and adopting the guise of a rational, disinterested, asocial seeker of truth. By stepping into an essayist literacy, writers sacrifice concreteness, empathy with discussed entities, and ways of representing change as a dynamic process. On the other hand, they gain the ability to discuss abstract things and relations, and to categorise, quantify and evaluate according to the perspectives of their disci-pline. Such gains, of course, are only perceived as such if students value what this literacy allows them to do and the kinds of people it allows them to be.

In fact, students often find that academic conventions do not allow them to represent themselves in their texts, suppressing the extent they can articulate a personal stance (Hyland, 2002). Ivanic (1998: 9) makes this clear in relation to mature students who often

> . . . feel alienated and devalued within the institution of higher education. Their identities are threatened and they respond either by attempting to

accommodate to the established values and practices of the context they are entering, or—more radically—by questioning and challenging the dominant values and practices.

In such situations, students are often uncertain about who they are expected to be and often feel more constructed by their texts than constructing them. We don't, then, blindly adopt such identities. Individuals do not define themselves only by one group membership but belong to different groups, so that their commitments and experiences often overlap and perhaps conflict. Socio-cultural factors such as gender, social class, age, religion, ethnicity, regional background and so on are key aspects of our experiences and can help shape our projection of an authorial identity.

The ways that writers present themselves and find themselves positioned in constructing a discoursal identity have been extensively discussed by Ivanic (Ivanic, 1998; Ivanic and Weldon, 1999). She argues that writers' identities are socially constructed by the prototypical 'possibilities for self-hood' available in the context of writing. Interacting with this are three inseparable aspects of the identity of actual writers when creating a particular text.

Concept 2.8   Ivanic on Writer Identity

1. **The autobiographical self** is the self which writers bring to an act of writing, socially constrained and constructed by the writer's life-history. It includes their ideas, opinions, beliefs and commitments: their stance. An example might be how a writer evaluates the quotes he or she brings into a text, or the topics he or she chooses to address.

2. **The discoursal self** is the impression writers consciously or unconsciously convey of themselves in a text. This concerns the writers' voice in the sense of how they portray themselves. An example is the extent to which a writer takes on the practices of the community he or she is writing for, adopting its conventions to claim membership.

3. **The authorial self** shows itself in the degree of authoritativeness with which a writer writes. This is the extent to which a writer intrudes into a text and claims herself as the source of its content. This would include the use of personal pronouns and willingness to personally get behind arguments and claims.

(See Ivanic, 1998; Ivanic and Weldon, 1999.)

This is a dynamic view of identity which emphasises the tensions which exist when individual writers meet the discourses of the institutions in which they write. People are constrained, but not determined, by the dominant disciplinary, professional, gender and political identities which are set up by the conventions of specific genres and the practices which surround any act of writing. We all bring multiple possibilities to any act of writing which carry the potential to challenge the pressures to conform to dominant identities.

2.5   English, Dominance and Writing

A final issue I want to address here is the language that we write in. About a quarter of the world's population now has some proficiency in English (Graddol, 2006) and the language has, quite clearly, firmly established itself as a global lingua franca in many domains, particularly published scholarship, higher education and international business. The vast majority of the research reported in this book relates to writing in English, for instance, and while the number of native speakers of English is declining as a proportion of all speakers, it is an official language of over 70 countries and studied as a foreign language by perhaps two billion people worldwide (Crystal, 2012a). This accelerating global spread of English raises huge questions concerning unequal access and opportunities, and issues related to indigenised varieties and standard language. Ammon (2001), however, asks what we mean by labeling English a *dominant language*: do we have in mind merely *prevalence*, the fact the language is used more frequently, or *domination*, that it has power and influence over others?

Originating with British colonialism and a global Empire, the spread of English became more prevalent after World War II, with the reach of American power (e.g. Ammon, 2001). It maintains this global status by taking on particular roles in government, trade and academia and through the consequent mushrooming of English varieties all over the world. Since the publication of Robert Phillipson's *Linguistic Imperialism* in 1992, debates have continued over whether the increasing presence of English as an international language should be seen as benevolent or malignant.

> **Quote 2.7   McKay on Three Main Problems of English Dominance**
>
> The main negative effects of the spread of English involve the threat to existing languages, the influence on cultural identity, and the association of the language with an economic elite.
>
> McKay (2002: 20)

Depending on one's perspective, English can be viewed as a neutral lingua franca, efficiently facilitating the free exchange of information and enabling communication between those who have no other language in common, or as an instrument of political hegemony, wiping out indigenous languages.

Certainly the massive expansion of English has had negative effects, such that in many countries, English plays gatekeeping roles regarding access to jobs, higher education and professional advancement (Phillipson, 2008). Countless students and professionals around the world must now gain fluency in the conventions of English writing to understand their fields, to establish their careers, or to successfully navigate their learning. Phillipson (1992: 47), in fact, argues that the current dominance of English is a continuation of linguistic imperialism planned through the English Language Teaching (ELT) policies. The World Bank, British Council, International Monetary Fund (IMF) and so on use ELT as a means of spreading capitalist ideologies and markets for Anglo-American companies, while ELT 'fallacies' such as the advantages of native speaker teachers, maximum exposure to English and early-start learning all helped to promote ELT into a multi-billion dollar industry.

Quote 2.8 **Benesch on ELT and Ideology**

EAP's discourse of neutrality has presented the history of this field as a consensual and inevitable chronology of pedagogical events rather than a well-crafted and organized effort on the part of governments, businesses, and foundations working together to promote English language teaching, conferences, publications, and faculty exchanges, ensuring that markets and labor would be available to promote their economic interests.

Benesch (2001: 34)

English monolingualism certainly has considerable limitations, even dangers, but while it undoubtedly benefits UK/U.S. interests and interlocks with a wider structure of U.S. dominance, it seems unlikely that there is a grand conspiracy behind its ascendancy. By emphasising the top-down imposition of English on reluctant nations, Philipson's account is over-deterministic, underplaying the role of agency and how users exercise choice. Many individuals and organisations in Asia, Europe and elsewhere are capable of making judgments about the benefits of adopting a language and using it to their gain, rather than being forced into adopting it. Nor is the spread of global English the direct cause of language endangerment, as the number of languages in the world has been falling throughout modernity and certainly before the rise of English as a global lingua franca. Nor is English the only language in global business, accounting for only around 30% of the world gross domestic product (GDP), and it is likely to account for less in the future.

Evidence for the prevalence of English in education and academia is everywhere, however, and this is where the danger of domain loss is very real. There has been, for example, a relentless shift to English as the preferred language of doctoral dissertations in Scandinavia through the twentieth century (Wilson, 2002; University of Oslo, 2006), and English has become a means of attracting fee-paying international students in many universities across Europe and Asia. Academics throughout the world are urged to publish 'their best in the west' to gain wider credit for their research. While complicated by geography and discipline (Kuteeva and Airey, 2013), academics all over the world are increasingly less likely to publish in their own languages and are likely to find their English-language publications cited more often. English is superseding many established languages, such as Swedish and Russian, for academic publishing (Hyland, 2015a). The situation in Africa, South America and Asia appears to be particularly bleak, as suggested, for example, by reports from Brazil (Meneghini and Packer, 2007) and Hong Kong (Li and Flowerdew, 2009), where many academics rarely write in any other language.

The fact that non-native speakers of English now outnumber native speakers by about four to one means that new varieties of English emerge which do not depend on either childhood acquisition or cultural identity, and which are used in contexts where no L1 English speakers are involved. This is referred to as *English as a Lingua Franca* (ELF), a variety of English which does not assume adherence to all Anglo communication conventions and where traditional native speakerness holds no advantages. Most ELF interactions take place among 'non-native' speakers of English who are not aspiring to speak or write a standard variety (Seidlhofer, 2005). What matters is clarity and comprehensibility, and L1 English speakers may need to adjust their language to new norms of international academic communication.

Quote 2.9   **Crystal: No Native Speakers on the Internet**

The internet changes everything, absolutely everything because of its anonymous character. You go to a chat room and, as soon as you're in there, the distinction between native and non-native speaker breaks down immediately because you have no idea who is there, what they're doing, what their background is, how much English they've got, where they've learnt it, or anything like that. All you've got is the evidence of the messages they have sent. Therefore, if someone uses a particular feature of English that isn't particularly standard, you don't know whether that is a learner at an early level, an advanced learner who is speaking a local variety of English or a native speaker who has made a slip: you have no idea what this is . . . what you see on the internet is a completely different scenario from what we've ever seen before; mixed standards, stylistically varied standards.

Crystal (2012b: 33)

Wikipedia is a good example of this, with the different styles of individual users contributing to the information on a page. In fact, the ubiquitous presence of the Internet in the communication practices of millions of people may be providing a new motivation for learning English, challenging the economic reasons which have generally driven learning.

In terms of spoken English, learners are increasingly likely to be less worried about sounding like a native speaker and more concerned with using English effectively in cross-cultural communication. Native-speaker norms are becoming less relevant as English becomes a component of basic education in many countries. In writing, the picture is less clear-cut, but a major challenge is the rhetorical standards demanded by editors, teachers, referees, examiners and other gate-keepers who frequently reject non-standard varieties of English. Tardy (2004), for example, found that L2 postgraduate science students felt frustrated in spending time to master a second language to communicate in English. Overall, a great deal of teaching and research writing is being done in English. Graddol (2006), in fact, argues that English is losing its position in the foreign languages curriculum, where it was taught mainly to teenagers and is now regarded as one of the basic skills students need to learn when first going to school.

It is obvious that the spread of English across the globe raises complex issues which demand a considered and sensitive response. Obviously we cannot see English as a hermetically sealed system unconnected to social, political and cultural issues, but equally it is unhelpful to regard ELF teachers as the unwitting agents of capitalist expansion.

2.6   Conclusion

This chapter has examined some of the key issues in writing today. Because it has been necessarily selective, I have chosen to look at topics which have not only motivated much recent thinking in the field but which also best illustrate where contemporary research into text and composition is going, and which reflect our current understanding about writing. Once again I have been concerned to highlight ideas which present writing as social and interactive rather than simply cognitive and individual. A text is always inextricable from the processes of production and interpretation that create it, and as we shall see in the next sections, the ways we teach and research writing have come increasingly to reflect this.

Note

1. http://www.readwriteweb.com/archives/fake_web_identity_poll_results.php retrieved 28 July 2008.

Further Reading

Barton, D. (2007) *Literacy: An introduction to the ecology of written language* (2nd edn). Oxford: Blackwell.

An exploration of competing definitions of literacy in contemporary society, and an examination of the language and learning theories which underpin new views of literacy.

Block, D. and Cameron, D. (2002) *Globalization and language teaching.* London: Routledge.

A series of papers documenting and reflecting on the impact of globalisation on language policies and practices around the world.

Clark, R. and Ivanic, R. (1997) *The politics of writing.* London: Routledge.

An absorbing discussion of issues of writer identity and writer–reader relationships.

Davies, A. (2003) *The native speaker: myth and reality.* Clevedon, UK: Multilingual Matters.

An examination of the concept of the native speaker and the kinds of knowledge this implies, concluding that the native and non-native speaker opposition is one of power.

Norton, B. (2013) *Identity and language learning: extending the conversation.* Bristol: Multilingual Matters.

A classic book which integrates research, theory and classroom practice.

3   Quandaries and Possibilities

This chapter will . . .

- follow up on some of the topics discussed in the previous chapter to explore their relevance for teaching writing;
- address a number of issues and options relating to writing instruction: *culture, digital technologies, plagiarism, error correction* and *automated marking*;
- set out the main points of these debates and their implications for teachers.

3.1   Writing Instruction and Culture

When discussing context and literacy in the previous chapter, it became clear that writers' linguistic choices are influenced by the practices they are familiar with, and this suggests that culture may play an important part in teaching, and learning, to write. Quite what these implications are for teachers, however, remain controversial.

Raymond Williams, a founder of cultural studies, said that culture was one of the most complex words in the English language (Williams, 1962). But while contested and uncertain, culture is generally understood as an historically transmitted and systematic network of meanings which allow us to understand, develop and communicate our knowledge and beliefs about the world (Lantolf, 1999). As a result, language and learning are inextricably bound up with culture. Not only are our beliefs and values reflected in and carried through language, but cultures make available certain taken-for-granted ways of organising perceptions and expectations, including those we use to learn and communicate. Language and writing are cultural phenomena and so are likely to vary in what members find familiar and acceptable. In writing instruction, this is the territory of intercultural rhetoric.

> **Quote 3.1**   **Connor on Intercultural Rhetoric**
>
> Intercultural rhetoric is the study of written discourse between and among individuals with different cultural backgrounds. By discourse I mean language use beyond the sentence as well as social and ideological

assumptions that are associated with communication. Intercultural rhetoric assumes that (1) the study of writing is not limited to texts but needs to consider the surrounding social contexts and practices (2) national cultures interact with disciplinary and other cultures in complex ways and (3) intercultural discourse encounters—spoken or written—entail interaction among interlocutors and require negotiation and accommodation.

Connor (2011: 2)

The field of intercultural rhetoric raises interesting questions for teachers about language and rhetorical choices in writing: it asks how features of discourse differ among language users and how these might influence writing in a second language. The basic idea is that students have certain preconceptions about writing, or schema, which they have learned in their own cultures or communities and which may influence how they write in English. Researchers have, however, come to be cautious in how they understand this relationship. An earlier understanding, known as contrastive rhetoric (Connor, 1996), drew on a somewhat static and deterministic view of culture and overgeneralised findings based on the writing of learners in isolation from other developmental and sociocultural factors that can influence writing (Casanave, 2004; Kubota and Lin, 2009). In Cassanave's (2004: 39) words, it ignored "the diversity, change and heteroglossia that are normal in any group of speakers or writers".

Cultures have been conflated with national entities; consensuality *within* cultures has been assumed and contrasted with differences *across* them (Atkinson, 2004). A 'received view' of culture makes it easy to see writing preferences as the outcome of fixed traits so that individuals can be lumped together and culture read off from written texts. In other words, we need to be cautious in making claims which see 'cultural patterns of rhetoric' in student texts and avoid attributing writing practice—and writing difficulties—to 'culture'. If we start with the assumption of difference, then we will invariably find difference and see writing problems as a negative transfer of L1 rhetorical patterns to L2 writing.

Quote 3.2 Canagarajah on Culture and Writing

Though difference is always going to be there in writing, and though much of it may derive from culture, the ways in which this influence takes place can be positive or negative, enabling as well as limiting, and teachers have to be aware of all these possibilities when they teach student writing. More importantly, teachers must keep in mind that no one needs to be held hostage by language and culture; students can be taught to negotiate conflicting rhetorical structures to their advantage.

Canagarajah (2002: 68)

It is, then, dangerous for language teachers to operate with a crude and un-nuanced view of culture, seeing it as a relatively stable, homogeneous and all-encompassing system of norms that determines how students write. Learners have different goals, motivations, abilities, knowledge and strategies which contribute to their success as writers and how much effort they invest in learning. However, while students will always write in ways that contradict stereotypes, it is not helpful to reduce a class full of students to a bunch of disparate individuals. To appreciate linguistic and cultural differences is to recognise that features in our students' essays may be evidence of alternative patterns and understandings, rather than of individual inability or poor study habits. Nor should we ignore research which points to differences in how group members organise their texts and achieve different rhetorical purposes.

Hinds (1990), for example, notes culturally related preferences for organising essays, with Japanese and Korean writers favouring an inductive rhetorical pattern and Anglo-American writers using a more direct, deductive style. The reason for this may be that there are greater expectations on writers to take responsibility for effective communication in English than languages such as Japanese and Finnish, where the onus is on the reader to dig out the meaning of a text. It is likely, for example, that English contains more metadiscourse signals which help guide the reader through a text (Hyland, 2005) by labelling text segments (*to conclude, in summary*), previewing text (*here we will discuss*) and explicitly structuring discussions (*I will make three points*).

Essentially, however, culture represents the lived experience of the individual and so builds on a range of sociocultural influences rather than simply national or linguistic cultures. Students have individual identities beyond the language and culture they were born into, and we should avoid stereotyping students according to crude cultural dichotomies. National cultures are themselves composed of many smaller professional, workplace, disciplinary, social and life-stage cultures which overlap, interact and may or may not influence writing. EAP, for example, has long argued the importance of specificity in writing and how genres are differently constructed in different fields of study using different argument patterns, tropes, jargon and ways of engaging with readers (e.g. Hyland, 2004a). The notion of culture therefore continues to be of considerable interest to teachers of writing because it shows us that particular writing preferences may be the result of prior learning and community expectations rather than deficit. It offers insights into writing practices and opportunities to understand students' literacy experiences.

> **Quote 3.3** **Linda Flower: Intercultural Inquiry**
>
> As an approach to talking across difference, intercultural inquiry is both an attitude and a scaffold created by literate practices. Partners in inquiry turn to literate strategies that help them to elicit something of the situated, affective, and embodied knowledge behind the speakers' words . . . to embrace these as rival interpretations; and to draw themselves into a joint, reconstructive negotiation with their own understandings. An intercultural rhetoric based on inquiry is, then, a deliberate meaning-making activity in which difference is not read as a problem but sought out as a resource for constructing more grounded and actionable understandings.
>
> Flower (2003: 40)

Turning to an emphasis on negotiation and accommodation between writers and readers of English brings us closer to how English is used as a lingua franca (part 2.5). In the classroom, teachers might use the notion of culture to generate questions for students, encouraging them to think about their educational backgrounds and writing experiences, about the sources of their writing preferences, and their beliefs, about good writing (Casanave, 2004: 53–4). Finally, a consideration of culture encourages us to reflect on our own writing practices and to see them as the result of historical and community factors rather than as a norm from which other patterns are merely deviations. The goal of L2 writing instruction can never be to bend the world's entire English-using population to the norms of a native speaker variety. Instead, teachers of writing need to be aware of different rhetorical conventions and to accept them in their learners' work.

3.2   Writing Instruction and Digital Technologies

Information and communication technologies, as discussed in Chapter 2, are having a massive impact on all aspects of writing. Reasons for writing, the genres we write, the language that we use and the nature of the audience are all changing rapidly and are being responded to by writing teachers in both first- and second-language classrooms.

Concept 3.1   Technology in the Writing Classroom

Many teachers today use commercial course management systems, such as Blackboard or Moodle, to display course materials and messages in one place and to encourage students to post online. Others have been using asynchronous (delayed) tools such as email or bulletin boards for many years to encourage student writing, and more are recognising the value of supporting students to develop and publish their own web sites so they can practice new online literacy skills. Class blogs have also been used by teachers to foster the expression of students' opinions in writing, creating both a sense of authorship and community (Bloch, 2008), while wikis are seen by some as encouraging research and collaborative posts (Beach, Anson, Kastman Breuch and Reynolds, 2014). Teachers have also turned to mobile technologies to exploit text messaging and micro-blogging and to social media as ways to engage students in authentic writing activities.

Any attempt to offer a state-of-the-art summary of information technology (IT) use in writing classrooms is doomed to fail, and overviews written just a few years ago (e.g. Warschauer, 2007) now seem dated and slightly quaint. Computers became generally available in language education in the 1980s, but today the range of technologies available has become so diverse and so much part of everyday practice that the use of the widely used term CALL (computer assisted language learning) may becoming obsolete (Dudeney and Hockly, 2012). A recent book published by the British Council on learning technologies (Motteram, 2013), for example, features case studies of a cornucopia of electronic features. While not all directly related to writing, these features include blogs, wikis, video conferencing, email, Second Life (a virtual world), talking books, Facebook and other social network sites, Skype, learner podcasts, audio blogs, online grammar quizzes and dictionaries, YouTube, Media Player, concordancers and online tools for making movies, cartoons, web sites and so on. Clearly, technology is having a profound effect on writing instruction.

Computer-mediated communication (CMC) was, until recently, mainly restricted to email (asynchronous) and instant messaging on MOOs (object-oriented multi-user dimensions/domains) or Internet Relay Chat (IRC, synchronous). Extensive research of both real-time and delayed modes has found a number of benefits for writing instruction. Not least, these tools help to foster collaboration among writers while providing students with an authentic audience and a purpose for their writing. By removing the teacher as the locus of control and encouraging more participation from less-confident students, CMC helps nurture students to develop texts which are both more accurate and lexically and syntactically more complex as well as covering a wide range of discourse functions (Warschauer, 2000). Email, because it allows time to compose a more considered response, seems to encourage greater participation among weaker writers and greater interaction between students and between students and teachers. Email also develops intercultural communication skills in writing by facilitating interaction among students of diverse backgrounds, languages and experiences (Cummins and Sayers, 1995).

The advent of the web provided teachers with a qualitatively different type of CMC, enabling students to engage in collaborative multimedia authoring rather than direct interaction. Initially, the web fulfilled a demand from teachers for authoring tools to transfer their paper tasks online, so that *Hot Potatoes* (Arneil and Holmes, 1998–2009), for example, provided templates for teachers to quickly create crosswords and tasks such as gap-filling, matching and jumbled sentences. While these tasks remain extremely popular with language teachers, many of them are now folded into virtual learning environments (VLEs) such as Blackboard and Moodle, which allow teachers to create online courses and peer communication (Suvorov, 2010). Increasingly, writing teachers have also encouraged their students to work together to create their own webpages (e.g. Bloch, 2008), some with extremely positive results particularly where students saw the task as relevant and integrated into a language programme (Warshaeur, 2000).

Concept 3.2   Web 2.0 Writing Tools

The term Web 2.0 became widespread from the mid-2000s to redefine the web as a social platform for collaboration, knowledge-sharing and networking, so that Web 1.0 was the *informational web*, and Web 2.0 is the *social web* (Pegrum, 2009: 18). The ever-growing diversity and flexibility of digital media and the ease with which they can be managed, has contributed to a massive expansion of options for teachers of writing (e.g. Thomas, 2009; Motteram, 2013). Tools such as wikis, cloud storage, teleconferencing, blogs and 3D virtual worlds like Second Life, which contains its own language school and hosts in-world annual conferences (Cooke-Plagwitz, 2008), are now common learning spaces for writing teachers.

In a survey of 2,500 U.S. teachers, the National Writing Project found overwhelming agreement that Web 2.0 tools encouraged students to be more invested in their writing by encouraging personal expression and providing a wider audience for their work, with 40% of teachers reporting that they had students share their work on wikis, web sites or blogs (Purcell, Buchanan and Friedrich, 2013). But while these tools enable students to research, present and share their projects either individually or collaboratively, 68% of the polled teachers believe digital tools make students more likely to take shortcuts and not put effort into their writing.

Tools for the collaborative creation of texts, such as Google Docs or wikispaces, are particularly productive resources for writing instructors. A wiki is a collaborative web space where pages can be created and edited by multiple users easily without any knowledge of web design. Wikis provide environments where the purposes for writing are authentic and audiences are real, while knowledge is accumulated collaboratively by groups sharing a common goal. Such groups, moreover, often expand beyond the class itself to other contributors, as Myers observes in discussing Wikipedia in Quote 3.4.

Quote 3.4   **Myers (2010) on Wiki Communities**

A sense of community is absolutely essential to Wikipedia. A look at the 'Talk' pages shows community at work, with shared norms, even if the definition of those norms is endlessly argued over. User pages show people rewarding others with recognition (often in the form of little primary-school stars) for their skills in starting articles, adding links, clearing up punctuation, getting them made feature articles or reverting vandalism. [. . .] The community around the article on a British city, Manchester, included not just local historians and enthusiasts, but contributions from around the world, many of them from people who haven't been to Manchester and know nothing at all about it, but who do hate to see a misspelling or a bad link.

Myers (2010:25)

Many teachers also now encourage their learners to blog, publishing their written work online to share their work with an audience beyond the teacher, and prepare them for post-education needs. Blogs, like wikis, allow for quick and easy publishing, but while the flexibility of wikis means they are good for project work, blogs are better as an ongoing record of classwork, as the latest work is always displayed at the top of the page. Blogs are essentially interactive, dynamic web pages. Teachers can include images they want their students to respond to, slide shows, podcasts, discussions, links, announcements, handouts, student writing or use them to create a class publication. Miller, Hafner and Ng (2012), for example, describe an EAP course project which involved students making use of a course blog along with video production and sharing software. Groups of students worked collaboratively to plan, film and share short science documentaries through video and Web 2.0. To participate, a student simply needs to sign up to a blogging web site such as *blogspot.com* or *blogger.com*. A particularly good site is *edublogs.org* because it is safe (moderated, education-specific and low risk from lurkers and stalkers) and contains instructions on how to create your own blog.

Quote 3.5 **A Writing Teacher on Blogs**

One way these tools help young writers is to see their work in another forum. Many students are used to only "desktop" publishing. They write on their desktop, finish their writing, and put it on the teacher's desk. I have found that students take a closer look at their writing when they know that the audience will include their peers. At RAW INK Online, their work is often seen by teachers and authors from outside of our school. So, students take a closer look at their blog posts and responses. Through having students share their writing with their peers in these modalities, I have seen them become more at ease with the writing process. They are more willing to put their ideas down in writing when writing for an authentic audience. The students begin to develop an awareness for the need to write/communicate in a way that makes sense to the reader and communicates clearly their intended message.

Purcell et al. (2013: 27)

Life is not always so rosy, however, and while participants in a recent survey of undergraduate teachers were interested in using blogs, some found its informal and unstructured character made it difficult to integrate into the organised flow of regular classroom teaching (Chen and Bryer, 2012).

Finally, it is worth mentioning here the growing importance of mobile technology in writing teaching (Pegrum, 2014). Portable devices such as tablet computers, smart phones and MP3 players (for podcasts) have particular value where teachers move between different locations and where learning occurs in isolated contexts. Mobile technologies free students from having to write at designated times or locations and instead allow them to write, capture, edit and publish while on the go, whether at a museum or on a beach. But while mobile assisted language learning (MALL) is growing as mobile devices become more central to our lives and evolve to perform more online tasks, their size places limits on their value as learning tools, while the willingness of students to use them for learning is greatly influenced by their ability to use necessary functions (Stockwell, 2013). Mobile devices do, however, have the potential to fit naturally into learners' everyday lives and so lower the barriers between classroom and out-of-class learning.

The last point to make is that while various Internet tools are now commonplace in many writing classrooms and are expanding rapidly, teachers remain central to instruction. In a two-year longitudinal study of an initiative by the Hong Kong government to help over 1,800 English teachers develop IT skills, for example, Wong (2013) found that the decisive factor for successful change resided with the teachers who implemented the changes in their classrooms. The advice Chapelle and Jamieson (2008) give for teaching writing with CALL thus seems appropriate in any writing classroom, whether digital technology is involved or not.

> **Quote 3.6**   **Chapelle and Jamieson on Tips for CALL Writing Teachers**
>
> 1. Select appropriate writing texts as models.
> 2. Choose CALL programs that teach genre as well as linguistic knowledge and strategies.
> 3. Teach learners how to benefit in terms of interactive help and feedback when using computers.
> 4. Create learners' opportunities to expand knowledge of English through writing and to write for real audiences.
> 5. Include explicit evaluation.
> 6. Help learners develop their writing strategies.

3.3   Writing Instruction and Plagiarism

While technology has dramatically influenced the ways we teach and understand writing, it also has its downsides, and one of the most significant of these is the role it can play in facilitating (or preventing) plagiarism.

Concept 3.3   Plagiarism

Plagiarism means using the words or ideas of another without giving appropriate credit. If exact words are used, the student must put the words in quotation marks and cite the source; and even if the student paraphrases the ideas in his/her own words, the source must be cited. It is often considered an academic 'crime', so that Plagiarism.org states, for example: "plagiarism is an act of fraud. It involves both stealing someone else's work and lying about it afterward". It therefore carries stiff penalties for both students and academics at universities, ranging from failing a course to expulsion. Nor are ignorance or lack of intent considered excuses in the eyes of the law, or by most publishers and academic institutions.

Plagiarism largely concerns writing in academia, journalism and the creative arts, so definitions are generally written to deny the 'ignorance' defence where an offender can say "I didn't know that wasn't allowed". Thus, University College London (2014) lists the following as plagiarism:

- turning in someone else's work as your own
- copying words or ideas from someone else without giving credit
- failing to put a quotation in quotation marks

- giving incorrect information about the source of a quotation
- changing words but copying the sentence structure of a source without giving credit
- copying so many words or ideas from a source that it makes up the majority of your work, whether you give credit or not

While this list only applies to words and ideas, plagiarism also includes copying or adapting pictures, data, diagrams, music or computer programmes without citing sources. As a result, it also has implications for teachers who may be used to copying a few pages from a textbook for a class or downloading pictures for a course web site.

There is, then, a sense in which plagiarism may be increasing, or at least getting more attention, with the term generating nearly 25 million hits in Google. There has been a massive growth in advice web sites and the use by universities of plagiarism detection software, such as Turnitin, which can check student written work for potential plagiarism using pattern recognition algorithms and generate a report almost instantly. Most teachers, however, probably recognise that a great deal of unattributed borrowing is evidence of lack of knowledge rather than deliberate intention to deceive. Bruton and Childers (2015) interviewees, for example, viewed most of the plagiarism they encountered as unintentional and penalised only what they considered to be extreme versions of intentional plagiarism. Yet it has been difficult to define plagiarism in a way which is unambiguous to students.

The concept of plagiarism obviously assumes that people can own ideas and combinations of words and that words can be original. The notion of 'intellectual property', however, is relatively new in the West and does not have a lot of meaning for many outside it. Pennycook (1996), for example, shows some of the complexities of Western views of textual borrowing and how culture influences the ways that students interact with texts. While it is impossible to attribute plagiarism directly to students' cultural traditions, the issue is obviously complicated by ignorance and lack of experience (Wheeler, 2009; Bloch, 2012). Moreover, the fact that plagiarism involves the re-appropriation of portions of an earlier text by a more recent one means that it is a form of intertextuality, although an unauthorised and highly stigmatising one. As discussed in Chapter 1, intertextuality refers to the relationship of a current text to prior texts and so is an inescapable aspect of communication, but it is one which requires careful handling with a repertoire of citing and referencing conventions and an idea about what constitutes an appropriate amount of borrowing and reconfiguring.

Although some students may buy off-the-peg assignments or pay for ghostwritten essays to attain unearned credit, many more commit plagiarism accidentally. They often have confused ideas about what it is, or they simply do not know how to make use of the information they find in the books they read and the web pages they access. In fact, the Internet, and particularly its evolution into the more interactive Web 2.0 form, is an environment which encourages sharing and reconfiguring content from various sources. As a result, plagiarism is easier to commit and more difficult to define. It also means that plagiarism is often not clear cut, with blurred boundaries between plagiarism and research, and between originality and authorship. A range of different kinds of practices have emerged, so that Turnitin, the producer of plagiarism-detection software, has identified a spectrum of ten distinct types which comprises almost all plagiarising strategies in student work (Turnitin, 2012).

Concept 3.4   Turnitin's Plagiarism Spectrum

Turnitin's (2012) spectrum is based on a study of thousands of plagiarised papers followed-up by a survey of 879 higher and secondary teachers regarding how prevalent and how severe these instances are. The types are tagged with Web 2.0 labels to both acknowledge the role that the Internet plays in instances of copying, and to make them meaningful for a generation of 'digital natives'. *Clone*, "an act of submitting another's work, word-for-word, as one's own", is ranked as the most common and the most serious in terms of intent. *Mashup*, which mixes copied material from different sources without citation, ranks second in prevalence but lower in the sale of severity, while *CTRL C* is the third most common and second in terms of seriousness

---

The proliferation of opportunities for students to compose texts by cutting and pasting from Internet sources creates serious problems for teachers and has come to undermine traditional views about the nature of authorship, so that individual creativity becomes *bricolage*, where the author doesn't so much *write*, but *assembles* a text from disparate sources. Over a decade ago, Bloch (2001: 225) suggested that in the future students may not need to learn these arcane rules about integrating sources but "cyberspace will have different rules regarding what is public and what is private", and this now seems to be coming about. At the same time, new conceptions of intellectual property which replace traditional copyright laws with greater opportunities for sharing work, like Open Source (*http://opensource.org/*) and Creative Commons (*http://Creative commons.org/*), are gathering momentum.

Certainly the Internet challenges teachers to consider their own position on textual borrowing and how they might best help their student writers survive in contexts where there are often strong sanctions about perceptions of plagiarism (Pecorari, 2013).

3.4   Writing Instruction and Error Correction

Perhaps no subject other than the explicit teaching of grammar has created so much controversy and disagreement in language teaching as error correction. A considerable amount of research has been invested in trying to find whether it works, what methods work best, and what students think of it. While students certainly value and want teacher corrections on their written work, and they believe that teachers who fail to provide it are not doing their job, evidence for its effectiveness in improving student writing is harder to come by.

One line of argument claims that feedback on errors to L2 students is discouraging and generally fails to produce any improvements in their subsequent writing (Polio, Fleck and Leder 1998; Fazio 2001). One reason given for this is that the teachers' feedback is often incomplete, idiosyncratic, arbitrary and, occasionally, incorrect (Zamel, 1985; Lee, 2004). This may be why some students do not pay attention to it or use it for revision or learning purposes, perhaps just checking the grade and moving on (Hyland, 2013a). In a well-known summary of the literature, Truscott (1996) saw very little benefit in this kind of feedback and argued strongly that it was the responsibility of teachers to change student attitudes regarding what they should expect from teachers. Instead, he advised teachers to adopt a 'correction-free approach' in their classes and use the time saved by dealing with errors on additional writing practice (Truscott, 1996; 2007).

Quote 3.7 **Truscott on Grammar Correction**

My thesis is that grammar correction has no place in writing courses and should be abandoned. The reasons are: (a) Research evidence shows that grammar correction is ineffective; (b) this lack of effectiveness is exactly what should be expected, given the nature of the correction process and the nature of language learning; (c) grammar correction has significant harmful effects; and (d) the various arguments offered for continuing it all lack merit.

Truscott (1996: 328)

Even though Truscott was referring only to correction which addressed grammatical errors to improve students' writing accuracy, teachers have been reluctant to follow this advice, feeling that something they spend so much time on must have some pay-off in terms of improvement. Like students, they know accuracy is important to avoid stigmatising writers when they communicate with academic and professional audiences. Research on student preferences has consistently found that students expect teachers to comment on their written errors and are frustrated if they do not (F. Hyland, 1998; Ferris and Roberts, 2001; Lee 2004). Nor is the research claiming the lack of effectiveness of error feedback as conclusive as Truscott claims (e.g. Chandler, 2003; Ferris, 2004). While there are undoubtedly variations in teachers' feedback practices, Lee's (2004) finding that half of her sample of Hong Kong teachers corrected errors inaccurately was based on a de-contextualised teacher correction task. Ferris' (2006) more naturalistic *in situ* study found teacher feedback to be overwhelmingly accurate.

It is, however, difficult to draw clear conclusions and generalisations from the literature because of varied populations, treatments and research designs (but see the discussion of Truscott, 2007, in part 6.6). Written feedback is obviously more than marks on a page and carries important information about interpersonal connections between teachers and students (Hyland and Hyland, 2001), yet research procedures often remove it from the real classrooms and teacher-student relationships within which it occurs (Goldstein 2005; Hyland and Hyland, 2006). Moreover, the view that there is no direct connection between correction and learning is greatly overstated. Ferris (2006), for example, discovered that about 80% of students in her L2 sample were able to successfully edit errors marked by teachers in a subsequent draft, with only 10% making incorrect changes. But demonstrating that a student can make use of teacher feedback to successfully edit from one draft to the next tells us little about the learner's successful acquisition of the linguistic features addressed by the feedback. It may be that writing improves by rewriting and is not evidence of *learning* (Truscott, 1996).

Concept 3.5   Treatable vs. Untreatable Errors

Ferris (1999) suggests that different types of errors "respond" differently to error treatment. Some errors, such as tenses, subject–verb agreement, run-ons, fragments, noun endings, articles, pronouns, and possibly spelling, can be considered "treatable" because they "occur in a patterned, rule-governed way". In contrast, errors such as word choice and word order are "untreatable" in that "there is no handbook or set of rules students can consult to avoid or fix those types of errors" (Ferris, 1999: 6). Teachers tend to mark "treatable" errors indirectly and "untreatable" errors directly, probably because they believe that students are unable to self-correct untreatable errors because they can't identify them.

The studies that have looked beyond immediate corrections in a subsequent draft, however, have noted improvements in students' language accuracy (Chandler 2003; F. Hyland, 2003; Bitchener, 2008). In a textual study of over 5000 teacher comments, Ferris (2006), for instance, showed that students made statistically significant reductions in their total number of errors over a semester in five major grammar categories with a particular reduction in verb and lexical errors. Students utilised more explicit 'direct' feedback more consistently and effectively than indirect types, partly as it involved simply copying the teacher's suggestion into the next draft, but less-explicit feedback also led to accurate revisions most of the time. These results underline the importance of general language proficiency and meta-lingusitic awareness in writing development so that both error correction and its effectiveness must be seen in the context of a student's evolving mastery of writing—basically, that improvement is likely to happen over time with regular writing practice, irrespective of correction.

Second-language acquisition (SLA) researchers, in fact, argue that mistakes are an important part of the complex process of acquiring the target language, which may not develop linearly but involve regression (e.g. Doughty and Long, 2003). In other words, we can't expect a target form to be acquired either immediately or permanently after it has been highlighted through feedback. Even though explicit feedback can play an important role in second-language acquisition, it needs time and repetition before it can help learners to notice correct forms, compare these with their own interlanguage, and test their hypotheses about the target language. Attempting to establish a direct relationship between corrective feedback and successful acquisition of a form is, therefore, over-simplistic and highly problematic (e.g. Ferris, Liu, Sinha and Senna, 2013).

While feedback alone will not be responsible for improvement in language accuracy, it is likely to be an important factor. One variable influencing this will be the interpersonal relations between teachers and students, and the kinds of feedback teachers give in response to particular students (F. Hyland, 1998; Hyland and Hyland, 2001). Another key issue is the type of error feedback that is given, and a number of researchers have compared the effectiveness of different teacher practices (see Concept 3.6).

Concept 3.6   What Feedback on Errors Seems to Work Best?

Based on an overview of research, Ferris et al. (2013) suggest these generalisations seem quite robust across a range of studies and contexts:

1. Focused corrective feedback, given to specific error types is more valuable than comprehensive correction of all errors noticed by the teacher (Ellis, Sheen, Murakami and Takashima, 2008; Bitchener and Knoch, 2010; van Beuningen, de Jong and Kuiken, 2012).
2. Indirect feedback, which calls the error to the student's attention but does not correct it, is more valuable for long-term improvement than where the teacher provides the right form (Ferris, 2006). This is probably because it requires students to reflect and solve the problem themselves, although where language acquisition, not writing development, is the goal, then direct correction may be more useful as it gives clear information about the targeted structures (Bitchener and Knoch, 2010; van Beuningan, et al., 2012).

> 3.   Feedback explicitly labeled with codes or other explanations may be more valuable than unlabeled feedback particularly where students have received a lot of formal grammar instruction and can make use of this meta-language (Ferris, 2006; Bitchener, 2008; Bitchener and Knoch, 2010).

Overall, students appear to attend to teacher error corrections, and in most cases use them to make accurate changes in their texts. This seems to facilitate student writing improvement both in the short term and over time, although it must be admitted that longitudinal studies rarely span more than one semester. Improvements seem to be more likely if feedback is related to instruction and if indirect feedback methods are used, so students are required to invest more effort in processing the input and noticing discrepancies in their own work and the correct pattern they are trying to employ. Importantly, however, much more research needs to be done before we have a clear idea exactly what effect teacher error feedback has on students' writing development.

3.5   Writing Instruction and Automated Marking

The importance which both teachers and students give to feedback means that responding and grading papers consumes large amounts of a teacher's time, especially with increasing class sizes and the advent of massive open online courses (MOOCs) through which universities reach out to huge numbers of students. One response to this challenge has been to develop software applications that can deliver computer-generated holistic and analytic scores derived from mathematical models based on combinations of organisational, stylistic and formal aspects of writing (Ware and Kessler, 2013).

Concept 3.7   Computer-Based Feedback

There are a number of computer applications which evaluate and score written work, some of which also provide formative feedback to the writer. These are generally known as *Automated Writing Evaluation* (AWE) systems (Warschauer and Ware, 2006) or robo-grading, and examples include *e-rater*, *MY Access*, *Holt Online Scoring*, *BETSY* and *Criterion*. Such programmes are claimed to save time, reduce costs and provide levels of reliability comparable to those attained by multiple human raters (e.g. Chapelle and Douglas, 2006; Coniam, 2009; Shermis and Hammer, 2012). It also has the potential pedagogical advantages of increasing both the frequency of feedback and widening the range of skills which are assessed (Bull and McKenna, 2004).

While automated grading systems for multiple-choice and true-false tests have been around since the very early days of CALL, the use of artificial intelligence technology to grade essays and offer feedback is relatively new. Early models calculated a score from word counts, spelling aberrations and sentence length, while current approaches are able to detect lexical-grammatical errors and organisational anomalies (Warschauer and Ware, 2006). Often programmes allow students to access planning templates and link to a range of resources while writing and then receive graphic displays and pop-up text boxes which explain how to address errors after they submit. Teachers have some flexibility by creating their own prompts and comments or selecting from those available in the programmes and classified by genre and proficiency level. Other settings, such as time limits on the writing and how many times students can revise, are also often available, as well as data storage allowing longitudinal tracking of students' progress.

Despite the apparent advantages of these automated marking and feedback programmes for teaching, research is divided on their success. Coniam (2009) and Shermis and Hammer (2012), for example, found close agreement between computer and human raters for scores awarded to exam scripts and essays, although more abstract qualities such as interest were given higher marks by humans. Perelman (2013), however, has been extremely critical of such studies, attacking Shermis and Hammer for flawed experimental design that privileged the machines. He has also gained some notoriety for writing nonsense essays that have fooled software grading programmes into giving high marks. This is possible because many computer algorithms cannot recognise the key features of good writing, such as tone, complex organisation, logical thinking, novelty and coherence (Byrne, Tang, Truduc and Tang, 2010). Instead the programmes over emphasise grammatical and stylistic errors (Cheville, 2004) and judge complexity by the average length or relative infrequency of words and average sentences per paragraph (Perelman, 2012b). Moreover, they seem unable to accurately score long and complex writing tasks which approximate to real-world writing conditions (Bridgeman, Trapani and Yigal, 2012; Perelman, 2012b; Condon, 2013).

Such programmes therefore appear unreliable as a means of measuring, and so promoting, authentic acts of writing. There is even an association in the U.S., Professionals Against Machine Scoring Of Student Essays In High-Stakes Assessment, which has collected some 5000 online signatures, including that of Noam Chomsky, opposing their use.

Quote 3.8 **Statement by 'Professionals Against Machine Scoring'**

Every year hundreds of thousands of students write essays for large-scale standardized tests. The scores are used in life-changing decisions. Students are accepted into, placed within, and rejected from educational programs.

Graduates are hired or not hired. Teachers are qualified, evaluated, promoted, and fired. Learning institutions are compared, accredited, and punished. Yet in a major disservice to all involved, more and more of these essays are scored not by human readers but by machines. Let's face the realities of automatic essay scoring. Computers cannot "read." They cannot measure the essentials of effective written communication: accuracy, reasoning, adequacy of evidence, good sense, ethical stance, convincing argument, meaningful organization, clarity, and veracity, among others.

(Retrieved from *http://humanreaders.org/petition/index.php*)

In terms of providing formative feedback, a possible advantage is that instant grading is obviously far better than traditional systems where students may wait weeks for feedback. The software can encourage students to re-take tests and re-write essays immediately to improve the quality of their answers—and the grade they get for it. Two large-scale studies of *Criterion*, which gives a holistic essay score and provides feedback on grammar, usage, mechanics and style, suggest something of this advantage. Attali (2004), for example, looked at 9275 essays by U.S. students and found that overall grades and organisation scores improved, and essay length increased, with revised submissions compared to first submissions following feedback from the programme. Ebyary and Windeatt (2010) collected qualitative data from 31 instructors and 549 Egyptian trainee EFL teachers, after which 24 of the trainees received computer-based feedback using *Criterion* on two essay drafts submitted on each of four topics. Results showed improvements in student writing and post-treatment questionnaires while interviews and focus groups revealed positive student attitudes towards the computer feedback. More recently, Li, Link and Hegelheimer's (2015) study suggests that *Criterion* can lead to increased revisions and improved accuracy from a rough to a final draft, although students' and instructors' views of the programme very much depend on the pedagogy employed.

However, while immediate feedback supports the conditions required for learning, teachers remain skeptical about its value as a grading tool (e.g. Fang, 2010) and Chen and Cheng (2006) report learners being dissatisfied with the grade they were awarded and with both the accuracy of feedback on content and the rhetorical aspects of their writing. One unrecognised danger is that when the scoring criteria of such programmes are made available, then it becomes an easy matter for writers (or perhaps automated writers) to create essays that are customised to please the grading bot. So while the technology is unlikely to teach people to write, it may teach them how to tune their writing to get the best grade.

Positive student and teacher perceptions, of course, may be greater where the software is used regularly for pre-writing and drafting. Some students, moreover, seem to respond to a computer as if it were a human marker when correcting very short texts of 20 words, while others seem very aware that they are being marked by a machine (Jordan, 2012). Ultimately, however, all an algorithm can do is quantify deviations from a benchmark: it cannot provide an emotional response to students' writing, however good it may be at analysing the structural elements. It remains unclear, then, whether students will be encouraged to rewrite an essay again and again for a machine, as the blogger in Quote 3.9 suggests.

Quote 3.9 A Blogger on Automated Marking

I wonder what the implications are (or will be) on students' motivation, and quality of their effort and work? Students spend time on writing essays, some more than others, yet for students to know that a real person will not be reading their essay, could impact many processes. My teenagers have been exposed to automated grading periodically at their high school and they both strongly dislike it (despise it is a more fitting term). They discount its value completely. I predict that teenagers and young college students will not be receptive to this type of grading. Why should they spend hours researching, writing and re-writing an essay when they know no one (a real person) will even read it? Even more so in a MOOC that is not for credit, why on earth would you write an essay for an automated grader?

(Retrieved from *http://onlinelearninginsights.wordpress.com/2013/04/12/ providing-student-with-feedback-instructor-or-machine/*)

There are, however, growing commercial and institutional incentives pushing automated marking, especially as a solution to growing class sizes and large numbers of distance students taking MOOCs. Harvard and MIT, for example, are part of a consortium offering courses on the Internet and have recently introduced an automated grading system which is available free on the web to any institution that wants to use it (Markoff, 2013). It is likely, therefore, that automated scoring will become an increasingly prominent feature of writing instruction and assessment in the future.

3.6 Conclusion

This chapter has explored some of the continuing challenges and dilemmas for teachers of writing. I have sketched what research has to say and what course developers and technology has to offer us as well as the potential of these offerings to address key issues in writing instruction. Some of these issues, of course, technology itself has exacerbated as well as sought to solve. While I have tried to set these issues out as fairly as I can, I have also taken a stance and expressed an argument which I hope readers will engage with and consider when planning their own courses, classes and research projects.

Further Reading

Bloch, J. (2008) *Technologies in the second language composition classroom.* Ann Arbor, MI: University of Michigan Press.

A comprehensive and accessible volume supporting teachers to adopt technologies in writing teaching.

Connor, U. (2011) *Intercultural rhetoric in the writing classroom.* Ann Arbor, MI: University of Michigan Press.

An accessible treatment of culture and how it can impact on writing.

Myers, G. (2010) *The discourse of blogs and wikis.* London: Bloomsbury.

An excellent textbook on the subject.

Pecorari, D. (2013) *Teaching to avoid plagiarism: how to promote good source use.* Maidenhead: Open University Press.

What it says in the title—a critical and interesting book on the notion of plagiarism and teaching to help students avoid it.

Section II
Researching Writing

4   Research Practices and Issues

This chapter will . . .

* introduce the key features and steps of small-scale writing research;
* outline some areas of writing which are amenable to small-scale research;
* provide an overview of the main approaches typically used in writing research;
* give advice on conducting research projects of your own into texts, writers and readers.

In Section I of this book I focused on areas of theoretical and practical concern, outlining what we know about writing, some of the things we don't know, and key issues these understandings raise for practitioners. I have said little, however, about how teachers, students and researchers go about studying writing. Teachers, in fact, often see teaching and research as entirely separate things, one practical and the other rather esoteric, so that research is regarded as an activity unrelated to their everyday work. They may even feel apprehensive at the prospect of it. Research, however, is a practical activity which, by revealing some of the mysteries of texts and how we write and use them, is central to what we do as teachers.

In other words, as Stake (1995: 97) observes, "research is not just the domain of scientists, it is the domain of craftspersons and artists as well, all who would study and interpret". Because it stimulates curiosity, clarifies classroom observations, and helps develop a critical perspective on practice, research is at the heart of professional development. It transforms personal understandings into informed awareness. This section therefore turns to look at research in more detail, providing something of a practical guide to some key methods and researchable areas, with this chapter introducing approaches to writing research.

4.1   Practitioner Research

Small-scale practitioner studies have always been important in writing research. Often these originate in the curiosity of individual teachers and a desire to understand something of the texts they present in their classes, the ways their students write, or how target communities use the texts that are important to them. The systematic study of practice therefore provides a basis for theoretical reflection and modelling which in turn feeds back into, and improves, that practice. This kind of enquiry is often called *action research.*

Concept 4.1   Action Research

Action research is the process of progressive problem-solving by collecting and analysing data to improve some original action. It is typically seen as 'empowering' teachers by giving them deeper insights and understanding of their practices. Unlike classic controlled experimental models of research which are based on objectivity and control, action research is often more pragmatic, employing methods which address issues of concern most effectively. This is not only a very accessible type of research for practitioners and students, but is also often regarded as an essential form of professional development as it encourages us to address problems in our own professional lives.

Burns (2013) points out that action research involves two related forms of activity: 'action', where participants enact plans embedded in their daily lives, and 'research', where they systematically investigate the impact and meanings of these plans. It is said to democratise research by putting it into the hands of teachers, and to professionalise teachers by giving them new skills and knowledge to enact syllabus or curriculum directives. Beyond this, however, we might want to consider topics which are not restricted to bringing about an improvement in the participants' work situation or enhancing collegiality in a workplace. The diversity of the research field suggests many potential areas of enquiry and lines of investigation which can involve methodologies which go beyond those of action research. These might include quantitative as well as qualitative methods and approaches which require the researcher to be an outsider rather than a participant in the context. It might generate theoretical as well as practical knowledge and may emerge from something we read as much as something we confront in our classrooms, beginning with our curiosity, interest or intuition rather than a practical problem to solve.

Here, then, I include not only problem-driven studies which have an immediate pay-off, but also studies motivated by simple inquisitiveness. My frame for this section therefore goes beyond action research as it is traditionally understood to consider a wider range of issues and a broader set of methods.

Cohen, Manion and Morrison (2013) provide some guidelines for those embarking on this kind of research:

1. Identify a problem you see as important.
2. Focus the issue and clarify objectives by talking to co-workers, administrators, etc.
3. Review what has already been written about the issue.

4. Restate the problem as a hypothesis or research questions.
5. Specify the research design in terms of participants, methods and data sources.
6. Clarify how you will evaluate the project.
7. Collect the data.
8. Analyse the data, draw inferences, and evaluate the results.

While there are other models, this list provides a helpful overview of the steps involved.

In addition, it is important to recognise that writing research does not simply involve fitting suitable methods to particular questions. Methods are inseparable from theories and how we understand writing itself. As I sketched out in Chapter 1, for some people, writing is an artefact of activity which can be studied independently of users by counting features and inferring rules. For others, it is a pattern of choices influenced by experience, purposes and contexts. Others see it is a kind of cognitive performance which can be modelled by analogy with computer processing through observation and recording what writers say when they write. Yet others understand writing as the ways we connect socially to construct our worlds, and still others see it as the carrier of ideologies and a system of control. In other words, while different methods will tell us different things about writing, they always start with our preconceptions.

Concept 4.2   Researching Writing

Research originates where theory and practice intersect, arising from a need to clarify what people do in certain situations and why. The ways individuals write, the issues they consider when composing, the texts they produce, the influence of contexts, purposes and creativity on style, and the strategies writers use to understand writing and improve their practices are all major areas of research. Our ability to answer these questions, and the bigger issues about expertise, literacy, community, pedagogy and genre which underlie them, is always going to be contingent on the context that is studied. This is the principle of 'it depends', and it informs all research. To be answerable, our questions must relate to specific students, writers, texts, users or practices, and this makes small-scale research as valuable to the accumulation of our understanding of writing as much larger government-funded projects. So in conducting small-scale research which focuses on the specific issues that concern us, we are also nibbling away at the larger questions which occupy our profession.

This chapter therefore turns to address research more directly, to offer something of a practical guide and overview on writing research. First I outline the features of research and the main ways that writing research is conducted, and then I go on to suggest some research topics.

4.2 Research Design

Research is a way of knowing which is seen as more reliable than everyday understandings and accepted truths. It often begins by isolating something that interests or worries us and then asking questions about it. We then go on to make those questions concrete by collecting and analysing data about the issue, what is often seen as the core of research. But while this is a common enough picture, there is no 'one-size-fits-all' formula to carrying out research on writing or on anything else. Nunan and Bailey (2009) provide a useful set of questions to guide the design of a research project (Concept 4.3).

Concept 4.3 Project Design (Based on Nunan and Bailey, 2009: 75)

Area	Question
Question	Is the question worth investigating? Is the question feasible? What are the constructs underlying my question? How will these be operationalised?
Design	Does the question suggest an experimental or a non-experimental design?
Method	What methods are available for investigating the question? Which of these are feasible, given available resources and expertise? Is it possible to use more than one data-collection method?
Analysis	Does my research involve statistical or interpretive analysis, or both? Do I have the skills to carry out this kind of analysis? What skills do I need?
Presentation	What is the best way for me to publish my research?

It is not only researcher preferences and preconceptions which influence research decisions, but also the topic studied, the context, the access one has to data, and the time and resources which are available to us. Despite differences, however, there are a number of key features of a good research project:

1. *Original*—The study is not aiming to tell us something we don't already know.
2. *Valuable*—It is worth doing, that the results will be useful or interesting in some way.

3. *Feasible*—It can be done. The project is realistic in the time frame and man-ageable given access to data and other resources such as time, money and literature, as well as the knowledge and competence of the research team.
4. *Ethical*—There are procedures to protect the participants, ensuring that they know the aims of the project, what information is sought, how it will be used and who will have access to it. They should also know that they have the right to anonymity, to withdraw, or to veto the release of data.
5. *Valid*—The research will answer the questions it has set itself, and the results can be trusted.

The question of *validity* is worth dwelling on for a moment as it refers to the appropriateness of the interpretations we make of our results and so the confidence we can have in our research. Together with *reliability*, which concerns how consistently the method comes up with the same findings across different repetitions of use, validity involves decisions about 'objectivity', rigour and generalizability and so raises some thorny issues for researchers. Practitioner research is often small-scale, local, under-resourced and unpredictable, and so it has trouble persuading others of its validity. Against this, champions of practitioner research argue that its validity is actually dynamic and subject to variation, determined by the changing directions of the research. The term 'validity', in fact, is associated with positivist views of research familiar to those working in the hard sciences which aim at securing objectivity by testing hypotheses through structured and controlled procedures. The researcher approaches an issue from the outside, working to discover facts about something that can be observed, measured and compared with precision, using quantitative methods which express results numerically.

Qualitative researchers, in contrast, argue that it is important to understand a situation from the participants' perspectives and is more inductive and exploratory. There is no attempt to control the situation because behaviour is seen as subjective and relating closely to its context, which means that the researcher focuses on instances and does not seek to generalise to other situations (Denzin and Lincoln, 2011). Instead of validity, then, researchers talk of 'credibility' or 'trustworthiness'.

Quote 4.1 Burns on 'Trustworthiness'

Trustworthiness refers to whether the data analyses, reports and interpretations constitute honest and authentic reconstruction of the research and of the knowledge that emerged in the social environment, while the value accruing to participants in undertaking the research contributes to its worthwhileness.

Burns (2010: 85)

In fact, writing studies often combine several methods to gain a more complete picture of a complex reality. The concept of *triangulation*, or the use of multiple data sources, investigators, theories or methods, is important as an alternative to traditional methods of validation by bringing greater rigour, complexity and depth to a study (Flick, 2007).

Certain methods suit some questions better than others, of course, so that exploring the effect of a writing prompt would suggest analysing student scripts and interviewing writers to see how they understood the prompt, while examining the effect of error correction codes on revision might involve an experimental study with a treatment group of writers receiving feedback with codes and a control group getting another kind of response. But it is also the case that different methods are associated with particular ways of understanding writing, so an intervention such as the feedback example assumes that we can isolate a particular feature and study it outside of contexts where it has meaning for participants. This contrast between *elicited* and *naturalistic* data is important in deciding research approaches; that is, whether data is to be gathered in controlled conditions or in everyday situations which are not specifically set up for the research.

Concept 4.4   Naturalistic vs. Experimental Research

Writing research tends to favour data gathered in naturalistic rather than controlled conditions. As a result, it differs from positivistic, more quantitative research in terms of how it views reality, the relationship of the researcher to the research subject, issues of generalizability, and causality. While methods that elicit data through questionnaires, structured interviews or experiments can provide interesting and useful insights into writing, data collected via observations or analyses of authentic texts are more common.

While no data can ever be free of the effects of the researcher collecting it, more interventionist research methods risk producing data that is simply the product of an artificially contrived situation. To avoid this, ethnographic methods have been used to collect data from real-life situations which are, as far as possible, undistorted by the researcher and faithful to the reality experienced by participants. Whatever the approach, however, the goal of research is to learn more about the topic under study, and this means letting go of our preconceptions and allowing ourselves to be surprised.

4.3   Research Methods

The main methods for researching writing are summarised in Concept 4.5 (based on Hyland, 2003: 253) and discussed briefly below.

Concept 4.5   Main Methods for Investigating Writing

Questionnaires: focused elicitations of respondents' reports about actions and attitudes

Interviews: flexible and interactive elicitations by respondents of beliefs and actions

Focus groups: specific issues discussed by participants in an interactive group setting

Tests: formal elicitation of language samples in constrained conditions

Verbal reports: introspective accounts made during or after composing

Written reports: diary or log accounts of writing or learning experiences

Auto-ethnography: self-reflection of researcher's personal experience

Observations: direct or recorded data of 'live' interactions or writing behaviour

Text analysis: study of authentic examples of writing from a natural context

Experiments: manipulation of a context to study a single feature under controlled conditions

Case studies: multiple techniques focusing on a single individual or situation

Ethnographies: various techniques to capture the experiences of participants in a situation.

Syntheses: systematic, empirical and evaluative review of past literature on a topic

---

4.3.1   *Elicitation: Questionnaires, Interviews, Focus Groups and Tests*

These are the main methods for eliciting self-report information and performance data.

Questionnaires are widely used for collecting large amounts of structured, easily analysable self-report data. The researcher does not manipulate the setting but seeks information about text users' characteristics, beliefs or attitudes, information that is not usually available from production data such as observation of their behaviour or texts. Like interviews, they allow researchers to tap people's views and experiences of writing, but they are more quantitative and conclusive. Questionnaires are particularly useful for exploratory studies into attitudes to writing and for identifying issues that can be followed-up later by more in-depth methods. They will often have both qualitative (open-ended) and quantitative (closed) components. One major use of questionnaires in writing research has been to discover the kinds of writing that target communities require. Evans and Green (2007), for example, used a questionnaire to survey

5,000 Hong Kong students about the difficulties they experience when studying through the medium of English, identifying problems of style, grammar and cohesion.

Interviews offer more interactive and less predetermined modes of eliciting information than surveys and so allow greater flexibility and potential for elaboration. Although sometimes little more than oral questionnaires, interviews generally represent a very different way of understanding human experience by regarding knowledge as generated between people rather than as objectified and external to them. Participants are able to discuss their interpretations and perspectives, sharing what writing means to them rather than responding to preconceived categories. This flexibility and responsiveness means that interviews are used widely in writing research to learn more about writing practices, such as what people do in approaching a writing task, about teaching and learning writing, and about text choices, to discover how text users see and respond to particular features of writing. Interviews are particularly valuable as they can reveal issues that might be difficult to predict, such as the kinds of problems that students might have in understanding teacher feedback (Hyland and Hyland, 2006), and they can be used to feed into questionnaire design.

Focus groups are groups of people with some similar characteristics who are brought together to discuss an issue in depth. They are more interactive than interviews as participants are free to talk with other group members, and they are generally seen as less-threatening contexts for gathering information about group perspectives and practices. So while they take some control away from the interviewer, they can produce richer data. One problem, however, is that what participants tell the researcher is shared with other group participants as well, raising privacy concerns and limiting the kinds of topics that the researcher can pursue. Usually conducted face-to-face, focus groups may also be held as synchronous computer-mediated sessions where transcripts can be saved and considered later. Groups have been used to discover students' academic writing needs (Zhu and Flaitz, 2005) and both students' and teachers' perspectives on a new programme in Hong Kong (Lo and Hyland, 2007).

Tests are perhaps the most common way that teachers elicit performance information from students, discovering what it is they know, can do or are able to remember in writing. By tests, I am including here one-shot essays and other short written pieces which are assigned to evaluate students. The information gathered from what students produce in response to a prompt or set of questions offers insights into students' writing ability and knowledge of genre, language forms and rhetorical understandings which can allow comparisons with other groups or previous performances or wash back into teaching practices. Indirectly, tests can also provide information about rater behaviour and judgements of good writing. Weigle (1999), for example, investigated how experienced and inexperienced raters scored essays written by ESL writers on two different prompts, finding that inexperienced raters were more severe on one prompt but that differences between the two groups were eliminated following rater training.

4.3.2 Introspection: Verbal and Written Reports

The use of verbal reports as data reflects the idea that the process of writing requires conscious attention and that at least some of the thought process involved can be recovered, either by talking aloud while writing or as retrospective recalls.

Think Aloud Protocols (TAPs) involve participants writing in their normal way but instructed to verbalise what they are doing at the same time, so that information can be recorded on their decisions, strategies and perceptions as they work. Think aloud data have been criticised as offering an artificial and incomplete picture of the complex cognitive activities involved in writing. For one thing, many cognitive processes are routine and internalised operations, and therefore not available to verbal description, while, more seriously, the act of verbal reporting may distort the process being reported on. But despite these criticisms, the method has been widely used, partly because the alternative— deducing cognitive processes from observations of behaviour—is less reliable. The technique has been productive in revealing the strategies writers use when composing, particularly what students do when planning and revising texts, so that de Larios, Murphy and Manchon (1999), for instance, used it to examine what students did when they were blocked by a language problem. Stimulated recalls, on the other hand, involve videotaping the writer while writing, then discussing the writer's thought processes while watching the video together immediately afterwards, such as Lei's (2008) study of student writing strategies.

Diaries offer another way of gaining introspective data. These are first-person accounts of a writing experience, documented through regular entries in a journal and then analysed for recurring patterns or significant events. Diarists can be asked to produce 'narrative' entries which freely introspect on their learning or writing experiences, or follow guidelines to restrict the issues addressed. These can be detailed points to note ('what do you think your readers know about this topic?') or a loose framework for response ('note all the work you did to complete this task'). Alternatively, researchers may ask diarists to concentrate only on 'critical incidents' of personal significance or to simply record dates and times of writing. While some diarists may resent the time and intrusion this involves, diaries provide a rich source of reflective data which can reveal social and psychological processes difficult to collect in other ways. Thus, Marefat (2002) used diaries to discover how her 80 Farsi-speaking undergraduates reacted to class events, materials and the instructor herself in an EFL writing course. The approach provided a rich account of students' reflections on particular areas of difficulty and interest, thus leading her to revise the syllabus and materials.

Auto-ethnography is a type of self-reflection that explores the researcher's personal experience and connects this to wider cultural, political and social meanings (e.g. Maréchal, 2010). Unlike ethnography, it focuses on the writer's subjective experience rather than the beliefs and practices of others. The potential benefits of auto-ethnography are that research of such a personal nature might provoke insight into often overlooked problems, such as the nature of identity, race, sexuality, life in academia, etc. While principally aimed at helping the researcher make sense of his or her individual experience, auto-ethnographies are also political, as they often challenge us to consider things or to do things differently. An example in writing research is the use of auto-ethnography by Chamcharatsri (2009), who found it to be a valuable tool for L2 learners, allowing them to explore and reflect on their cultural background and identities in a U.S. university. He found, citing Canagarajah (2002: 149), that it gave the learners an opportunity to explore and value their own experiences ". . . [to] liberate them and make them 'truly creative in ˙integrating experience, imagination, and knowledge . . .'"

4.3.3   *Observations*

While elicitation and introspective methods provide reports of what people *say* they think and do, observation methods offer actual evidence of it by systematic documentation of participants engaged in writing. They are based on conscious noticing and precise recording of actions as a way of seeing these actions in a new light. Once again, the researcher can impose different degrees of structure on the data, from simply checking pre-defined boxes at fixed intervals or every time a type of behaviour occurs, to writing a full narrative of events. The most highly structured observations employ a prior coding scheme to highlight significant events from the mass of data that taped or live observation can produce (see Hyland, 2003, for examples). All observation will privilege some behaviours and neglect others, as we only record what we think is important; but while a clear structure is easier to apply and yields more manageable data, such pre-selection may ignore relevant behaviour that wasn't predicted. Hopkins (2008) gives several examples of classroom observation studies, but this is often combined with other methods, as in Louhiala-Salminen's (2002) study of a business manager's discourse activities through one day. In addition to observation, oral encounters were tape-recorded and copies were taken of the written materials, and these data were supplemented with interviews.

4.3.4   *Text Data*

A major source of data for writing research is writing itself: the use of texts as objects of study. Texts can be approached in a variety of ways: to see how they operate as systems of choices, how they embody and realise institutional power and ideologies, how they differ across languages and the first language of their authors, how they express group membership and social identities, and how they combine and link to other texts.

Quote 4.2 **Connor on Text Analysis**

Text analysis describes texts and evaluates their quality, both from the viewpoint of texts that learners produce as well as the kinds of texts they need to learn to produce. Text analysis can help ESL researchers, teachers, and language learners identify rules and principles of written or spoken texts at a variety of levels: sentences, sentence relations, and complete texts. This research orientation differs from traditional linguistic analysis in two major ways: (a) It extends analysis beyond the level of sentence grammars, and (b) it considers the multidimensional, communicative constraints of the situation.

Connor (1994: 682)

Text analysis embraces a number of different tools and attitudes towards texts. Sometimes researchers work with a single text, either because it is inherently interesting or because it seems to represent a particular genre. A major policy speech, a newspaper editorial or an essay can offer insights into forms of persuasion, particular syntactic or lexical choices, or the writer's use of particular strategies to engage readers. Bhatia (1993) and Bawarshi and Reiff (2010) suggest steps for conducting genre analyses, emphasising the importance of locating texts in their contexts. While it is not necessary to follow all the stages, nor in the order suggested, it is a useful heuristic when considering text research following an English for Specific Purposes (ESP) approach.

Quote 4.3 **Bhatia on Doing Genre Analysis**

1. Collect samples of a genre that interests you—more samples show features more clearly.
2. Use your background knowledge to put the text in a context—where the genre is used, by whom, who for and why it is written the way it is.
3. Survey the existing research literature to learn more about it.
4. Refine your understanding of the community that use the genre—what are their goals?
5. Decide what you want to study (moves, lexis, cohesion, etc.) and analyse the text.
6. Check your analysis with a regular user of the genre to confirm your findings and insights.

Bhatia (1993: 22–34)

Analysis of a single text can reveal important features, but representative-ness is strengthened if evidence can be secured from several texts, and corpus analysis is helpful here as it represents a speaker's experience of language in some restricted domain, thereby providing a more solid basis for text descrip-tions. A corpus provides an alternative to intuition by offering both a resource against which intuitions can be tested and a mechanism for generating them. The key starting points are *frequency* and *association*. *Frequency* is the idea that if a word or pattern occurs regularly in a genre, then we can assume it is significant in that genre. *Association* refers to the ways features combine or are normally found together in collocational patterns, pointing to common usage in the genre.

4.3.5 *Experimental Data*

Experimental methods are set up to discover if one variable influences another by holding other factors constant and varying the treatment given to two groups. Statistical tests are then carried out on the data to find if differences between the control and the experimental groups are significant. Writing research largely tends to be dominated by a 'relativist' orientation which rejects this 'rational-ist' position in favour of more qualitative, natural and 'thicker' data collection techniques. There are, however, contexts in which they may be appropriate. One example is Truscott and Hsu's (2008) study of the influence of corrective feedback on learning. In this study, learners wrote an in-class narrative which they revised during the next class. Half the students had their errors underlined and used this feedback in the revision task while the other half did the same task without feedback. Results matched those of previous studies in that the underline group was significantly more successful than the control group. One week later, all students wrote a new narrative as a measure of short-term learn-ing, but the two groups were virtually identical in the change in error rate from the first narrative to the second. This suggests that improvements made during revision are not evidence of learning.

While this is a good example of how experimental research can apply to writing and so feed back into teaching, results of experimental studies should be treated cautiously. Classrooms are not laboratories, and there are serious difficulties of holding all non-experimental variables constant in natural set-tings. Differences in teaching styles, learner preferences, teacher attitudes, peer relationships, and so on can all influence results, and experimental meth-ods are best combined with other forms of data if used at all.

4.3.6 *Case Studies*

Case studies are not an actual method but the investigation of a single instance, usually a writer, a context, or set of texts, explored as a totality using a range of methods. Case studies attempt to provide a rich and vivid description of real people acting in real situations, blending description and analysis to understand actors' perceptions and experiences. Their strength lies in their potential for revealing the complexity and interactions in a context, and although this often means they are of limited generalisability, others may recognise them as representing aspects of their own experience. On the minus side, the very richness and variety of the data collected can mean that cases are difficult to organise and keep track of (Cohen, Manion and Morrison, 2013). Case studies can comprise various methods and are often closely associated with ethnographic approaches, although they do not always carry the researcher's commitment to research which 'will convey the subjective reality of the lived experience of those who inhabit' the research site (Pole and Morrison, 2003: 16).

An example of a case study is Yi's (2007) examination of one Korean high school student's composing practices outside of school. The findings revealed the diversity and richness of her involvement with multiple literacies and genres in her voluntary composing practices. In presenting the student's story as a case study, the research helps to build an understanding of out-of-school writing as experienced by students with immigrant backgrounds.

4.3.7 Ethnography

Ethnography focuses on the direct observation of behaviour within particular settings to understand that behaviour and reality from the perspectives of those involved in it. It is labour-intensive and requires plenty of time, energy and resources (Hesse-Biber and Leavy, 2006). Ethnographic research seeks to provide a rich (or 'thick') description and interpretive explanatory account of what people do in a classroom, lab, cattle auction or whatever, as well as the outcome of their interactions in that setting and how they understand what they are doing.

> **Quote 4.4** **Harklau on Ethnography**
>
> The term ethnography refers to a range of diverse and ever-changing research approaches . . . characterised by first-hand, naturalistic, sustained observation and participation in particular social setting. The purpose of ethnography is to come to a deeper understanding of how individuals view and participate in their own social and cultural worlds.
>
> Harklau (2005: 179)

Ethnographic approaches thus take a more contextual view of writing than positivist approaches and presuppose a more prolonged engagement with the research site (Pole and Morrison, 2003). They also use different methods, favouring descriptive observation, participant observation, reflective and indepth interviews, focus group discussions, narrative diaries, and the analyses of documents and texts. An important dimension of any ethnographic study is obviously the part played by language, but language is considered within the context of its production and reception, rather than in isolation simply as text. Studies with an in-depth emphasis on the latter have become known as *textographies* (Swales, 1998). It also involves collecting and analysing this data without any pre-set categories or explicit hypotheses, typically following a general interest in an issue or problem. While sometimes criticised for a lack of generalizability to other settings, a strength of this kind of research is that it allows for a detailed explanation and understanding of what is specific to a particular group. This also encourages us to take research out of the classroom and into the community, investigating people's everyday writing practices.

4.3.8   Research Syntheses

A research synthesis, or systematic review, aims to provide an exhaustive summary of current literature relevant to a research question. It differs from a traditional literature review by adopting an empirical perspective, being as exhaustive as possible, and not taking the claims of report authors at face value. It uses an explicit approach and aims to identify what can reliably be said on the basis of these studies, recording why papers may have been screened out and what criteria were used to evaluate those included (Petticrew and Roberts, 2006; Wardlaw, 2010). They therefore go beyond the individual results contained in the original studies to produce synthetic findings. Essentially the method has a positivist and quantitative orientation (Ortega, 2015) which reflects its origins in the social sciences and wide use in assessments of clinical trials in health care. The *Cochrane Handbook* gives steps for preparing a review and a guide to a typical structure.

Quote 4.5   **The *Cochrane Handbook* Steps for Conducting a Review**

1. defining the review question(s) and developing criteria for including studies
2. searching for studies
3. selecting studies and collecting data
4. assessing risk of bias in included studies
5. analysing data and undertaking meta-analyses
6. addressing reporting biases
7. presenting results and "summary of findings" tables
8. interpreting results and drawing conclusions

Higgins and Green (2011)

The need for appropriate methods for syntheses of qualitative studies have been proposed, such as Noblit and Hare's (1988) *meta-ethnography*, and a number of systematic meta-analyses of writing, particularly the effect of feedback, have been conducted (e.g. Truscott, 2007). Norris and Ortega (2006) have published a collection which exemplifies the methodology for conducting synthesis research in applied linguistics.

4.4   Research Topics

While research on writing can be done in a variety of ways and for different purposes, it essentially seeks to discover what texts are like and how people write and use them in specific contexts. Some topics will be more relevant in first-language contexts and others in L2, but research is almost certain to address questions in one or more of the areas of the framework of text, writer and reader outlined in Chapter 1. While research in one area can clearly illuminate another, this is once again a useful way of exploring potential research topics.

4.4.1   *Researching Texts*

Perhaps most current research on writing looks at describing and explaining how texts work, largely driven by the massive increase in second-language writers who are required to produce work in English for their work or study. Texts can be explored in various ways, including the frequency and use of specific features such as tense, lexis or cohesion; they can be examined for particular discourse features such as interpersonal marking, hedging or move structure; and they can be measured for the quality of student writing or its improvement over time. We can examine a text in isolation or as a sample from a single genre, a single discipline or a single writer, and we can compare the work of writers of different proficiencies, genres, time periods, first-language backgrounds or social contexts. Some of these issues are very tricky to operationalise in a study: how do we ensure that the genres we are examining from different cultures are comparable (Cassanave, 2004)? How do we identify moves in a text (Hyland, 2004b)? How can we measure linguistic accuracy (Polio and Shea, 2014) or writing improvement (McCarthey, Guo and Cummins, 2005)?

Researchers examine students' writing for various reasons, but a common one is to study the effect of some intervention, such as the impact of different essay prompts on linguistic performance (Kuiken and Vedder, 2008), the type of feedback given (Bitchener and Knoch, 2010), the professional development of teachers on writing (Johnson, 2011), or the impact of peer-response training (Min, 2006). Such studies often use an *experimental* design to test the impact of the independent variable (such as the peer-feedback training) on the dependent variable (the improvement of texts). Other research of this type is *correlational* in that the researcher seeks to measure the relationship, or co-variation, between two or more dependent variables, such as students' ability to speak French and their ability to write it. An example is Helms-Park and Stapleton's

(2003) study which found little evidence of a relationship between features of L1 'voice' and the quality of L2 academic essays as rated by three raters.

Text research, however, also draws heavily on genre and corpus analyses, examining either individual texts or collections of texts to find salient patterns or features, or how particular functions, such as making claims or changing a topic, are expressed. Again, teachers often undertake such research to describe the texts their students need to write to succeed in their studies or their future jobs. Recent topics of interest in the corpus study of texts include exploring the phraseological competence of L2 writers (Adel and Erman, 2012; Bestgen and Granger, 2014) and the creation of discipline-specific word lists based on the most frequent words in a specialised corpus such as nursing (Yang, 2015) and engineering (Ward, 2009). Finally, there is enormous scope for new researchers to usefully replicate studies they find in the literature. Replication studies repeat, either exactly or approximately, a previous study to discover if its findings are reliable and/or can be generalised to other participants and circumstances (Porte, 2012).

Concept 4.6   Some Researchable Questions on Texts

- What writing tasks are typical in a particular context (e.g. a workplace or classroom)?
- How are the genres linked together in a context and how do they relate to speech and reading in that context?
- What are these texts like in terms of their typical lexical, grammatical or discoursal features?
- How are particular meanings typically expressed in this genre?
- What is the purpose of a given genre (persuasion, description, explanation, entertainment, information), and how is this achieved through its structure and language?
- Does a genre in one context, such as a course or discipline, differ from the same genre in another?
- What can specific text features tell us about the assumptions or identities of the writer?
- What can text features tell us about the contexts in which the text is used?
- Do the target text(s) exhibit intertextuality and what is the source of this?
- What writing features are typical of a particular group of writers?
- Do these features differ from those in texts produced by other writers?
- Can these differences be explained by reference to language proficiency or L1 conventions?
- What teaching interventions might best assist learners towards producing better texts in a given context?

4.4.2 Researching Writers

In addition to knowing *what* written texts are like, research also addresses *what writers do* when they write, and often too, *how* they can be helped to do it better. This involves focusing research more on the writers themselves, and so on some part of the writing process, rather than on the outcomes of writing; and this means asking different questions and using different methods. While intervention studies are employed here to examine the effects of instructional treatments on writing behaviour, most of these studies involve the researcher in observing writers at work and collecting self-report data of various kinds to understand their perceptions of what they are doing. While many of the research methods used to investigate writers originated in psychology, they are now widely used to explore how contextual factors shape writing decisions and practices. Semi- and un-structured interviews, Think Aloud Protocols, stimulated recalls, reflective diaries, observations, and analyses of peer or teacher–student interactions now represent standard practices in writing research. These qualitative methods allow researchers to explore the context-dependent nature of writing events as they occur, or soon after they are completed, examining what is regular and what is idiosyncratic about them.

Quote 4.6 **Denzin and Lincoln on Qualitative Research**

Qualitative research is a set of interpretive, material practices that make the world visible. These practices transform the world. They turn the world into a series of representations, including field notes, interviews, conversations, photographs, recordings and memos to self . . . qualitative researchers study things in their natural settings, attempting to make sense of or interpret phenomena in terms of the meanings people bring to them.

Denzin and Lincoln (2011: 3)

Research on writers has been considerable, but because each situation is different and because contextual factors play such a large part in what happens when individuals sit down to write, it is always possible to say more. In particular, there is still much to learn about what writers do in different situations, and how contextual factors such as proficiency, prior learning, cultural background and first language can influence writing processes. In the classroom there are opportunities to discover aspects of writing and learning. For example, Sabbaghan's (2013) stimulated recall study compared peer–peer and expert–novice interactions during the replay of participants' writing processes using a keystroke recording programme and how this affected subsequent revisions. Willey and Tanimoto (2013), on the other hand, used protocol data to investigate the anxieties of English teachers acting as 'convenience editors' for publishing scientists.

Interviews are another popular method in process research, of course, and have been used to explore issues such as the strategies used by L2 scientists to write academic papers in English (Okamura, 2006), how students choose topics during a writing exam (Polio and Glew, 1996), and how teachers make use of computers in their English classrooms (Wong, 2013). As mentioned above, technology has also been employed to explore the writing process, with keystroke recording during composing. Software such as *Free Keylogger* or *REFOG Key-logger* can be installed to register all keystrokes, including all pauses and revisions, during a writing session so that the entire text can later be replayed exactly as it was created to give insights into thinking and revision (e.g. Sullivan and Lindgren, 2006). Overall, research on writers is valuable because the more we learn about writers in the contexts in which they write, the fuller our understanding of writing becomes more generally.

Concept 4.7   Researching the Writing Process

- What strategies does a group of writers employ in accomplishing a given writing task?
- How do they interpret prompts, plan, draft, edit, etc.?
- What use do writers make of written sources, notes, and other students when writing?
- Do the strategies of experts differ from novices and in what ways?
- Do L2 learners transfer composing strategies from their L1?
- What role does talk play in the writing process?
- What role does reading play in the writing process?
- Where do students find source materials for writing and how do they use them?
- How do students understand plagiarism?
- How do the experiences of writing in social media impact on students' writing practices?
- What strategies do writers use when revising their texts?
- What is the focus of their revisions (sentence level, meaning, formal conventions, organisation)?
- Does technology and CALL change writing practices, and in what ways?
- What use is made of feedback, in what areas, and from what sources?
- How do students give peer feedback, and is it effective in encouraging revisions or learning?
- Are there differences in L2 students' revising strategies in their L1 and in their L2?

In addition to research on writing and revision practices, writer-oriented research also addresses the impact of particular teaching methods on the writing process and the use that writers make of various kinds of feedback. Experimental techniques have been used in this regard, particularly when seeking to evaluate the relative claims of different teaching practices on learners' writing. This is often done by randomly assigning students to two groups, providing different instruction to each group, then testing to discover which method was more effective. This was the approach adopted by Song and Suh (2008), for example, in determining the relative effectiveness of two types of writing tasks in noticing and learning the conditional.

Experiments have also been massively popular in feedback studies. The study by Truscott and Hsu (2008) mentioned earlier is one example, as is that by Lundstrom and Baker (2009) on whether giving or receiving peer feedback is more beneficial. Here the *givers* reviewed anonymous papers but received no peer feedback over the course of the semester, while the *receivers* received feedback but did not review other students' writing. An analysis of writing samples collected at the beginning and end of the semester indicated that the givers made more significant gains in their own writing over the semester than did the receivers, and that lower-proficiency givers made the most gains.

Generally, more qualitative research has dominated intervention studies, particularly into the effects of teacher and peer feedback. Lee and Shallert (2008), for instance, used interviews, class observations and writing samples with teacher-written comments to understand the influence of the teacher–student relationship on a teacher's written feedback and in how students responded to this feedback in their revisions. Jones, Garralda, Li and Lock (2006) used transcripts of face-to-face tutoring sessions and logs of online sessions conducted by the same peer-tutors to compare the interactions of face-to-face and online peer-tutoring, finding more hierarchical relations in the former and less emphasis on "global" writing concerns. Needless to say, this kind of qualitative, interpretive research confronts the researcher with an enormous quantity of unpredictable data which has to be organised, analysed and categorised in some way. Moreover, researchers often have to face the need to reconsider procedures mid-study and the challenge of the idiosyncratic nature of each project they undertake. Studying writing processes therefore requires a necessarily provisional approach to draw inferences from observations and reports.

Concept 4.8   Researching the Effects of Instruction

How is teacher feedback given and responded to?

- What are the effects of teacher-written and/or oral feedback on writers' behaviours?
- What kinds of response styles do teachers use and how do they influence revision?

- What do teachers focus their feedback on?
- What kinds of feedback are most effective in improving drafts in a given context?
- What kinds of feedback, if any, produce long-term learning gains?
- What interactions occur in teacher–student conferences and how do these influence revision?
- How does mitigation influence revision?
- What individual/cultural/proficiency differences influence feedback?
- What kinds of feedback do particular learners prefer and why?
- Is oral conferencing more effective than written feedback in improving student texts?
- What impact does online feedback have on writers and how does it differ from face-to-face feedback?

How is peer feedback given and responded to?

- What are the effects of peer-written and/or oral feedback on writing?
- What does peer feedback focus on and what do revisions address?
- What kind of response sheets are most effective in encouraging peer comments?
- Does proficiency make a difference in peer interactions and uptake on comments?
- What differences does training make on peer comments and revision practices?
- Is oral or written feedback more effective in changing revising behaviour?
- Are there cultural differences in giving and responding to peer feedback?
- What interactions take place in peer conferences and how do these influence revision?
- Do learners prefer teacher or peer feedback and why?
- Is teacher or peer feedback more effective in improving writing processes and texts?

Finally, writer-oriented research has also explored how people write and participate in literacy events in going about their everyday lives. This social-literacies approach (discussed in part 2.2) links writing with local contexts and examines how the activities of reading and writing are located in particular times and places, looking at events as diverse as writing job applications, texting and creating web pages. Research methods here take considerable pains to capture an understanding of the participants, the setting, the materials involved, and the activities participants perform. This 'visible evidence' helps the researcher infer the knowledge, feelings, purposes and so on which lie beneath the surface and inform the context. Ethnographic methods, which include conducting interviews, taking photographs, observation and the study of texts are therefore valuable in understanding the meaning of activities that form the participants' perspectives. Barton summarises these steps in Quote 4.7.

Quote 4.7 Barton on Researching Literacy Practices

1. Identify domain or domains
2. Observe visual environment
3. Identify particular literacy events and document them
4. Identify texts and analyse practices around texts
5. Interview people about practices, sense making

Barton (2000: 170)

Some studies have already been mentioned in part 2.2, but people participate in literacy practices in many ways which can be investigated as small-scale projects. Hamilton (2000), for example, discusses how photographs can provide evidence of a range of everyday uses of literacy, from words on clothing and tattoos to people interacting around texts. Barton mentions numerous studies conducted by students (Barton, 2000: 171) and current projects can be seen on the Lancaster Literacies Log[1].

Concept 4.9 Researching Social Literacies

- How are texts produced and used in a particular social context?
- How do the writing practices of specific writers connect people with each other?
- What languages do people use for different writing activities?
- How are complex writing tasks organised?
- How is writing related to other events and goals in the writers' domains of activity?
- How is writing related to reading and speech in specific contexts?
- What are writers' attitudes toward writing and its role in their lives?
- How do writers express their individual identity and group membership in a context?
- How do writers feel about the institutional genres in which they participate?
- Which writing practices are privileged (and which ones less so) in different contexts?

4.4.3   Researching Readers

Compared with research on texts and writers, issues concerning audience, or what readers expect to find in texts, are relatively unexplored. This is despite the fact that a developed sense of audience is essential to successful writing, and that student writers often have problems shaping their ideas for readers: What will readers find familiar and persuasive? What stance should I take? How will readers respond to my message? How formal should I be? Research therefore seeks to understand how writers understand their readers, how they construct texts to express these understandings, and how these rhetorical features might best be taught. Studies have mainly focused on what faculty require students to write and how the faculty react to it, the reading practices of professional academics while writing, how writers routinely address readers by repeatedly drawing on same rhetorical and linguistic features, and the evaluation of teaching practices designed to raise student awareness of audience.

Once again, the method adopted will largely depend on the questions asked and the orientation of the researcher. Questionnaires have been widely used to collect data on what genres teachers require their students to write, for example, so Jenkins, Jordan and Weiland (1993) collected questionnaires from faculty members to determine the role of writing in graduate engineering schools. Protocols have been used to explore writers' mental representations of their intended audience as they write (Wong, 2005) and interviews to discover what faculty intend to achieve through their feedback to writers (Hyland, 2013c). Researchers have also analysed reader comments to compare L1 and L2 evaluations of student writing (Hinkel, 1994).

Corpus studies have been used to analyse the writing tasks that are set at university, so Nesi and Gardner (2011), for example, conducted a large-scale study of the British Academic Written English (BAWE) undergraduate corpus and distinguished 13 "genre families", ranging from case studies through empathy writing to research reports, which differ in social purpose, generic stages and the networks they form with other genres. Experimental methods have also been used to study writers' awareness of readers. Roen and Willey (1988), for example, used an experimental study to see if focusing on audience before or during revising influenced writing quality, while Schriver (1992) conducted an experiment to assess the effects of reader protocols on the ability of L2 writers to anticipate readers' comprehension problems. As noted earlier, it is difficult to hold everything constant to study one variable in natural settings, and so writing experiments have often been conducted in artificial contexts. Because of this, researchers conducting classroom experiments may need to draw on several data collection methods to get a complete picture of the phenomena they are studying.

In fact, it is probably a good rule of thumb for researchers to collect as much contextual information as possible, including the views of the participants they have studied, in any research. Researchers must manage the complex task of juggling multiple methods. Different methods have different affordances and tell us different things about texts and the ways they are used in real life. So, by analysing texts and conducting interviews or focus groups, by distributing questionnaires and observing actors writing or learning to write, by studying photographs or artefacts and asking writers to tell us what they are doing as they write, we can build more robust understandings of writing or learning to write.

Concept 4.10   Some Researchable Issues on Readers

- Who are the target audiences for a particular group of writers?
- What kinds of genres and features do these readers expect to find?
- What do these readers typically look for in a text and how do they read it?
- What do writers need to know about the target audience to write successful texts?
- What interactional features are important to engage a particular audience?
- How is the discourse community represented in a particular genre?
- How do writers achieve particular rhetorical effects such as persuading, engaging or informing readers?
- How do considerations of audience influence writing?
- How do these considerations differ between experienced and novice writers?
- What do readers see as an effective text in a particular context?
- Are there general principles of audience that writers can transfer across contexts?
- What help can we give students to accommodate audiences in their writing?

4.5   Conclusion

To summarise some of this discussion: there is a need for research that tells us about the features of specific text types, the practices of specific writers, and the relationships between instructional practices and writing effectiveness. Research conducted by teachers and students can illuminate each of these areas, contributing to what we know about writing by exploring and validating existing practices and analyses, and grounding them in specific contexts. More immediately, it can also have great practical pay-offs for individual practitioners, both for our understanding of the kinds of writing that we encounter and the contribution this understanding can make to our professional practices.

Note

1. The Lancaster Literacies Log is at *http://literacieslog.wordpress.com/*

Further Reading

Burns, A. (2010) *Doing action research in English language teaching: a guide for practitioners.* New York: Routledge.

An accessible, step-by-step overview, with lots of examples of action research projects, aimed at teachers new to doing practitioner research.

Cohen, L., Manion, L. and Morrison, K. (2013) *Research methods in education,* 7th edn. London: Routledge.

Clearly written, authoritative and wide-ranging discussion of major issues and approaches.

Edge, J. (2001) *Action research.* Alexandria, VA: TESOL.

Contains plenty of ideas based on reports of different action research studies.

Litosseliti, L. (ed) (2010) *Research methods in linguistics.* London: Bloomsbury.

Ten chapters on key issues in the design, collection and analysis of language data.

Nunan, D. and Bailey, K. (2009) *Exploring second language classroom research.* Boston: Heinle.

A comprehensive introduction to research methods for teachers with lots of examples.

Paltridge, B. and Phakiti, A. (eds) (2010) *Continuum companion to research methods in applied linguistics.* London: Continuum.

An excellent one-volume resource setting out methods with clear examples.

5   Research Cases
Observing and Reporting

This chapter will . . .

*   give concrete expression to some of the methods discussed in the previous chapter by presenting five published research projects based on data collected through observation and self-report methods;
*   use these cases to examine some central themes and good practices of recent writing research;
*   suggest how researchers might develop the methods and results of these cases for projects of their own.

In Chapter 4 I outlined the main research methods that have been used to study writing and suggested some issues that can usefully be tackled by small-scale projects. In this chapter and the one that follows, I will flesh out these methods and topics with some examples of successful cases, all of which have the potential for further research or replication. I have selected these cases to represent a range of different research areas and methodologies, taking in research on writers, texts and readers. Like action research projects generally, these examples centre on local, concrete issues of relevance to practitioners and generally occur in natural settings (Burns, 2010). They are all initiated by a question, supported by data and interpretation, and conducted by researchers, teachers or students. In this chapter I focus on research methods which might be more familiar to teachers: those which involve observing what people do and recording what they say.

5.1   Questionnaire Research on Faculty Beliefs and Practices

Summary

Jackson, L., Meyer, W. and Parkinson, J. (2005) A study of the writing tasks and reading assigned to undergraduate science students at a South African university. *English for Specific Purposes*, 25: 260–81.

> This study surveyed faculty members in 14 science disciplines at three campuses of a large South African university to discover the reading and writing tasks assigned to undergraduate students. Questionnaire results provided data on teachers' views on academic literacy and the main genres that students were required to read and write.

Surveys of academic writing can play an important role in understanding what readers want from a text and the features they expect to find in them, and so they can help teachers to develop appropriate course material for both L1 and L2 writers. Jackson et al. became interested in this issue through teaching academic literacy on a year-long Science Foundation Programme designed to prepare students who do not qualify to enter first-year tertiary studies. These are largely Black African students from disadvantaged backgrounds and poor schools who are required to study courses in Mathematics, Chemistry, Physics, Biology and Communication to improve their knowledge and skills so they are ready for first-year studies. This study is part of the preparation for redesigning the academic literacy courses so the information gained would ensure that their courses would be grounded in a solid research base.

5.1.1   *Aims*

The main goal of this study was to determine the kinds of writing and reading required and the literacy expectations of science lecturers. The questionnaire addressed three main areas:

1.   The amounts of reading and writing science students were expected to do;
2.   The nature of this reading and writing and the difficulties for students as seen by the lecturers;
3.   The lecturers' personal perceptions of students' academic literacy problems.

5.1.2   *Methodology*

The questionnaire covered the three issues above in just six questions. The first asked respondents how much guidance and feedback they gave students on different aspects of writing, with the option to indicate whether they corrected, gave brief or extensive written comments, verbal feedback or no comments at all. The next question asked lecturers to indicate, on a four-point scale, the extent to which poor performance in organisation, grammar, referencing, plagiarism and style affected students' marks. The remaining questions concerned the frequency and type of writing tasks the lecturer had set the previous semester, the frequency of reading tasks, and their perception of how well students generally performed the written tasks.

The categorisation of the writing tasks was based on those used by Braine (1995) and Horrowitz (1986). These were: summary of/reaction to readings, experimental (laboratory) report, experimental report (design), case study (knowledge of a theory to solve a problem) and research paper (combines information from a number of sources), to which they added the essay genre, which is often used in the science faculty. The questionnaires were sent to lecturers from the science faculties at three campuses of a large South African university. A total of 47 questionnaires were returned (25% of those distributed), representing 14 disciplines from the three campuses. Most responses concerned first-year courses, but some referred to second- or third-year teaching. The responses were analysed only descriptively, and no tests of statistical significance were calculated.

5.1.3   Results

The results showed that lecturers set between three and four pieces of writing on average per semester and that the nature of these assignments depended on the discipline. *Report* is the most common genre in science, comprising 66% of assignments, followed by summaries of readings (16%) with essays being relatively rare (10%). Academics in the experimental sciences expected a lot of writing, largely in the form of laboratory reports, while staff in maths and physics set very little and awarded grades based on mathematical accuracy rather than writing.

In terms of awarding grades, the lecturers appeared to value the organisation of written assignments above other aspects, followed by attention to referencing conventions and avoidance of plagiarism. Grammatical accuracy influenced students' marks to a lesser extent, and tone and style only marginally. Feedback on student writing mainly took the form of brief written comments, with corrections to the grammar also being common. The final question concerned reading tasks and revealed that the textbook was the most common source of reading material for science students, closely followed by photocopied readings of chapters from other textbooks. Students were almost never assigned journal articles to read.

Concept 5.1   Questionnaire Research

Questionnaires can be useful for collecting self-report data on writing and reading practices and have been used extensively in research on reader preferences, attitudes and judgements. They have the advantage of being easier and quicker to administer than interviews, and the responses of far more informants can be gathered. Data are more amenable to analysis and quantification, and because the information is controlled by the questions, they allow considerable precision and clarity. We need to remember, however, that questionnaires only provide reports of what people say they think or do and not direct evidence of it, and they may need to be validated with other methods, typically by following up with in-depth interviews with a sample of respondents. In any case, questionnaires need to be carefully constructed and piloted to ensure reliability, to avoid ambiguity, and to achieve a balance between having sufficient data and not overburdening respondents.

Statistical tests are often used to establish the significance of results. Lomax and Hahs-Vaughn (2012) and Hatch and Lazaraton (1991) are straightforward and accessible sources of information on different kinds of statistical tests in applied linguistics research. In small-scale studies, however, researchers often simply use descriptive measures, such as means and percentages, to identify general features.

5.1.4 Commentary

This study is a good example of both the strengths and weaknesses of questionnaire research. The information gathered provided the researchers with valuable information about the writing needs of their students and the expectations of their immediate audience. From their results they learnt that the lab report is the main way that students learnt about scientific writing, and that there was a serious discrepancy between this writing assignment and the kinds of reading the students did. Textbooks proved very poor models for writing lab reports, as these are far more similar to a research article in terms of audience interactions and stance (Hyland, 2004a). On the other hand, the absence of any follow-up interviews and lack of provision for open-ended comments on all but one question meant that respondents were strait-jacketed into the initial perceptions of the research. No rubrics or texts were examined and the self-report data were not supplemented by other forms of evidence. Nesi and Gardner (2011), for example, explored undergraduate writing demands through corpus analysis. Finally, several interesting issues, such as the fact form and content of the laboratory reports differed across disciplines, were not followed up, and the specific characteristics of particular writing assignments were not clarified or explored.

5.1.5 Further Research

Jackson et al. give a clear account of their research, and their questionnaire is appended to their paper for use by others. The study could therefore be replicated in other contexts to provide information about the views and practices of teachers working with students outside the writing classroom. Students in different disciplinary areas and at different levels of education need different kinds of help with writing, but the writing requirements and problems of many student groups remain unknown. This is a very fruitful area for further research, and similar studies would be useful to determine the tasks, evaluation criteria and audience expectations in other contexts.

Such studies are not only likely to show us what the important writing issues for our students might be, but also raise the awareness of subject lecturers concerning the importance of writing and their own practices, perhaps leading to greater cooperation between subject tutors and academic literacy tutors in providing students with authentic writing experiences. More generally, surveys of this kind are very valuable in building up a picture of discipline-specific writing practices and how these might vary in different institutions. This kind of information can contribute to what we know about variations in disciplinary writing, faculty attitudes and practices, and the need for specifically tailored writing programmes.

Equally, survey studies can also help target more specific reader-oriented features of context. It would be useful, for example, to know what it is our students actually have to write, so we can go beyond generic labels to the specific tasks required. This means exploring audience perceptions of exactly what constitutes a '*term-paper*', an '*essay*' or a '*laboratory report*' in different fields; the differences they perceive in the writing of L1 and L2 students; and the relative importance they assign to different features of student writing. Surveys alone, however, cannot give us all the information we need and might be usefully complemented with other approaches. Interviews with selected respondents, the study of departmental documents and style sheets, and analyses of target discourses could also be used with questionnaires to tell us a great deal more about the relationship between what we teach, what writers do and what real audiences want.

5.2   Experimental Research on Peer-Response

Summary

Lundstrom, K. and Baker, W. (2009) To give is better than to receive: the benefits of peer review to the reviewer's own writing. *Journal of Second Language Writing*, 18(1): 30–43.

This study examined peer review from an unusual angle: looking at whether benefits mainly accrued to the provider of feedback or to the recipient. The researchers used an experimental methodology which divided students in nine writing classes at two proficiency levels into two groups: those who reviewed anonymous papers but received no peer feedback over a semester, and those who received feedback but did not review other students' writing. An analysis in the gains in writing ability over the semester showed that the givers made more significant gains in their own writing than did the receivers, especially at the lower proficiency level.

Originating in process teaching, peer response is now widely used in writing instruction in both L1 and L2 contexts to improve writers' drafts and raise awareness of readers' needs (see part 1.2). Peer response enables writing teachers to help their students receive more feedback on their papers as well as facilitate students' meaningful interaction with peers and a greater exposure to ideas. Peer reviewing may also help students learn critical evaluation skills which are necessary to effectively review texts and see logical gaps, problems with organisation, and other weaknesses, making them better writers and better able to review their own papers as they write. Previous studies have suggested that when two novice learners are paired together, they are able to support each other's writing and learn from each other (e.g. De Guerrero and Villamil, 2000; Teo, 2006). The benefits of peer review to the reviewer, however, have not been thoroughly investigated in second-language writing research, and this study set out to fill this gap.

5.2.1   Aims

The purpose of this study was to determine which is more beneficial to improving student writing: giving or receiving peer feedback. It addressed the following questions:

1. Do students who review peer papers improve their writing ability more than those who revise peer papers (for both beginning and intermediate students)?
2. If students who review peer papers do improve their writing ability more than those who revise them, on which writing aspects (both global and local) do they improve?

   This is perhaps the first rigorous study conducted in L2 research to address the issue of whether the act of reviewing peer-written work improves students' ability to critically evaluate writing, an ability which may then transfer to the students' own writing process.

5.2.2   Methodology

Concept 5.2   Experimental Research Methods

Experimental research is a way of determining the effect of something on something else, such as a teaching technique on test scores, error correction or writing improvement, and so on (Gass, 2015). It is a deductive method in that the researcher comes up with a theory and tests this through applying some treatment to one group and not a control group, while holding other factors constant. The two groups are then given a post test to see the effect of the treatment. Statistical tests are then carried out on the data to find out if differences between the control and the experimental groups are significant.

The study was conducted with 91 L2 students in nine sections of writing classes at an English Language Centre at a U.S. university. Forty-five of the participants were at a "high-beginning" level and 46 were in "high-intermediate" writing classes. At both levels, students were divided into two groups. The first was a control group of two high-beginning and three high-intermediate classes which received peer feedback but did not review peers' papers. The second was the experimental group, comprising two high-beginning classes and two high-intermediate classes, who reviewed peer papers but did not receive peer feedback. Four times throughout the semester, participants received training on peer review in addition to their normal writing curriculum. Both groups were asked to look at the same issues in the same anonymously written sample essay, but the receivers were given training on how to use feedback to revise the paper, whereas the givers were given instruction on how to give feedback on it. Other than this, the two groups of students received similar instruction.

To assess whether there were any changes in their writing ability, all students were asked to write a 30-minute timed essay at the beginning and end of the semester. These pre- and post-test essays were rated by seven experienced teachers working at the English language centre using an established grading rubric. This allowed for an analytical assessment of both the global and local aspects of writing, in addition to providing a holistic, overall final assessment score. Validity was established by having all raters attend moderation sessions in using the grading scheme and ensuring that they reached agreement on sample essays before reading the pre- and post-tests. Each test essay was graded by at least two readers, and the different scores were averaged with a third marker adjudicating if the first two raters disagreed by more than one point in any of the seven criteria of an essay. Finally, to ensure that all the scores used to calculate gain were valid and consistent, the data were run through a statistical programme called FACETS.

5.2.3 Results

Analysis in the gains in writing ability measured from writing samples collected at the beginning and end of the semester indicated that while both groups improved, students who focused solely on reviewing peers' writing made more significant gains in their own writing over the course of the semester than did those who focused solely on how to use peer feedback. The results of a repeated measures analysis of variance (ANOVA) also indicated that givers at the lower proficiency level made more gains than those at higher proficiency levels, and that slightly more gains were observed on global than on local aspects of writing.

The researchers acknowledged that the gains found for the giver group over the receiver group may have been the result of factors other than differences in treatment, such as the quality of teaching, individual student differences or different experience from pretest to post-test. While these factors can't be completely discounted, however, they point out that:

1. Although eight different teachers and their students participated, the findings show that students in all the giver group classes made significantly greater gains than those in the receiver group classes.
2. The same kinds of gains (global) were made by both beginning and intermediate group 'giver' students who had no previous peer review experience; but if other factors were at play, we would not expect all the giver groups to make the same types of gains.
3. The intermediate students in the giver group who had never been exposed to peer review differed considerably in gains from similar students in the receiver group. This points to the treatment as a key factor.

5.2.4   Commentary

This case is a good example of how research has both the possibility to reveal something surprising and the potential to wash back into practice. Lundstrom and Baker's study addresses an important classroom issue with clear relevance for teachers, suggesting that although L2 students in the receiver group improved over the semester, students can improve their own writing by transferring abilities they learn when *reviewing* peer texts, and that this advantage is greater than if students are taught to *use* peer feedback. This improvement may be because students learn from these activities to critically self-evaluate their own writing in making appropriate revisions. Moreover, the beginning givers improved significantly more than the receivers in all global writing aspects (organisation, development and cohesion) while the gains made by the intermediate giver students over receivers was less dramatic. One possible reason for this is that students at the beginning level had more room for improvement than those who were more proficient, and so they had a greater relative improvement in their writing ability. It may also be that the intermediate group was developing skills that take longer than one semester to mature, so the benefits would take longer than a semester to become apparent.

5.2.5   Further Research

This study suggests a number of areas for further investigation. First, the study could be replicated with other learners in other contexts to see how far these findings apply to them, and to reveal more precisely the relationship between the processes of reviewing and of revising texts following review. Such research might tell us what kinds of instruction on peer review work best with students of different learning backgrounds and proficiency. It would also be interesting to see whether similar benefits are found for different aspects of writing, such as grammar, vocabulary or rhetorical structure. Nor is it clear whether the benefits of training persist over time or whether these advantages fall away, so the impact of training needs to be monitored beyond a single essay.

Clearly, the conditions of this study differ from those of an authentic class-room context, as the students who received peer review did not themselves review peers' texts, so further research might explore both aspects of peer review. This might also help us see what occurs in peer negotiations, how these differ between trained and untrained students, how trained responders draw on their instruction in these discussions, and the effects the training has on revisions. Obviously, more qualitative approaches are needed to obtain this kind of data. Research here could employ observation techniques, perhaps using video recordings of peer-response sessions, interviews with participants focusing on the interactions which occurred, scrutiny of interview or conferencing transcripts, and close analysis of student drafts in the light of this spoken data.

5.3   Interview Research on Scientists' Writing Practices

Summary

Okamura, A. (2006). Two types of strategies used by Japanese scientists when writing research articles in English. *System*, 34(1): 68–79.

This study examined how some writers succeed in mastering scientific discourse in English used in a non-English speaking environment. Okamura interviewed 13 Japanese researchers of varying experience, focusing both on their difficulties and on their strategies to cope with them. The results showed that identification of their audience and their learning strategies distinguished established researchers from others. While all read academic texts in their field to learn typical writing patterns, only five sought to master English speakers' language use.

English is now unquestionably the language of international scholarship and an important medium of research communication for non-native English speaking academics around the world. Non-English-speaking scientists often face enormous difficulties, however, and interviews and questionnaires have been used with both experienced and novice researchers to discover what difficulties they have. However, most academic communities contain individuals who are successful in publishing in English and have overcome these difficulties. This study examines differences among researchers in a linguistically less advantageous environment, Japan, where English is taught as a foreign language from secondary school. The study focuses on junior, middle-ranking researchers and established global players in the sciences to reveal something of how they survive and succeed when writing research articles, despite their linguistic handicap.

5.3.1   *Aims*

The study aimed to identify Japanese researchers' language difficulties in relation to experience, then compare the strategies that helped them to cope with these difficulties in writing research articles. It addressed two main questions:

1.   What kinds of difficulties are non-English-speaking professional researchers aware of when writing research papers?
2.   What learning/writing strategies do they employ to cope with these difficulties?

5.3.2   *Methodology*

Concept 5.3   Interview Research

Interviews enable participants to discuss their interpretations of the world and to express how they see situations. The method acknowledges that human interaction is central to understanding, and emphasises the social situatedness of research data. Interviews have been widely used in writing research and have three main purposes: as the principal source of gathering data; as a means of testing hypotheses or generating new ones; and as one method with others to triangulate information or cross-check data. They can be characterised on a spectrum of formality. These include 1) a structured format where the researcher has an agenda and works through a set of predetermined questions; 2) a semi-structured pattern where the researcher knows where he or she wants the discussion to go but allows the respondent considerable freedom in getting there; and 3) an unstructured format where the interview is guided by the responses of the interviewee rather than the agenda of the researcher, enabling unanticipated themes and topics to emerge.

Cohen, Manion and Morrison (2013: 267–72)

Okamura interviewed 13 Japanese researchers (two lecturers, three associate professors, and eight professors) in science and engineering departments in major research universities. All were educated in Japan to the Ph.D. level and were actively publishing in American, European and Japanese journals in English. Three professors had spent two to three years working outside Japan and had been invited to international conferences as leading figures in their fields. Okamura therefore categorised respondents into three groups: five junior researchers (the lecturers and associate professors), five mid-ranking researchers (five professors) and three established researchers (three professors). Participants provided copies of two of their published papers, which were referred to in the semi-structured interviews. The interviews lasted 45 to

90 minutes each and were conducted in Japanese in the researchers' offices. The use of the native tongue, the fact that the interviewer was not an English speaker, and the interviewer's obvious interest helped create rapport when talking about their difficulties in writing in English.

5.3.3   Results

All of the writers in this study mentioned their lack of vocabulary, which created difficulties in describing their results and staking a claim. Two biologists believed this was likely to be more a handicap in their discipline, which relied less on mathematical formulae than other sciences. They also recognised less tangible difficulties. Although all agreed that they had to consider the readers to be accepted by their target journal, the junior and middle-ranking researchers stated they did not have specific readers in mind, and that they were unable to think of subtle linguistic forms that would persuade readers. Two junior researchers, in fact, said they were so preoccupied with grammatical accuracy that they did not consider their readers when writing. The three established writers, in contrast, were able to talk about their target readers and describe strategies to draw their attention.

To improve their writing, all the writers adopted 'subject knowledge-oriented strategies', such as reading and collecting useful phrases, at an early career stage. After internalising set phrases, they tended to become ambivalent about the need to achieve native-like fluency in writing, recognising that time pressures meant they could not spend extra time polishing their English. They also commented that, with experience, they realised the discourse community was tolerant of non-English speakers' writing. Seven of 13 writers therefore showed no interest in going beyond using short sentences and simple structures, while the remainder continued to develop their writing skills, often by contacting English speakers about the use of English in research articles. In addition to learning strategies, the writers also differed in their use of writing strategies, with the junior and middle-ranking researchers reporting that they thought mainly in Japanese but wrote only in English, and the established researchers did both their thinking and writing only in English.

5.3.4   Commentary

This is an uncomplicated but effective study of the writing practices of a specific group, identifying some of their difficulties and describing the coping strategies they used when writing scientific papers in English. The research shows that while the junior or middle-ranking researchers were aware of the need to convince their fellow researchers that their findings were worth publishing, they had difficulty in visualising readers. Established researchers, on the other hand, were not merely concerned with getting published, but by being read by their target audience. These differences in experience seemed to affect the learning and writing strategies they used to overcome their difficulties, with most writers happy to work within their limited English, because they saw no reason to go beyond it. While it is not possible to conclude that success is related to English skills, the interviews suggest that adopting language-oriented strategies seems necessary for success in academic writing.

5.3.5   Further Research

While this research identifies some of the difficulties that Japanese researchers experience and describes the coping strategies they used when writing scientific papers in English, it is essentially preliminary and exploratory. The idea that the writer's experience in the discourse community can play a part in perceiving language problems and adopting strategies is interesting, however, and worth further study. It might be worth exploring experiences and background with other groups of writers to discover the strategies they use to overcome any disadvantage. The views of writers in other disciplines and language groups, for example, could offer interesting comparisons with the Japanese writers and also help teachers become aware of their learners' professional experience and the kinds of guidance different students might need, perhaps feeding into teaching of localised strategies for writers.

5.4   Protocol Research on the Writing Process

Summary

Wong, A. (2005) Writers' mental representations of the intended audience and of the rhetorical purpose for writing and the strategies that they employed when they composed. *System*, 33(1): 29–47.

This paper studies the composing strategies employed by four advanced L2 writers as influenced by their mental representations of the intended audience and rhetorical purpose for writing. The writers were asked to verbalise all the thoughts that went through their minds when they wrote an assignment, and the video protocols were transcribed, coded and analysed in conjunction with the drafts they produced and their follow-up interviews. Wong found that while the writers used a similar range of composing strategies, they used them differently and to serve different purposes at different junctures of the composing process.

This study is in the tradition of cognitive research which has helped us to understand the strategies writers use in the writing process (see part 1.2.2). This research has shown that writing is not simply a series of actions, but a series of decisions which involves setting goals and selecting strategies to achieve them. Wong was interested in understanding something of these strategies in the writing of L2 graduate students, looking in particular at whether there is a correspondence between how they compose and their perceptions of the rhetorical purpose for writing and of the intended audience.

5.4.1 Aims

This study sought to discover how far the writers' perceptions of writing purposes and target audience impacted their composing strategies. Specifically, Wong wanted to answer the following questions:

- What strategies do advanced L2 writers employ when they write in an academic context?
- Do advanced L2 writers have different mental representations of the target audience and of the rhetorical purpose for performing the writing task? If so, in what ways are these representations different?
- Is there a correspondence between advanced L2 writers' mental representations of the target audience and the purpose for performing the writing task and the composing strategies they use?

5.4.2 Methodology

Four Chinese L1 English major student-teachers with similar academic backgrounds and near-native-speaker proficiency in English were given a writing task that required them to reflect upon their experience of teaching. They were given the topic only at the start of the writing sessions, but were told beforehand that the task would be on the teaching of grammar and that they should bring relevant reference materials with them. They were told that there was no time limit and the suggested length of 500 words could be taken flexibly. Data were collected by asking them to verbalise all the thoughts that ran through their minds while they composed. The Think Aloud Protocols were triangulated with data from the video recording of the writing behaviour of the writers, follow-up interviews, and analysis of the writing plans and drafts produced during the composing sessions.

Following some short training and warm-up tasks, the participants were given the following set of instructions:

1. Say whatever is on your mind. Don't hold back hunches, guesses, images and intentions.
2. Speak as continuously as possible. Say something at least once every five seconds, even if only, "I am drawing a blank".
3. Speak audibly. Watch out for your voice dropping as you become involved.
4. Speak as telegraphically as you please without worrying about complete sentences or eloquence.
5. Don't over-explain or justify. Analyse no more than you would normally do.

6. Don't elaborate past events. Get into the pattern of saying what you are thinking now.
7. Verbalise in English, Cantonese, or mixed code as you prefer.

The sessions were video recorded with one camera focused upon the writer full front and the other capturing the writer's pen movement on paper. Following the composing session, the observation notes were used as a basis for an interview to discover why the writers behaved in certain ways during composing, why they adopted certain composing strategies, what they saw as the purpose of the assignment, and who they had in mind for the audience when they composed. The protocols themselves were coded using a scheme adapted from Raimes (1987) and 10% were selected and coded by another rater to ensure inter-rater reliability. As described in part 1.2.2, protocols have been criticised for their artificiality, their incompleteness, their heavy reliance on inference and the fact that they may even distort writers' normal composing processes, but it is a method which produces extremely rich data.

Quote 5.1   **Smagorinsky on Protocol Analysis**

Often represented as a mechanical procedure conducted by automatons on information-processing subjects, it is in fact an essentially human experience, fraught with the potential for mishap through personal flaws and vagaries and the fragility of social interactions, and dogged throughout by agonizing decision making at every level. Researchers who understand the magnitude of their task and account for the potential perils to the greatest extent possible can provide a rich source of data that, when seen in the context of validating research, can provide a unique and important view of composing processes.

Smagorinsky (1994: 16)

5.4.3   *Results*

The results of this study show that the four writers displayed a richly diverse repertoire of mental representations of audience. Typical of school-sponsored writing and knowledge display, two writers perceived their course lecturer as their audience, one trying out ideas to solicit feedback and the other relating to the teacher as an evaluator. Another saw his students as the primary audience and wrote with simpler English than his counterparts, focusing on grammar and seeking to help the reader learn more about auxiliary verbs. The final writer perceived the rhetorical purpose as reflecting on her own experience in order to improve her teaching, and so wrote as if she was the audience of her own text, finally sharing it with peers towards the end. This suggests that the mental representations of audience may have an influence on shaping writing decisions.

The protocols showed that writers used a range of common strategies such as reading and re-reading, planning or goal setting, editing and revising, but in addition they also used questioning and self-assessment to facilitate their writing. Wong also discovered a correspondence between how the writers saw the context and their strategies, with the student writing for the lecturer-evaluator employing a narrower range of strategies with lower incidence of use to 'get it right the first time she put words on paper'. The writer addressing the lecturer as coach saw the assignment as an opportunity to try out ideas to solicit feedback, and so produced a high incidence of major text revisions. The student who invoked his students as the intended audience attached great importance to planning at the rhetorical level when he constructed the plan of the assignment, while the more reflective writer made use of the broadest range of composing strategies and with the highest frequencies.

5.4.4 Commentary

This study highlights some of the complex operations of composing, pointing to the multi-layered considerations which occupy students as they write. In particular, it suggests that the perception of rhetorical purpose and audience influences particular composing strategies. For teachers, this suggests that it may be important that the intended audience should be clarified and explained to students, replicating what happens in real-life language use. Interestingly, the participants seemed to become far more aware of their composing strategies as a result of verbalising their thoughts while composing and reflecting on their composing behaviours. This may encourage teachers of writing to employ a limited amount of think aloud activities in writing programmes. This kind of research is therefore valuable for increasing our understanding of what can occur when we write and why we do what we do. Protocol analysis, however, needs to be carefully handled, particularly in L2 contexts where reporting and writing simultaneously may overburden novice writers.

5.4.5 Further Research

Many process research methodologies are easily adapted for the classroom. Through Think Aloud Protocols, we can 'listen in' on students' writing processes to see how they handle the tasks we give them, the effects of different prompts, or the choices they make at given points in writing. Protocols are also useful for examining the ways that writers plan and revise their work, respond to feedback, integrate source material into an essay, select themes and arguments, or draw on prior rhetorical experiences. In addition to helping us learn more about writing processes, protocols can reveal the effects of our teaching on composing strategies or the particular social factors which influence writers' goals and strategies. These might include the rhetorical context, prior instruction, knowledge of academic conventions, earlier experiences with the genre, and so on. As we have seen here, the technique can be particularly useful when examining the importance of audience to writers, identifying the points where they anticipate the expectations of readers.

5.5   Diary Blogs Research on Drafting a Research Paper

Summary

Li, Y.-Y. (2007) Apprentice scholarly writing in a community of practice: an interview of an NNES graduate student writing a research article. *TESOL Quarterly*, 41(1): 55–79.

This research examined how a novice Chinese scholar, working in a non-Anglophone context, went about writing a research article for publication in an English-medium journal. The writer's blogs were the main source of data, supported by analysis of his developing text, his bulletin board message exchanges and post-hoc interviews. The study shows how the apprentice writer engaged with the local research community, the laboratory, his own experience of writing research articles, and the global specialist research community.

This study, like the previous one, employs introspective research techniques to explore writing practices, mainly drawing on a writing log. The case study explores the writing processes of a third-year doctoral student of Chemistry at a major university in China writing a first draft of a research article for publication in an international journal. Publishing in English-medium journals is a graduation requirement for doctoral students in the sciences at this university and typically presents a major challenge for Chinese students, as their study of English has generally involved grammar tests and essays on current affairs topics rather than conventions of disciplinary rhetoric. Before he wrote his first article in English, this student had not taken any academic writing courses but had learnt by reading and emulating specialist journal articles.

5.5.1   *Aims*

The major aim of this study was to track this student's activities as he wrote the first draft of his third first-authored article. It was undertaken to learn more about L2 writing practices in disciplinary, high-stakes genres outside Anglophone settings and to develop knowledge of these situations to inform the instruction of advanced academic literacy. The study also sought to put more flesh on the idea of situated learning (Brown, Collins and Duguid, 1989), a concept which emphasises that learners best acquire local expertise by participating in the learning activities of a community. Lave and Wenger (1991) describe this kind of learning as *legitimate peripheral participation* through which novices gradually acquire full membership in a *community of practice.* Li sought to document this student's experience of acquiring disciplinary literacy expertise through the process of engaging with a community while writing a paper for publication.

5.5.2   *Method*

Concept 5.4   Diaries/Process Logs

Bailey (1990: 215) defines diary studies as 'a first-person account of a language learning or teaching experience, documented through regular, candid entries in a personal journal and then analysed for recurring patterns or salient events'. Writers are encouraged to enter all relevant activities on a regular basis. When a substantial amount of material has been produced, the researcher examines the log for patterns, which are then interpreted and discussed with the writer. Logs can provide valuable insights into both social and psychological processes that might be difficult to collect in other ways.

Li's main source of data was process logs, or diary entries, which her case-study subject wrote in Chinese as blogs and posted in the 'Friends' Zone' of his university's bulletin board. Diary studies are not commonly used to study writing, but logs are important introspective tools in language research and can provide insights into the ways individuals write, or learn to write, that would be otherwise difficult to obtain. Unlike think aloud methods, logs are retrospective and therefore offer the benefit of hindsight and reflection on writers' practices, suggesting why they acted as they did and their perceptions of the contextual influences on them. Li believes that process logs offer an ideal tool for tapping into the writer's perspective, obtaining an *intraview* (Walker, 1985) of the writer's process, harnessing the power of introspection. The advent of the Internet, and the popularity of weblogs (or *blogs*), has given diary studies a new lease on life as well as given researchers an easily accessible source of naturalistic data.

The student in this study was used to posting blogs on this site as a way of sharing news with his friends and recording his feelings, but Li provided him with a process log guide sheet which asked him to record progress, difficulties, strategies and feelings about writing. She advised him that this was merely a loose reference to help him reflect on his experience, but he could go beyond them to record what he felt most strongly about during the writing process. Together with his friends, she was able to access the blog area at any time and respond to his entries, showing her appreciation of the content and sometimes following up with questions.

Because a blog contains only a part of the events that occurred in the process, the researcher supplemented these entries with bulletin board correspondence between them, posting draft interviews which clarified specific points and verified interpretations and with copies of the student's developing draft. Together, these sources allowed her to discuss progress and decisions he was making on the paper while it was being written. Analysis of the logs themselves was a recursive process of noticing trends and then looking more closely at the data to see how stable, frequent or striking those patterns were. This process resulted in a preliminary set of themes which Li then revised, clarified and verified in further data collection.

5.5.3   Results

The blog entries provided rich information about the writer's attitudes and concerns as he wrote as well as data on his decisions, actions and reasons for acting as he did. It also revealed something of how he negotiated a way towards structuring his argument and organising his material through a learning process which involved engagement with his community of practice, which involved four categories: the laboratory data, his experience of writing articles, the local research community, and the more global specialist research community. During the writing process he gained a deeper understanding of his data, identifying its limitations, deciding what data to focus on and how to make his claims by reference to other articles and his growing awareness of readers in a global scientific community.

5.5.4   Commentary

This is an interesting piece of process research which focuses on a largely unexamined aspect of student perceptions and writing. It provides a detailed behind-the-scenes look at the different assumptions and strategies that a novice scientific author draws on in writing for publication in a second language. The student's recourse to mother tongue in this process is interesting here, reinforcing other studies on academic writing (e.g. Shaw, 1991; Gosden, 1996). More interesting is the writer's engagement with the local and global research communities, which illustrates the social nature of his apprenticeship into scholarly writing. The student increasingly addressed the more global context of the research community rather than the local disciplinary community and was well aware of the need to impress the referees by highlighting the significance of his work through self-citation and framing the topic to address an international audience (see also Hyland, 2015a). It is also interesting to note that this writer did not reach his current level of awareness about academic writing for publication until he had worked on his third English article in the doctoral programme.

The fact that the researcher offered the student articles on the rhetorical structure of scientific articles when he struggled with the Results and Discussion sections underlines the value of such assistance to novice L2 writers. In addition, Li found that the student benefited from keeping a record of, and posting, his writing process as it facilitated reflection on his decisions and a critical awareness of the genre.

5.5.5   *Further Research*

Research into the ways that students write or carry out particular writing tasks, the factors that influence their strategies, and the assumptions they hold about each of these are clearly important for both our understanding of writing and our success in learning to write. While this study focused on a student writing for publication, there are obvious possibilities for further research in this area with other students and other types of writing. Moreover, a series of studies using logs or a more prolonged engagement with a student can provide insights into how strategies and attitudes develop, or comparisons can be made between students to identify something of how age, proficiency, type of instruction or different prior learning experiences influence the ways students interpret and perform writing tasks.

While the topic is important, Li's use of a relatively little-used methodology is equally instructive. Diary writing, or blogging, is a method of collecting data inherent to the interpretative research paradigm and is particularly suited to contexts where the researcher is also the classroom teacher (Sa, 2001). Through learners' process logs we can discover students' beliefs about the writing they do, the tasks they are set and the teaching they receive, while gaining insights into their composing strategies. It is, then, an instrument for conducting research on affect and practice, as well as cognition. Logs have also been used as introspective tools by teachers to record their own writing experiences or the effects of their classroom practices on students' writing improvement. Effective writing teaching cannot be based solely on the implementation of abstract theoretical principles but needs to be grounded in local knowledge of what works with particular students.

The information gathered from diaries therefore offers both a rich source of research data into the writing process and a means of privileging the writer's perspective when seeking to solve the problems of teaching and learning to write.

5.6   Keystroke Logging Research on Writing Strategies

Summary

Leijten, M. and van Waes, L. (2013) Keystroke logging in writing research using Inputlog to analyze and visualize writing processes. *Written Communication*, 30(3): 358–92.

This study sought to reconstruct the writing strategies and cognitive processes of writers as they composed, using keystroke recording software combined with other observational techniques: TAPs and eye-tracking data. The texts were professional tweets and emails and involved accessing information on the web.

A final observational method worth mentioning briefly in closing this chapter is that of keystroke logging. With writing practices now largely focused on writers' interactions with the keyboard and screen, the computer recording of their actions offers a less obtrusive way of observing writing processes than a researcher looking over a writer's shoulder, as well as an alternative to introspective methods such as Think Aloud Protocols. This approach utilises software which allows researchers to record and then play back the actions of writers as they are engaged in producing text at the keyboard, logging and time-stamping keystroke and mouse activity to reconstruct and describe text production processes. Closely associated with psycholinguistic aspects of writing, keystroke logging is a means of exploring the complex cognitive activities involved in writing and theorised by Flower and Hayes (1981), Kellogg (1994) and others; these cognitive activities potentially involve planning, problem-solving and decision-making with clearly defined goals. The non-linear, recursive and interactive processes with which the writer struggles in creating texts leave traces in the deletions, revisions, pauses, cursor movements and bursts of writing which are recorded, potentially providing access to these deeper processes.

5.6.1 Aims

In this study the researchers wanted to explore the complementarity of the keystroke recording method with Think Aloud Protocols and eye-tracking software to reveal how a group of master's students and experts used sources when writing short texts. The research set out to describe and understand writing processes such as searching, reading and copying from multiple digital sources. The secondary purpose was to illustrate the value of keystroke logging data to describe how these writers went about writing in a digital context in which writers had easy access to a wide variety of resources.

5.6.2 Methodology

In the first part of the study, 47 master's students were instructed to inform their followers by Twitter about an upcoming communication conference. In the second part, 10 other participants (five professionals and five master's students) performed two writing tasks, first tweeting the conference information and then sending an email on the same topic to a more restricted group of colleagues. It was expected that they might search for additional information, but in a different way, because the task had a different focus.

Eye-tracking data were collected to investigate what the writers were reading/searching for during inactive writing periods; and Inputlog (www. inputlog.net), a keystroke recording programme, was used to observe their writing and surfing activities. Inputlog not only logged the text development in a Microsoft Word document but also registered all windows accessed during the writing process. Each switch from one application to another represented a 'focus event' or change in the writer's attention from text production to reading a source. Researchers could therefore track the writer's search and consulting behaviour and gather data about the use of sources, the time and keystrokes in each source, and the interaction between sources. It then generated information for graphic output for analysis.

Quote 5.2   **Spelman Miller et al. on Keystroke Logging**

The observation of writing by means of this method provides researchers with detailed information concerning aspects of the planning, formulation, and revision processes . . . the potential uses of logging not only include reaching writers' processes but also as a pedagogic tool given that its replay facility allows access to information about aspects of the writers' attention and strategies as they write.

Spelman Miller, Lindgren and Sullivan (2008: 433)

While keystroke tracking software has been around for many years, it has generally been difficult to link the data it provides to underlying cognitive processes (Spelman Miller and Sullivan, 2006; Latif, 2009). The development of more articulated theoretical frameworks and recent technological advances have led to an improvement in both the logging measures and how they are analysed, making keystroke logging a useful way of collecting writing process data. The log files contain a wealth of information concerning operations on the text, however, and this data, as well as the statistical methods for interpreting them, can be daunting for the uninitiated. The 'analysis' component of the programme, however, allows the user to pull out interesting patterns based on algorithmic processing of the raw logging data and to see things from a variety of perspectives: product/process, pauses, revisions, and multiple sources.

5.6.3   *Results*

The eye-tracking and keystroke logging data revealed how the writers interacted with sources in creating the short texts. Thus, one case study student writer switched 68 times among the various sources, interrupting her writing flow about four times per minute to move from her document to other sources. About half of these switches had only a technical function and were caused by transitions between the sources (taskbar, Windows Explorer, etc.). Ignoring these transitions, the interaction rate was reduced to 35 switches among three sources. The writer spent over 20% of her time on other sources (this was 48% in the Twitter task), underlining how much attention to external sources is part of digital writing and a major cause for writing task fragmentation. The composing process that characterised the tweet design shows that, having accessed the Twitter page, the writers Googled the conference name and engaged in intensive interaction between the tweet and the conference website, using other sources while composing the message.

5.6.4   *Commentary*

This research suggests that keystroke logging can be a useful tool in describing and analysing writing processes, either as a stand-alone application or in combination with other observation methods such as eye-tracking and think aloud recording. Combining research methods provides a more solid basis to achieve results, although this is a complex approach for teachers to use. The value of the method is that it can show how a writer juggles the complex web of interacting cognitive activities in real time, planning content, choosing forms, considering audience and style, and so on. These tasks, of course, are more difficult for those writing in a foreign language or in an unfamiliar genre, as their attention to lower-level linguistic demands may take up a large amount of their working memory, leaving less capacity available for higher-level considerations such as content, audience and style. The method can, however, reveal the degree of automaticity of composing as writers become more familiar with a genre or more fluent in writing.

5.6.5   *Further Research*

Research into the ways that students perform particular writing tasks is clearly important, both for our understanding of writing processes and the behaviour of particular groups of students engaged in specific kinds of writing tasks. Keystroke recording can provide information about what learners or experts focus on when composing, how they interact with online resources, the ways they go about revising, how they develop content, and how their production processes develop over time. Interestingly, the method also has potential pedagogic uses, not only in offering teachers a diagnostic instrument to help monitor students' writing development, but also in developing learner autonomy and helping them to notice their own language performance. Teachers have used the approach to indicate to L2 writers how they might engage in more global planning and less sentence-level revision (e.g. Whalen and Ménard, 1995), while several studies have shown how replaying the writing event can stimulate students to reflect on and evaluate their writing (Sullivan and Lindgren, 2002). The effects of this methodology suggest avenues for further research.

5.7   Conclusion

Throughout this book I have tried to emphasise the importance of research to both our understanding of writing and to the practices involved in teaching it. This research is often conducted on a small scale by teachers, students, trainers or other practitioners interested either in texts, composition, or the teaching and learning of writing. Because of this, I have focused here on how projects might be effectively carried out by novice researchers working in their own professional contexts and using cases which might be familiar to them. In the next chapter I turn to another group of methods which typically work by combining these and other approaches to gain a fuller picture of writing and writing practices.

Further Reading

See also the recommended texts in Chapters 6 and 7.

Brown, J.D. (2001) *Using surveys in language programs.* Cambridge: Cambridge University Press.

What it says on the cover—a guide to questionnaire research in language teaching.

Brown, J.D. and Rodgers, T.S. (2002) *Doing second language research.* Oxford: Oxford University Press.

A comprehensive guide to conducting research on L2 students.

Dornyei, Z. (2007) *Research methods in applied linguistics: quantitative, qualitative, and mixed methodologies.* Oxford: Oxford University Press.

A practical book looking at quantitative, qualitative and mixed methods research written in an accessible and hands-on style.

Hatch, E. and Lazaraton, A. (1991) *The research manual: design and statistics for applied linguists.* Boston, MA: Heinle & Heinle.

A key text for quantitative applied linguistics and TESOL research.

Mackey, A. and Gass, S. (2012) *Research methods in second language acquisition: a practical guide.* Oxford: Wiley-Blackwell.

A hands-on book covering a range of research approaches and topics.

6 Research Cases
Texts and Contexts

This chapter will . . .

- present summaries of six research projects which exemplify some of the main methods used to research writing by studying texts and contexts;
- evaluate the projects and draw out implications for novice researchers;
- examine some central themes and good practices of contemporary writing research;
- consider the extension of these studies to other topics of research.

In Chapter 5 I presented some sample studies based on methods which principally involved collecting data through observation and self-report techniques. In this chapter I turn to approaches which may be less familiar to novice researchers but which are nevertheless widely used in studies of writing research. Teacher education courses have only recently begun to include skills such as compiling corpora, analysing texts and investigating interaction, perhaps because these are more challenging for researchers as they often combine several data collection methods in a single study. Such methods, however, are also demanding as they require reflection and the ability to step back to conduct a detailed interrogation of talk, text and communication. As in Chapter 5, each case in this chapter begins with a brief context for the research and is followed by a summary of its aims, methodology and results, then a commentary on its design and contribution to our understanding of writing. I conclude each case with some brief suggestions for further research, which, while not intended to restrict possible approaches and topics, might stimulate readers into extending and adding to what we know about writing.

6.1 Genre Research on Scientific Abstracts

Summary

Ayers, G. (2008). The evolutionary nature of genre: an investigation of the short texts accompanying research articles in the scientific journal *Nature. English for Specific Purposes,* 27(1): 22–41.

This study analysed the short texts accompanying research articles in the journal *Nature* from 1991 to 2005, focusing on their move structure and promotional elements and how these changed over the time period. The findings showed that these texts differed from prescriptive models of abstracts, but that they changed following the introduction of the e-version of the journal in 1997 to become more standardised and concerned with the 'general reader', indicating a kind of 'democratisation' of the scientific community.

Abstracts are one of the most studied genres in writing research; their brevity and clear purpose, features which often make them difficult for students to write, make them ideal for study. Several researchers have noted that abstracts do not merely summarise the research which follows but also 'sell' that research, encouraging the reader to continue into the main paper. This is typically done by a structure which foregrounds important information for easy access and grammatical features, which highlight novelty and immediacy. This study was undertaken to trace any changes over time in the abstracts accompanying articles in *Nature,* the world's top multidisciplinary scientific journal.

6.1.1 Aims

This study follows the genre tradition discussed in part 1.1.2 and was designed to provide a fuller understanding of the abstract in a single, highly prestigious journal, and how it might have evolved over a period of 14 years. In particular, the author was interested in the following questions:

1. How far do abstracts today differ from those 14 years ago?
2. In what ways have the abstracts changed since the introduction of the e-version of the journal?

The study, then, was both descriptive, exploring *what* these texts were like, and *explanatory*, seeking to account for any changes in them over this period.

6.1.2 Methodology

The researcher collected two small corpora of texts to reflect pre- and post-1997 practices: 61 abstracts from copies of *Nature* published during 1991–1996 and 32 abstracts from Internet copies of *Nature* from 1999–2005. Since abstracts after 1997 were double the length of the earlier ones, the two samples contained an equivalent amount of text. Analyses revealed that moves were generally signaled by the use of tense, voice and lexis, and their relative brevity often meant that the introduction and methods were conflated into a single move in the earlier texts. The post-1997 abstracts were more complex, and difficulties in identifying moves were often resolved by appealing to the accompanying text. Steps or sub-moves were then identified, and these often followed the directions in the "Guide to Authors". The textual analyses were supplemented by interviews with the journal's executive editor and four scientists from different fields.

Concept 6.1   Genre Analysis

Because g*enre* is understood in different ways, there are several ways of approaching analysis. Some of these focus exclusively on text structure, some give greater attention to sociocultural factors, some examine the practices of writers, and others explore the expectations of readers. They also reflect an interest in either adding to an understanding of language use which links language to contexts and is rich in social, cultural and institutional explanation, or which describe conventionalised aspects of texts and so have practical relevance for teachers. Essentially, genre analysis seeks to:

- identify how texts are structured in terms of functional moves
- identify the features which characterise texts and help realise their purposes
- examine the understandings of those who write and read the genre
- discover how the genre relates to users' activities
- explain language choices in terms of social, cultural and psychological contexts
- provide insights for teaching language

6.1.3   Results

This study found that these texts deviated considerably from 'textbook' models of abstracts and that they had undergone further recent changes. Up until 1997, the texts (called 'headings' in the journal) emphasised more news value than is generally recognised in abstracts, achieved through the manipulation of structure and tense, the use of persuasive language and the removal of hedging. Following the introduction of the e-version of the journal in 1997, texts became more traditional, with the new label 'summary/abstract', the extension of the text from 50–80 words to 150–180, and a more self-contained, stand-alone relationship to the main paper to summarise the paper explicitly for readers outside the field. The two versions remained similar in terms of tense, with the predominant use of the Present, and persuasive lexical items, such as the use of descriptive adjectives, which indicate a continued concern for the promotional content of the text.

However, the post-1997 abstracts displayed greater efforts to 'explain' by making clear to the reader the importance of a particular study, the greater standardisation of structure, the elimination of methods, the incorporation of the results into the conclusion move, a greater amount of commentary in the conclusion move, expanding discussion of the study's effect on the field, and the inclusion of definitions. Together, these changes promote the aims of the journal by showing how a study 'moves the field forward'. Ayers suggests that this demonstrates a growing concern for the general reader and the multidisciplinary nature of the journal. Methods have become far more numerous and specific in the sciences, making them too complex and specialised to be relevant to the average *Nature* reader. At the same time, the expansion of the results into the conclusion move, where they are interpreted for the non-specialist reader, and the growth of definitions in the introduction, all suggest a greater concern for the general reader.

6.1.4   Commentary

In many ways this paper is exploratory since the samples are small and the study is confined to a single journal. *Nature* is perhaps an unusual choice because it occupies a niche position among the top-ranked journals, being both multidisciplinary and having high prestige among scientists. This may largely explain these recent attempts to make it more reader-friendly and to promote its findings to a wider public, but while Ayers suggests this represents a 'democratisation' of the scientific community by extending the audience for research, it seems equally likely to be yet another promotional strategy by appealing to the press—to whom it looks to carry research as news to a wider audience. The study does raise interesting points which confirm observed tendencies in scientific publishing, revealing how writers use textual and rhetorical features to respond to the distributional impact brought about by e-publishing, to the greater specialisation of science, and to the need to include an ever-wider readership. These changes underline and reflect social changes, which mean the audience to whom information about methods is meaningful is shrinking, and the academic and career pressures to reach ever-wider audiences is growing.

6.1.5   Further Research

While this looks like a complex piece of research, it is a relatively straightforward study which could easily be replicated with other texts. Most obviously, it might be asked whether the features found by Ayers have found their way into more mainstream science journals, or into the abstracts of articles in other disciplines. With more time and resources, it would be possible to collect comparative data to count the features Ayers identifies and track any changes that may occur between two dates. Perhaps more relevantly for many teachers, we might want to investigate the texts our students have to write, looking at company sales letters, internal emails, engineering reports, history essays or other genres. Such research has a pedagogic pay-off by providing writers in different academic, workplace or professional contexts with the communicative resources they need to interact effectively in these genres.

6.2   Corpus Research on Learner Uses of Modality

Summary

Hyland, K. and Milton, J. (1997) Qualification and certainty in L1 and L2 students' writing. *Journal of Second Language Writing*, 6(2): 183–205.

This study examined a computer corpus to compare the expression of doubt and certainty in the examination scripts of Cantonese school-leavers writing in English with those of British learners of similar age and education level. The analysis found that the Cantonese learners used a more restricted range of epistemic modifiers and had considerable difficulty conveying the appropriate degrees of qualification and confidence.

This study arose from the concern of my co-author and I about the difficulties our students seemed to have in expressing doubt and certainty appropriately when writing in English. Our impressions were that Hong Kong learners often overstate their claims and are generally unable to control features of 'hedging' and 'boosting' in academic writing. We were also concerned by the fact that L2 writers' efforts to master these forms are often measured against unrealistic standards: the requirements of an academic community to which they do not belong and of which they have little experience. We therefore decided to compare features in texts written by Hong Kong students with those of British students of comparable age and educational level in a similar context. This study therefore draws on principles of intercultural rhetoric, looking at the ways people write in a second language, and learner corpora, or authentic language data produced by second-language writers of English for academic purposes.

6.2.1   *Aims*

This study focused on issues in both discourse analysis (part 1.2) and intercultural rhetoric (part 2.3) and addressed three principal questions:

1.   What are the most frequent forms used by each group to express doubt and certainty?
2.   To what extent does each group of students boost or hedge its statements?
3.   Are there differences in how these two groups handle these meanings?

The purpose of the study was therefore to determine the ways the two groups presented their statements in academic English.

6.2.2   *Method*

One of the most significant innovations in writing research in recent years has been the ability to compile corpora of students' writing. L2 learners admittedly share a number of difficulties with novice native writers, but they may also have their own distinctive issues which a careful corpus-based investigation can help uncover. Corpora can provide insights into authentic learner language, telling us how particular groups of students typically express certain meanings or approach rhetorical problems. To do this, however, we need reliable comparative data of the ways analogous target groups write; then we can identify which features students typically over- or under-use in their writing or seem to use in idiosyncratic ways. In other words, we can compare particular learners' uses with native-speaker uses to identify potential difficulties or infelicities in their work.

This study consisted of two large corpora. The first was a collection of 900 essays written by Hong Kong students for the high-school matriculation General Certificate of Education (GCE) A level 'Use of English' examination consisting of 500,000 words which had been graded by markers into six ability bands. The second corpus, also of 500,000 words, was transcribed from GCE A level General Studies scripts written by British school-leavers of similar age and education level. A list of 75 of the most frequently occurring lexical expressions of doubt and certainty in native-speaker usage was compiled from the research and pedagogic literature. The corpora were then examined to determine the frequency of these words in each grade of the Use of English corpus and in the GCE data. Fifty sentences containing each of those items (if there were 50 occurrences) were randomly extracted from each grade and from the L1 sample using a text retrieval programme. All target items were analysed in their sentence contexts by both researchers, who worked independently to ensure they expressed the writer's certainty or doubt. Figures were then extrapolated for the entire sample.

Quote 6.1 **Leech on Learner Corpora**

Let us suppose that higher-education teacher X in a non-English speaking country teaches English to her students every week, and every so often sets them essays to write, or other written tasks in English. Now instead of returning those essays to students with comments and a sigh of relief, she stores the essays in her computer, and is gradually building up, week by week, a larger and more representative collection of her students' work. Helped by computer tools such as a concordance package, she can extract data and frequency information from this 'corpus', and can analyse her students' progress as a group in some depth. More significant are the research questions which open up once the corpus is in existence.

Leech (1998: xiv)

6.2.3 Results

Overall the results of this study showed that both student groups depended heavily on a narrow range of items, principally modal verbs (might, may, should) and adverbs (probably, perhaps), and that the use of these features was particularly problematic for the L2 students. The Hong Kong learners employed syntactically simpler constructions, relied on a more limited range of devices, and exhibited greater problems in conveying a precise degree of certainty. Most importantly, the results confirmed that the academic writing of these learners was characterised by firmer assertions, a more authoritative tone and stronger commitments than the writing of native English speakers. The UK group used more markers of tentativeness and caution than the Hong Kong students, with about two-thirds of the modifiers serving to hedge, compared with only a third of the Hong Kong students' choices. Interestingly, the essays of the weaker Hong Kong students contained fewer devices overall and were characterised by far stronger statements. Thus, the more proficient were the writers in English, the more they approximated the writing of the native speakers, thereby suggesting that the main reason for these differences is proficiency rather than 'culture'.

6.2.4   Commentary

Our analysis of the learner corpora revealed that the difficulties our students seemed to have expressing appropriate degrees of conviction and certainty were widespread among Hong Kong secondary school students and differed considerably from comparable L1 usage. While both groups relied on a limited number of forms, the L2 writers used hedges and boosters very differently and displayed less awareness of relevant discourse conventions. The literature suggests it is unlikely that Hong Kong students differ greatly from other L2 learners in this regard, although English language teaching and research agendas have largely overlooked the importance of epistemic language. The differences revealed in this study are partly attributable to this neglect and underpin the need for teachers to have a clear idea of how their novice writers differ from comparable L1 language groups.

6.2.5   Further Research

Corpus research has a great deal to offer the study and teaching of language, particularly where students are required to write for academic purposes, as it replaces evidence with intuition, indicating what is frequently used and how it is used. By studying learner corpora and comparing features in them with those in some equivalent target corpus, we can discover developmental issues or misconceptions among writers regarding how language is used, thus informing instruction and learning. Further research can exploit learner corpora in various ways. We can, for instance, exploit longitudinal corpora to explore the writing of the same students at different stages of development, or of different individuals, or, as above, of writing from comparable learner groups. This allows instruction to be focused where it is most needed and, more generally, helping us to understand learner preferences or how L1 features might be transferred into L2 writing.

Although the compilation of learner corpora can be a painstaking and time-consuming business, numerous corpora are now available online. Some are listed at the end of this book.

6.3   Case-Study Research on Students Writing from Sources

Summary

Li, Y. and Casanave, C. (2012). Two first-year students' strategies for writing from sources: patchwriting or plagiarism? *Journal of Second Language Writing*, 21(2): 165–80.

This case study looked at the writing strategies and understandings of plagiarism of two first-year Hong Kong undergraduates doing the same writing assignment using sources. The study drew on textual comparisons between student texts and source texts, interview data and observation notes. These data suggested that while both students appeared to understand the university's plagiarism policy, their texts were characterised by patchwriting and inappropriate citation. Only one student's problems were spotted by the lecturer and checked with Turnitin, while the other's was hidden to the lecturer. The authors discuss issues related to students' writing from sources such as the difficulty level of sources for assignments in introductory courses, the complexities of attribution, and patchwriting in the work of novice writers.

Assignments which require students to write using sources are common in universities but often raise significant issues of plagiarism for both teachers and students. While students are often aware of regulations regarding plagiarism and are taught the technical skills of paraphrasing and citation to represent source material appropriately, they typically lack the disciplinary content knowledge needed to do this skillfully. As a result, they turn to patchwriting as a coping strategy, which involves "copying from a source text and then deleting some words, altering grammatical structures, or plugging in one-for-one synonym substitutes" (Howard, 1993: 233). The Internet makes a seemingly unlimited range of sources temptingly accessible, although these are not always appropriate and may encourage poor writing strategies.

6.3.1   Aims

This case study examines how students understand plagiarism and the strategies they use to write one short assignment actually assigned as part of their classwork, not as a research task. It therefore treats writing as a situated act (part 1.2.3) by exploring three questions:

1. How do the students understand 'plagiarism' at their university?
2. What strategies do they use as they write an assignment that requires sources?
3. What are the textual results of their strategies and the instructor's response to each text?

6.3.2   Methodology

Concept 6.2   Case-Study Research

A case-study is 'an instance in action', a means of portraying what a particular situation is like by capturing the close-up reality of participants' lived experiences and thoughts about a situation. It is concerned with a rich description of events and blends this description with interpretive analysis that draws on participants' own perspectives. A key issue is the selection of information, for while it may be useful to record typical actions, infrequent but critical incidents or events crucial to understanding the case may also be highlighted by the researcher. Case-studies typically represent research in a more publicly accessible form than other methods as they are often less dependent on specialised interpretation.

Cohen, Manion and Morrison,(2013)

Plagiarism and students' writing strategies have been studied in a variety of ways: through questionnaires (e.g. Selwyn, 2008), interviews (e.g. Shi, 2010) and case studies (e.g. Pecorari, 2006). Research on individual students in a particular context, what university policies mean to them, and how their writing strategies may be perceived by teachers concerned when Turnitin is used as part of the assessment process, however, is rare. This study adopted a naturalistic methodology focusing on an authentic introductory linguistics assignment, collecting the following types of data over a one-month period:

- the students' texts and most of the source texts they used
- six interviews conducted and recorded with one student and five interviews with the other student, each ranging from 30 minutes to one hour
- two interviews with the teacher soon after he had graded the papers to elicit his views on the two students' work
- observation of the students as they worked at the computer on the assignment
- research notes and profiles of the students

Data analysis involved reading the students' texts against source texts, examining interview and observation data for evidence of the students' decisions about how they located and cited sources and of the instructor's responses to the essays, and referring to background information in the research notes and profiles.

6.3.3   *Results*

The researchers found that both students were able to say what plagiarism was, although both borrowed and cited sources inappropriately despite claiming they did not intend to plagiarise. Both used a limited number of sources for the assignment and relied heavily on patchwriting. One completed the task in about two hours, using a keyword Internet search on the essay topic and relying on three main sources: a PowerPoint lecture slide, and cut-and-paste passages from two articles. She edited by removing sentences that seemed irrelevant and hard to understand and changing active to passive voice. The second student worked on the essay over several days, citing the textbook twice in his essay ("to give the lecturer a message that I've read the textbook") and putting nine references totaling 400 words into footnotes to save space and come in under the 700-word limit for the paper. Like the first student, he also engaged in textual borrowing, but from a variety of sources including Wikipedia and links from a Wikipedia entry. His integration of patchwork material was more skillful than that of the first student, reusing technical terms, using extensive metadiscourse connectives, and adding his own interpretations.

Because of the paper's overall coherence, the borrowing went unnoticed by the teacher, who thought the sources were well-integrated and gave the paper an A grade. He didn't run it through Turnitin as he did with the first student's essay, which he found "quite mixed up and confused" and he suspected the student of plagiarising. Turnitin revealed approximately 25% overlap with her sources.

6.3.4   *Commentary*

This case study highlights a number of issues taken up by the authors themselves:

First, they point out that these kinds of essays are fairly typical in introductory undergraduate courses where they are intended to 'deepen understanding' as well as assess students' disciplinary knowledge and rhetorical competence. Both students, in different ways, however, saw the task as 'collect and display' rather than an opportunity to study and understand information on their topic. These cases suggest that discussions of plagiarism need to consider the role of reading in source-based assignments and how the task itself might encourage this kind of surface textual borrowing.

It may have been that the texts themselves, being too difficult for the students to fully understand, encouraged a cut-and-paste approach. The authors suggest that students should be given greater guidance on how to search for and select appropriate sources, shown how to distinguish between primary and secondary citations, and taught that patchwriting is generally unacceptable. They further argue that given its ubiquity as a first-stop shop for students, EAP courses should offer training in how to use Wikipedia to assist learning and writing. The authors make the point that while patchwriting is unacceptable, it is not plagiarism or cheating. Students are not trying to pass others' work off as their own but resorting to a strategy to compensate for their lack of knowledge of their topic and with little experience writing academic papers from sources. For these reasons, patchwriting deserves attention from teachers and researchers. Making assignments more non-standardised and localised may help to discourage shallow information searching and mechanical copying by students, and foster deeper reading and understanding of material.

6.3.5 *Further Research*

Questions of validity and reliability are often raised in relation to the findings of small-scale case studies such as this, but Li and Casanave's multifaceted and detailed approach helps overcome the deficiencies of any particular method as well as offering a way of cross-checking data. The study thus provides a clear model for achieving internal consistency in further research and shows how sufficient information can be provided for readers to draw informed conclusions. The research also suggests how valuable small-scale studies can be in revealing how our students understand the tasks we ask them to do and how they actually carry them out, and there is considerable scope for further studies like this, exploring what students do when they create texts for us. Such studies can also be extended to recover teacher understandings of student texts and how they view student writing processes such as those revealed here. Attending more closely to such processes may make us more sympathetic to student difficulties and identify new ways to support student writing.

Such research, however, presents considerable challenges, not only in terms of the time involved in collecting and analysing qualitative data, but also in overcoming the potential threats students might perceive to their face. Impersonal surveys or one-off interviews offer fewer terrors than being closely observed when writing, particularly when something as sensitive as plagiarism is under scrutiny, and it may be difficult to encourage students to open up and feel comfortable in discussing their strategies and decisions. Such research, however, is crucial if we are to fully understand student writing practices and to make more fine-grained distinctions of the kinds of textual borrowing that it often entails.

6.4   Ethnographic Research on Teacher-Written Feedback

Summary

Hyland, F. (1998) The impact of teacher written feedback on individual writers. *Journal of Second Language Writing*, 7(3): 255–86.

This research investigated six ESL writers' reactions to, and uses of, teacher-written feedback in two courses at a New Zealand university. Hyland used a longitudinal approach which drew on a variety of data sources including observation notes, interview transcripts, Think Aloud Protocols and written texts. Her results show not only the value students place on feedback, but also the ways that they respond to and use it in their subsequent writing.

Giving effective feedback is a major concern for writing teachers and an important area of both L1 and L2 writing research (part 1.2). However, much of this research has involved artificially constructed experimental studies and tended to focus narrowly on error correction. There is still a need for more research which examines the effects of feedback within real classroom contexts and this study was an early attempt to do this, employing ethnographic techniques. Hyland's study addresses this need by providing in-depth information about the effects of feedback on individual L2 students over a 14-week course preparing them for academic study in English.

6.4.1 *Aims*

In this study, there were four main research questions:

1. What were the students' attitudes and expectations about the purpose and value of feedback and did these change over the course?
2. How did the students interpret and use the written feedback on their writing?
3. Were there individual differences in the way students responded to feedback and what might have accounted for these?
4. What types of revisions were made and which revisions could be linked to a feedback source?

6.4.2 *Methodology*

Two classes were studied and six students participated as case-study subjects. All written teacher feedback and students' revisions were catalogued and analysed to investigate the relationship between feedback and revision. Measures taken to ensure reliability included triangulation and respondent validation or 'member checking' of interpretations. While Hyland would not claim the research represents a full ethnography of events, the study has clear ethnographic aspects and conforms to general characteristics of the approach.

Concept 6.3   Ethnographic Research

Collaborative	The research entails the involvement of various participants, including the researcher, the teachers, and the students.
Contextual	The research is carried out in the context in which the subjects normally work.
Emic	The researcher adopts methods which privilege the perspectives of participants.
Interpretive	The researcher carries out interpretation of the data.
Longitudinal	The research takes place over several weeks or months.
Organic	Generalisations and hypotheses emerge during data-collection and analyses rather than being predetermined.
Unobtrusive	The researcher avoids intruding on the subjects or manipulating the phenomena.

The research employed data from the following sources:

- researcher's participant knowledge as a teacher of earlier courses;
- pre- and post-course questionnaires to all students in the classes;
- collection of class documents and observations of writing workshops;
- pre- and post-course interviews with the case-study participants and the two teachers;
- Think Aloud Protocols given by teachers as they marked assignments;
- retrospective interviews with students immediately after they had revised that assignment;
- analysis of all forms of feedback on drafts, from both teachers and peers;
- analysis of all students' written drafts and revised versions of these following feedback;
- all-day observations of classes and participants' out-of-class activities.

Each instance of teacher feedback was categorised according to its purpose, the degree of intervention, its focus (meaning, form or academic issues), and its span over the text. All student revisions in second drafts were also identified and categorised according to focus, span and the extent to which they improved the quality of the text. The 'usable' feedback points were then cross-linked to the student revisions to see how feedback triggered revision and in what areas. Detailed information about the role of teacher feedback in each writer's development came from a longitudinal examination of all student writing and feedback over the complete course. The interviews, questionnaires and observations were used to refine and validate the analyses and to provide a detailed contextual description.

6.4.3   *Results*

The findings showed that students tried to incorporate most of the usable teacher feedback when revising their drafts, but that this varied greatly according to their individual needs, prior experiences and approaches to writing. Many revisions either closely followed the suggestions offered, acted as an initial stimulus which triggered changes beyond the point addressed, or simply prompted deletions. A considerable number of the revisions, however, seemed not to be related to the written feedback at all, and originated from self-evaluation, peers or other external sources. Interestingly, the data also revealed that despite different stances on feedback, both the teachers tended to concentrate on *form* and that this encouraged revision at the same level, but did not appear to have a long-term developmental effect. In contrast, a very small proportion of the feedback addressed academic issues, even though this kind of feedback was more extensively used in the revisions and the knowledge gained appeared to be transferred to later pieces of writing. The fact that the study revealed communication breakdowns partly due to basic differences in the value that teachers and students placed on written feedback suggests the need for an open dialogue concerning the kinds of feedback students want and what teachers will give.

6.4.4   *Commentary*

In the best traditions of practitioner research, Hyland's study is concerned with ways of improving writing teaching based on a specific classroom issue with both practical and theoretical implications. In practical terms the results indicate the need to be sensitive to individual students' perceptions on what constitutes useful feedback and the need to gain an understanding of their past experiences, expectations and requirements. More widely, the research underlines the importance of examining feedback as part of a whole teaching and learning context rather than simply as an isolated event in the writing–revising cycle. This research is useful for teachers of both L1 and L2 writers as it encourages teachers to see feedback from the learner's perspective as part of a wider context of learning to write. It also urges teachers to help students develop their own sources of feedback and strategies for revising by monitoring their own revision practices.

6.4.5   *Further Research*

This study could be usefully replicated in other contexts, but it also highlights several areas for further research in both feedback and revision practices. In terms of feedback, Hyland's work indicates that the teachers were aware of individual students and their possible responses to feedback when they gave comments and that they tailored their feedback according to this awareness. Researchers might wish to extend this to investigate the relationship between teachers' personal conceptions of students and the amount and type of feedback they offer. Another line of enquiry would be to begin with the students and to study their independently selected sources of feedback, such as friends or partners, and how these interact with teacher feedback. Neither of these areas has been considered in L2 feedback research, yet both are highly significant factors in writing development and would be a valuable extension of this study.

An important conclusion of this study is that the relationship between teacher-written feedback and the ways that students respond to it in their revisions is highly complex, and this opens up a number of interesting areas for small-scale research into the influence of different learner variables. The part played by prior experience, proficiency level or various aspects of affect, for example, are clearly worth further study. Most importantly perhaps, research that looks at cross-cultural differences in attitudes to written feedback and its use is also needed. A greater understanding of what students bring with them to writing classes through comparative studies of the ways writing teachers in different cultures and settings provide feedback would be extremely useful for teachers working in EFL contexts. Smaller-scale studies than this one could therefore produce important results with a narrower focus. More research is also needed to establish what problems limited linguistic resources can cause outside EAP classes and what areas feedback should target to have the greatest effect.

6.5   Literacy Research Among Disadvantaged Adults

Summary

Barton, D., Ivanic, R., Appleby, Y., Hodge, R. and Tusting, K. (2007) *Literacy, lives and learning.* London: Routledge.

This book reports a major research project which explored the literacies in people's lives and their engagement in learning at different adult education sites. Drawing on various qualitative methods in a series of case studies, the research takes a literacy practices view of writing and reading to understand the complexity of different contexts and the factors which impact on choices. In particular, the methodology sought to be collaborative, by engaging those participating in a context, in order to explain the meanings of that context for those involved.

One important way for us to increase our understanding of writing is to research the everyday literacy practices of those around us (see part 2.2). The study of how people make use of literacy in their everyday lives provides insights into how writing works and the situated meanings it has for them, underlining the fact that a study of language needs to be both a study of texts and those who use them. This example of research moves away from the small action-oriented projects discussed in other cases to present a major study into the connection between people's lives and their participation as adults in formal learning. While focusing on learning, the study offers insights into both what writing means to people and how it might be studied.

6.5.1 Aims

Barton et al. were aiming to understand something of the meanings and connections that adults make between learning and their everyday lives, taking account of social and economic factors. This wider project focused on adults whose education had been interrupted and were attending classes in English for Speakers of Other Languages (ESOL), literacy or numeracy, but also addressed people's everyday literacy practices, how they used literacy to manage and enjoy their lives, and the meanings these had for them. Consequently, they asked:

1. What is the significance of literacy for people in their everyday lives?
2. What range of uses of literacy practices do they engage in?
3. How is literacy learned though participation in everyday activities?

6.5.2 Methodology

Quote 6.2 **Barton et al. on Researching Literacy Practices**

To draw upon the richness and complexity of people's lives and social practices we used many tools common in qualitative research. These included participant observation with detailed field notes; in-depth and repeated interviews, both structured and unstructured; case studies which focused on particular issues in detail and over time; photography and video-recording people's practices and working with them to record their own; collecting images and documents, as well as examples of free-writing, poems and rap. This enabled us to gather different types of data and allowed us to see complexity, multiple values, different positions, opposing perceptions, and different identities in different contexts.

Barton et al. (2007: 39)

The research was conducted in adult literacy, numeracy and ESOL learning classrooms in colleges and community adult education venues, such as a drug support and aftercare centre, a young homeless project, and a domestic violence project, all in the north of England. It involved collaboration with six teachers and over 30 learners who formed the longitudinal cohort of the study. The participants typically had unconventional educational experiences and felt excluded from or disaffected with mainstream culture and conventional educational discourses. One element of the literacy practices element of the research was to focus on five people and how they used literacy outside their classes. The research methods typically employed in literacy studies are a mixture of observing particular literacy events and asking people to reflect on their practices.

An important aspect of the methodology was its emphasis on situated practice, which entails explaining the meanings of what is involved for those engaging in the practice. As the authors of the study point out, this cannot be achieved without collaboration with the participants. It also involves a certain degree of responding to the situation as it evolves and making the results useful to those involved.

6.5.3   Results

Barton et al. found that these men and women of different ages and with diverse life circumstances and experiences used literacy in a variety of different ways, although for three broad purposes:

- *For finding out and learning about things*: all the subjects had hobbies or interests, such as wrestling stars or model aircraft, which they discovered more about by reading books, magazines, adverts and the Internet. One participant followed-up her reading by writing applications for grants and voluntary work posts.
- *For life purposes*: this included everyday activities such as reading food labels and participating in chat rooms. While some participants read avidly and kept in touch with family and pen-friends through emails and letters, others read little apart from functional texts, such as bus timetables, and wrote only short message service (SMS) messages or shopping lists. One created hand-made greetings cards; another kept a diary, wrote poems and found it easier to communicate with peers through writing than speaking; and a third catalogued his CD collection on a computer.
- *For literacy learning through everyday events*: using reading and writing to get things done provides many opportunities to expand literacy, and participants used a variety of strategies to do this. One struggled with formal spelling conventions and frequently used previous pages in record books to see how words had been spelt or to ask for 'acceptably difficult words' like *diarrhoea* to be spelled. Another participant learnt web page creation from the scaffolding of her grandfather and another learnt through routinely emailing a close friend.

Reading and writing therefore offered these individuals important options for self-expression and pleasure, interaction with others, and learning, while revealing how these vary from person to person. The book in which the study is reported goes on to document how a wider group of people used literacy for learning and life purposes as well as the practices they had to engage with when dealing with bureaucracy and employment demands.

6.5.4 Commentary

Through their observations and conversations with these adults about their writing and uses of literacy, the researchers came to understand the importance of writing in their lives: as personal statements, as tools for learning, as aspects of their work, and as intimate exchanges of friendship. More generally, these vignettes helped to reveal how literacies fit into a larger picture of peoples' interests, identities, sense of self and imagined futures. For these individuals, their writing practices were vehicles for accomplishing personal goals and sustaining relationships; it shows, in other words, not only that literacy mediates social life in various ways, but that it is often a highly collaborative activity which draws us into relationships with others.

6.5.5 Future Research

This research highlights both the academic and personal value of researching local literacies, as it not only increases our understanding of literacy as a plural and social concept but can also help us to reflect both on our own ideas and the lives of those around us. The links between writing and its meaning in the regularities of cultural life offer a rich source of research, and detailed studies of various domains can yield important insights into literacy practices. Equally, however, it brings to the awareness the richness and value of the writing culture of students, perhaps forcing us to review unexamined beliefs, widely held in education, which see vernacular discourses as rebellious or inadequate. Taking literacy variations seriously shows such vernacular discourses to be more than simply deviations from legitimate forms and reveals the ideological underpinnings of dominant literacies.

This kind of research, moreover, need not start with individuals in a particular context. Instead it might take a particular text such as a church notice, or a type of text such as a betting slip or a benefit-claim form, and examine the practices associated with it, tracing the ways it is used, discussed and responded to. Alternatively, research can focus on the vernacular practices of particular groups, such as taxi drivers or canteen workers, or detail the writing that occurs in particular places, such as a pub, a job centre or video store. Another departure point might be to look at certain routine activities, such as buying a lottery ticket, celebrating Christmas or writing to a newspaper, and breaking them down into sets of literacy practices. There is also enormous potential for research into bi-cultural communities and groups and the ways they use writing in their daily lives. Studies into any of these areas are likely to uncover many seen but unnoticed acts of reading and writing, and reveal a surprising degree of literacy.

When analysing data such as this, concepts from a social theory of literacy are crucial to interpreting what is going on. This might involve examining the particular roles participants take, looking at gender, class or age differences, studying how various media interact, or researching how a particular practice has developed over time or is acquired by users.

6.6   Synthesis Research on Written Corrective Feedback

Summary

Truscott, J. (2007) The effect of error correction on learners' ability to write accurately. *Journal of Second Language Writing*, 16: 255–72.

This systematic review of the literature evaluates and synthesises research on the controversial issue of how far written corrective feedback (WCF) affects learners' ability to write accurately. The study combines qualitative analysis of relevant studies with quantitative meta-analysis of their findings. Truscott concludes from the existing research that: (a) correction has a small negative effect on learners' ability to write accurately, and (b) any benefits are very small.

Another form of textual research is to analyse what has already been said about an issue, and this is the approach adopted by John Truscott to discover the value of correction in writing classes. This is a topic which has been hotly debated (e.g. Truscott, 1996; Ferris, 2004) and remains a contested issue. Teachers spend considerable amounts of their professional lives correcting papers and sincerely hope their efforts are bearing fruit in terms of producing better writers as well as better texts, although this hope may be based more on wishful thinking than hard evidence. Truscott therefore sought to update the empirical case for or against the practice and introduce a more quantitative dimension to the discussion, using a small-scale meta-analysis.

6.6.1   Aims

The overall objective of the study was to establish the effectiveness of correction by systematic analysis of relevant prior research. This entailed two sub-goals, each involving quantification of the research findings: (1) to find the best estimate of the overall effect of correction on accuracy by averaging the results of all the relevant research; and (2) to determine a probabilistic upper limit on how helpful correction might be based on a degree of confidence that any benefits of correction are no greater than 95%. Thus, Truscott (2007: 256) established the overall goal as follows: "Based on existing research, the best estimate of the effect of correction on students' ability to write accurately is X, and we can be 95% certain that any benefits produced by correction are no greater than Y".

6.6.2   *Method*

> **Quote 6.3**   **Ortega on Research Syntheses**
>
> Research syntheses refers to a continuum of techniques and research procedures that have been developed by social scientists with the aim of reviewing past literature systematically. Simply put, the methodology produces contemporary literature reviews that differ from traditional literature reviews in taking an empirical perspective on the task of reviewing. Syntheses investigate and evaluate past findings in a systematic fashion, always explicating the methodology followed in the review so as to enable replication by other reviewers.
>
> Ortega (2015: 111)

The researcher selected the studies to review from published sources, relying mainly on reviews by Ferris (1999, 2003, 2004) and Truscott (1996), for sources which focused on whether correction should be used in L2 writing classes. All the studies reviewed used authentic writing samples for their measures, rather than grammar exercises, and looked at writing ability over a period of months, because these provide the most clearly valid tests for the value of correction. Studies that examined only one-shot experiments looking at revisions following feedback were excluded, as Truscott claims they offer no measure of changes in students' ability to write accurately, i.e. their learning. Studies that failed to fully describe their methods or results were also excluded.

Meta-analysis is the best known technique for synthesising quantitative research. It involves determining one or more effect sizes for each study reviewed, measuring how large an effect the independent variable (correction) had on the dependent variable (accuracy of students' writing). Truscott employed Cohen's d for this, which takes the number of standard deviations by which the means of two groups differ. Thus, if an experimental group's mean is one standard deviation above that of a control group, the resulting d will be 1.0 (Cohen, 1992). A d of .20 to .50 is a small effect; 50 to .80 is a medium effect; and .80 and up is a large effect. Negative values are interpreted as a harmful effect. When averaging the overall estimate of the effect of correction across all the studies, the results are given together with a confidence interval to show the precision of the estimate, so an average effect size with a 95% interval has only 5% likelihood that the actual value lies outside the range. Because the reviewed research literature did not allow Truscott to distinguish evaluations of different types of grammatical errors, a meta-analysis of different error types was not possible.

6.6.3   *Results*

Results from six studies which met the selection criteria and used controlled experiments to compare the effects of correcting errors with those of not correcting them all produced negative means, suggesting that correction had a very small harmful effect on accuracy. So it was possible to say with 95% confidence that correction had no better than a small beneficial effect on accuracy. Truscott then turned to examine uncontrolled experiments of correction, or those studies which did not include a control group but only looked at absolute gains made by groups receiving correction. Such studies, of course, are not reliable indicators of the effect of correction. Not only is it impossible to determine if any gains are the result of feedback or of other factors, but also gains cannot be quantified in a way that allows comparison with gains expected in the absence of correction. The six studies in this category looked at the impact of correction on a variety of grammatical forms, but when Truscott compared accuracy before and after the correction and combined these findings with primary evidence from the controlled experiments, he found that the results were consistent with the negative findings from the controlled experiments and lent further support to those findings.

6.6.4   *Commentary*

Truscott's meta-analytical study of the experimental literature is an interesting and valuable approach to what can often be seen as a mass of contradictory and confusing research. His findings show that even the most optimistic interpretation of these studies is that correction of students' writing has only a negligible effect on the improvement of accuracy beyond a second draft. Referring to the individual studies he examined, he suggests that there may be two key factors which have systematically biased their findings in favour of correction groups, making them look better than they actually are. One is that measurements of improvement in accuracy are often taken with only a short delay following the correction, leaving no time for students to forget the feedback and so failing to allow for long-term decline. A second possible source of bias is that students may not know how to apply the corrected form in other contexts (Truscott, 1996) and so tend to shorten and simplify their writing to avoid using the construction, thus hiding their weaknesses. Uncorrected students are likely to show avoidance to a lesser extent as they are not pushed by correction to focus on their errors. In other words, research often overestimates corrected students' ability and improvement.

The finding that absolute gains in writing accuracy made by corrected students are limited, even when beneficial extraneous factors are not controlled, is perhaps depressing news for teachers who spend considerable time marking student drafts. The research, however, is restricted to the lack of improvement in accuracy in writing and has nothing to say about the effects of comments on content and clarity, which teachers also give and which may well be effective. It is also worth noting that experimental studies do not replicate authentic situations and the teacher–student relationships which exist in real classrooms. Teachers give feedback to students, not to texts, and actual correction given in such contexts may be more effective than that which is given in contexts set up for research purposes.

6.6.5   Further Research

This research method is likely to be unfamiliar to many researchers and requires some statistical expertise, or at least a passing knowledge of a statistics package such as NCSS or PSPP, is needed. Because meta-analysis is a quantitative methodology which involves mathematically summarising past findings, however, such a synthesis can only be used where the research to be synthesised is itself quantified. This means experimental or quasi-experimental reports must be in sufficient numbers to address the same question. Literature which offers descriptive, qualitative or mixed-methods data cannot be evaluated and synthesised statistically to show cause or effect but may, of course, be systematically reviewed in traditional ways. Synthetic findings go beyond the results of individual studies to show something new which is a trustworthy and significant finding.

6.7   Conclusion

The range of topics and methodologies described in this chapter and Chapter 5 suggest how rich and varied the topic of writing is. My aim here has simply been to suggest some topics which are representative of central themes in contemporary thinking on writing, and to illustrate how these can be tackled using current research approaches. I hope to have captured some of the variety and flavour of research in this field and perhaps to have encouraged readers to contribute to our growing understanding of writing.

Further Reading

See also the recommended texts in Chapter 5.

Barton, D., Hamilton, M. and Ivanic, R. (eds) (2000) *Situated literacies: reading and writing in context*. London: Routledge.
An excellent collection of studies offering insights and guidelines for further literacy research.
Hyland, K. (2004) *Genre and second language writing.* Ann Arbor, MI: University of Michigan Press.
Includes ideas for research and discussion of methods for studying written genres.
McKay, S. (2006) *Researching second language classrooms*. London: Routledge.
An introduction to classroom research for teachers.
Paltridge, B. and Phakiti, A. (eds) (2015) *Research methods in applied linguistics: A practical resource*. London: Bloomsbury.
A series of accessible chapters, each with a sample study, covering many of the approaches in this chapter.

Section III
Teaching Writing

7   Approaches to Teaching Writing

This chapter will . . .

*   explore some of the implications for writing instruction suggested by the main approaches discussed in Chapter 1;
*   outline the kinds of knowledge and skills involved in writing instruction;
*   develop some general principles for writing teaching through a critical analysis of the main classroom orientations.

   This chapter follows up on the broad approaches to understanding writing outlined in Chapter 1 to discover the teaching practices implied by seeing writing in terms of either texts, writers or readers.

   It sets out to provide a broad outline of methods and to show that while teaching may, in part, be an application of practical knowledge gained through hands-on classroom experience, it is always informed by our theories and beliefs about what writing is and how people learn to write. These assumptions underlie everything that goes on in the classroom, from selecting materials through sequencing learning to assigning tasks and assessing outcomes.

> ### Quote 7.1   Jack Richards on 'Methods'
>
> Methodology in teaching is the activities, tasks, and learning experiences used by the teacher within the teaching and learning process. Methodology is seen to have a theoretical basis in the teacher's assumptions about (a) language and second language learning, (b) teacher and learner roles, and (c) learning activities and instructional materials. These assumptions and beliefs provide the basis for the conscious or unconscious decision making that underlies the moment-to-moment processes of teaching.
>
> Richards (2001: 167)

Richards therefore suggests that the way we choose to teach writing is not a set of fixed procedures that we carry out like following a rule book, but more of an exploratory process that changes and grows as we learn more about ourselves, our students and our profession. Awareness of the options we have and how these are related to different understandings of writing can therefore help us to reflect on our assumptions, assist our teaching and enable us to approach current methods with an informed and critical eye. Here, then, I follow the pattern of Chapter 1 and look in turn at text-, writer- and reader-oriented approaches to writing to see what options they make available to teachers.

7.1   Text-Oriented Approaches to Teaching

Approaches to teaching which view writing as texts, or artefacts of activity rather than the activity itself, probably form the basis of most writing instruction around the world. Methods are likely to vary depending on whether texts are seen as rule-based objects or as writers' attempts to create meaning though discourse.

7.1.1   *Texts as Objects*

Conceptualising writing in this way directs attention to products and encourages a focus on formal text units or grammatical features of texts. Learning to write becomes an exercise in acquiring linguistic knowledge and gaining control over vocabulary choices, syntactic patterns and cohesive devices. The goal of writing instruction is training in accuracy, stressing the importance of formal aspects of writing with the prized goal of avoiding error. As a result, writing is essentially an extension of grammar teaching. Informed by a behavioural, habit-formation theory of learning, guided composition and substitution exercises are the main teaching methods with little concern for a communicative context beyond the classroom. The teacher is an expert passing knowledge on to novices following a prescribed view of texts: there is one right way to write a letter, for example.

This view of writing is still very much alive in many classrooms around the world, especially where English is taught as a second or foreign language. In many schools, writing classes are grammar classes in disguise and students are asked to write simply to demonstrate their knowledge of syntactic rules. In these situations, grammatical accuracy and clear exposition are often the main criteria of good writing. Following this perspective, teachers tend to focus on correcting errors and identifying problems in students' control of language rather than seeing how they are trying to convey their meanings.

Concept 7.1   A Product Approach to Teaching Writing

An emphasis on language structure as a basis for writing teaching is typically a four-stage process:

*   ***Familiarisation***: learners taught certain grammar and vocabulary, usually through a text

- *Controlled writing*: learners manipulate fixed patterns, often from substitution tables
- *Guided writing*: learners imitate model texts
- *Free writing*: learners use the patterns they have developed to write an essay, letter, etc.

Because texts are essentially regarded as a series of appropriate grammatical structures in this model, instruction may take a 'slot and filler' approach where students are presented with gaps to fill or sentences to complete, varying the words in the slots to generate different meanings. The goal is to achieve accuracy and avoid errors, so good writing is restricted to demonstrating a knowledge of forms and the rules used to create texts.

This autonomous, decontextualised view of writing also carries over into the design of many large international exams. Indirect assessments, typically multiple choice, cloze or error recognition tasks, are widely used in evaluating writing. But while they are sometimes said to be reliable measures of writing skill because they ensure consistency across test takers and occasions (e.g. Alderson, Clapham and Wall, 1995), they have little to do with the fact that communication, and not accuracy, is the purpose of writing. Moreover, even direct writing tasks, which require students to write one, or sometimes two, timed essays of a few hundred words, provide little information about students' abilities to produce a sustained piece of writing for different audiences or purposes.

In fact, focusing on accuracy is exactly the wrong place to look for writing competence, as there is little evidence to show that either syntactic complexity or grammatical accuracy are the best measures of good writing. Many students can construct syntactically accurate sentences and yet are unable to produce appropriate written texts. Moreover, while fewer errors might be seen as a marker of progress in a student's writing skills, this may merely indicate his or her reluctance to take risks and reach beyond a current level of competence.

What this means for teaching is that no particular feature can be said to be a marker of good writing because what is 'good' varies across contexts. We can't simply list the features needed to produce a successful text without considering appropriate purpose, audience, tone, formality and so on. Simply, students don't just need to know how to write a grammatically correct text, but how to apply this knowledge for particular purposes and genres.

7.1.2   *Texts as Discourse*

While students need to have an understanding of appropriate grammar and vocabulary when learning to write in English, these are a means to a communicative end of some kind. In deciding which structures to teach in a writing course, it is important to consider how these structures relate to the functions students need in their writing and the genres they need to write. Functions are the *means* for achieving the *ends* (or purposes) of writing and are typically taught together with the genres they help realise. As discussed in Chapter 1, genres are recognised types of communicative actions, and to participate successfully in any social event, individuals must be familiar with the genres they find there.

Concept 7.2   Advantages of Genre-Based Writing Instruction

Explicit—makes clear what is to be learnt to facilitate the acquisition of writing skills

Systematic—provides a coherent framework for focusing on both language and contexts

Needs-based—ensures that course objectives and content are derived from students' needs

Supportive—gives teachers a central role in scaffolding students' learning and creativity

Empowering—provides access to the patterns and possibilities of variation in valued texts

Critical—gives students the resources to understand and challenge valued discourses

Consciousness raising—increases teachers' awareness of texts to advise students on writing

---

In the genre-oriented writing classroom, teachers often discuss models based on analyses of texts and adopt a highly interventionist role, acting as guides to lead students through the typical rhetorical patterns of the genres they need to produce (Hyland, 2004c). Like the earlier views of writing as texts, there is an emphasis on writing as an outcome of activity rather than as activity itself. But while the focus has shifted from autonomous meanings to discourse, and from isolated sentences to the ways in which language creates texts, writing largely remains the construction and arrangement of forms.

But while genre is a central organising principle in many writing classes, it remains controversial for some who see it as imposing models on students. There is also the question of which genre approach to adopt, as it is customary to identify three approaches in writing instruction (Hyon, 1996; Johns, 2002):

a)   the Australian work in the tradition of *Systemic Functional Linguistics*
b)   the teaching of *English for Specific Purposes (ESP)*
c)   the *New Rhetoric* studies developed in North American composition contexts

I will elaborate a little here on these broad distinctions.

a) Systemic Functional Views: In the Systemic Functional Model, genre is seen as "a staged, goal oriented social process" (Martin, 1992: 505), emphasising the purposeful and sequential character of different genres and reflecting Halliday's concern with the ways language is systematically linked to context.

Genres are social because members of a culture interact to achieve them; they are goal-oriented because they have evolved to achieve things; and they are staged because meanings are made in steps, and it usually takes writers more than one step to reach their goals. When a set of texts shares the same purpose, they will often share the same structure, and thus they belong to the same genre. Concept 7.3 shows some features of two school genres.

Concept 7.3   Some Primary School Genres

Explanations	**Procedures**
Social function	**Social function**
Explanations account for why things are as they are or how/why something occurs.	Procedures tell how something is to be accomplished through a series of steps or actions
Explanations usually consist of:	**Instructions usually consist of:**
a general statement to introduce the topic a sequenced explanation in logical steps and perhaps with sub-headings	Goal—the desired outcome Materials—listed in relevant order Steps—needed to achieve the goal
Explanations are usually written with:	**Instructions are usually written with:**
the simple present tense technical vocabulary relative clauses to expand meaning of technical vocabulary passive voice temporal and/or casual conjunctions	Imperative mood Technical words Non-human, concrete participants rather than individuals Adverbs describing how to carry out actions, etc.

Government of South Australia (2014: 16)

This approach is perhaps the most pedagogically well-articulated of the three orientations, having had an enormous impact on first-language and migrant writing in Australia. It reminds us that successful writing demands an awareness of both rhetorical structure and control of grammar. This, however, is not the old disembodied grammar of the writing-as-object approach, but one linked to the specific purposes of a genre (Hyland, 2004c).

Quote 7.2   On Genre-Based Grammar in Teaching

Grammar is a name for the resource available to users of a language system for producing texts. A knowledge of grammar by a speaker or a writer shifts language use from the implicit and unconscious to a conscious manipulation of language and choice of appropriate texts. A genre-based grammar focuses on the manner through which different language processes or genres in writing are codified in distinct and recognisable ways. It first considers how a text is structured and organised at the level of the whole text in relation to its purpose, audience and message. It then considers how all parts of the text, such as paragraphs and sentences, are structured, organised and coded so as to make the text effective as written communication.

Knapp and Watkins (2005: 32)

b) English for Specific Purposes (ESP): This orientation follows SFL in the emphasis it gives to the formal properties and communicative purposes of genres, but it differs in adopting a much narrower concept of genre. Instead of seeing genres as the resources available in the wider culture, it regards them as the property of specific discourse communities.

Quote 7.3   **Swales on Discourse Communities and Genres**

Discourse communities evolve their own conventions and traditions for such diverse verbal activities as running meetings, producing reports, and publicizing their activities. These recurrent classes of communicative events are the genres that orchestrate verbal life. These genres link the past and the present, and so balance forces for tradition and innovation. They structure the roles of individuals within wider frameworks, and further assist those individuals with the actualisation of their communicative plans and purposes.

Swales (1998: 20)

The idea that people acquire, use and modify the language of written texts in the course of acting as members of academic and occupational groups is central to ESP. Genre here, then, comprises a class of communicative events employed by specific discourse communities whose members share broad communicative purposes (Swales, 1990: 45–7). These purposes are the rationale of a genre and help to shape the ways it is structured and the choices of content and style it makes available. It is a view of language motivated by pedagogical applications and descriptions of different genres that have been widely used in methods and materials for university students and professionals (e.g. Hyland, 2003; Swales and Feak, 2013).

Perhaps the best-known ESP genre model is Swales' (1990) description of research article introductions where writers 'create a research space' (CARS) to justify their work.

Quote 7.4   **Swales' CARS Model for Academic Introductions**

Move 1   Establishing a territory
               Step 1 Claiming centrality and/or
               Step 2 Making generalisation and/or
               Step 3 Reviewing previous research

Move 2   Establishing a niche
               By counter-claiming, indicating a gap, question-raising, or continuing a tradition

Move 3   Occupying the niche
               Step 1 Outlining purposes or announcing present research
               Step 2 Announcing principal findings
               Step 3 Indicating structure of the article

Swales (1990: 141)

Writers compete for attention for their research, and the introduction attempts to hook readers using three main moves, each of which can be expressed in a number of different ways. It first attracts readers by foregrounding what is already known, then establishes an opening for the current work by showing that this prior knowledge is somehow incomplete, as in this example from my research article corpus in Mechanical Engineering, where the second sentence establishes that the author has something new to say:

> (2) Stiffened planes are commonly used in many engineering structures (e.g. bridge decks, ship superstructures, aerospace structures, etc). Despite their wide application, little is known about their behaviour.

The writer then goes on to the third move which 'occupies the niche' by stating the contribution of the current paper.

Describing these moves has greatly contributed to teaching writing in ESP courses, but teachers need to be cautious in both oversimplifying text structures and presenting them as one right way of creating meanings. Materials have not only drawn on analyses of genre structures, but also sought to characterise particular genres in terms of the features they contain and the ways they combine with other features, stressing the importance of lexical bundles like *as a result of, it should be noted that,* in academic texts (Hyland, 2008a). Genre text research of this kind has helped replace intuitive understandings with evidence of how language works and informed classroom practices. In the classroom, teachers use a variety of methods, although these almost always seek to expose students to a range of genres and require them to reflect on their genre practices. There is, then, a stress on rhetorical consciousness-raising through analyses of the genres students need to write, often by comparing texts and producing mixed-genre portfolios (e.g. Johns, 2002; Swales and Feak, 2013).

c) The 'New Rhetoric': This approach diverges from the previous two in seeing genres as more flexible and less straightforward to teach. Greater emphasis is given to the ways that genres evolve and exhibit variation, and this leads to a far more provisional understanding of the concept (Freedman and Medway, 1994). The focus is less on forms than the actions these forms are used to accomplish, and so practitioners use qualitative research methods which explore connections between texts and their contexts rather than those which describe their rhetorical conventions.

Quote 7.5   **Coe on the New Rhetoric Genre**

Genres are a motivated, functional relationship between text type and rhetorical situation. That is to say, a genre is neither a text type nor a situation, but rather the functional relationship between a type of text and a type of situation. Text types survive because they work, because they respond effectively to recurring situations.

Coe (2002: 197)

As a result of this focus, research has examined issues such as the historical evolution of genres (Atkinson, 1999); the processes of revising and responding to reviewers in writing scientific articles (Berkenkotter and Huckin, 1995); the social impact of transferring genres into new contexts with different purposes (Freedman and Adam, 2000); and the study of genres in the workplace (Dias, Freedman, Medway and Paré, 1999; Paré, 2000).

New Rhetoric also has a distinctive view on genre pedagogies. It criticises ESP and SFL approaches for removing genres from their complex, dynamic contexts (Freedman, 1994); for locating the study of genres outside their authentic situations of use (Bleich, 2001); and for limiting the understanding of genres to features that writers already recognise (Bazerman, 2004). Genres are said to be too unstable and the classroom context too artificial to teach genre forms, and instead students should be given opportunities to observe genres in their actual situations of use. Students should therefore learn at least one genre in each course actively, by investigating it themselves through the use of "mini-ethnographies", or focused studies that explore a particular event in a community (e.g. Devitt, Reiff and Bawarshi, 2004). Writing classes which link observation and interviews with analyses of genres can therefore be used to give students access to authentic contexts for language use.

Quote 7.6   **Mary Jo Reiff on New Rhetoric Genre Teaching**

As a first assignment, I have students research a field site and observe and describe the participants and their interactions. The following assignment asks students to analyze the language patterns and genre use within that site. For the third assignment, students interview members of the community, culminating in a final ethnographic project that synthesizes the previous research. . . . Making genre analysis the focal point of ethnographic inquiry—having students examine an organization's newsletter or the employee manual at a business—ties communicative actions to their contexts and can illustrate to students how patterns of rhetorical behaviour are inextricably linked to patterns of social behaviour.

Johns et al. (2006)

In other words, emphasis is given to raising students' awareness of contextual features of genres and of the communities who use them. It is knowledge of the social contexts which give life to texts, and this is more important than their formal patterns. It is important, however, not to overestimate genre flexibility. Genres are supported by powerful interests and so change only slowly, while the extent that individuals, particularly students, are able to manipulate established forms is limited. New rhetoric advocates are correct, however, in cautioning us to be aware of the degree of genre differentiation. As noted in Chapter 1, moves can overlap, recur or appear in different sequences. Writers make different choices from optional genre elements and particular communities may emphasise different aspects of the genre that override common structures.

More serious variations are the result of interdiscursivity (or the use of conventions from other genres), particularly the increasing intrusion of promotional elements into genres often considered non-promotional (such as job announcements which advertise the hiring company) and the growing 'synthetic personalisation' of formal public genres (such as letters from companies which seem to be from close friends) (Fairclough, 1995). Mixing genres in this way blurs clear distinctions, sometimes to the extent that new genres become recognised in a community (e.g. *infotainment*, *advertorial* and *docudrama*). Ultimately, however, genres are the ways that we engage in, and make sense of, our social worlds, and our competence to use them does not lie in our ability to identify monolithic uses of language but to modify our choices according to the contexts in which we write.

7.2   Writer-Oriented Approaches to Teaching

The second broad teaching orientation takes the writer, rather than form, as the point of departure. For teachers, Furneaux (1998) suggests this helps to shift an emphasis on the product of writing (what have you written?) to the way it might be developed (how can it be improved?). The three broad theoretical conceptions which collect around this idea (discussed in part 1.2), emphasising personal creativity, cognitive processes and the writer's immediate context, tend to produce similar classroom approaches. There is, therefore, considerable overlap in the methods discussed in this part.

7.2.1   *Writing as Personal Expression*

Some writing teachers, following composition theorists such as Elbow (1998) and Murray (1985), see their goal as fostering students' expressive abilities, encouraging them to find their own voices to produce writing that is fresh and spontaneous. Classes focus on students' personal experiences and opinions, and regard writing as a creative act of self-discovery. This can help generate self-awareness of the writer's social position and literate possibilities (Freire, 1994) as well as facilitate "clear thinking, effective relating, and satisfying self-expression" (Moffett, 1982: 235). From this perspective, writing is learnt, not taught, and so instruction is non-directive and personal, and writing becomes a way of sharing personal meanings.

Teachers adopting this approach see their role as providing opportunities for students to make their own meanings within a positive and co-operative environment which minimises teacher intervention and avoids offering models or suggesting responses to topics beforehand. Instead, they seek to stimulate the writer's ideas through pre-writing tasks, such as journal writing, and responding to the ideas that learners produce, rather than dwell on formal errors. Students are given considerable opportunities for writing and are urged to be creative and take chances through free writing. Where exercises are used to support writing, these may attend to features such as style, wordiness, clichés, active vs. passive voice and so on.

Teachers who focus on expressive discourse assign writing only about personal experiences rather than about information, data or ideas to become more engaged in writing and to help dispel fears of writing. Quote 7.7 shows typical writing rubrics in this approach. Both ask students to read personal writing extracts, respond to them as readers, and then to use them as a stimulus for writing about their own experiences.

> **Quote 7.7**   **Expressivist Essay Topics**
>
> In his article, Green tells us that Bob Love was saved because "some kind and caring people" helped him to get speech therapy. Is there any

example of "kind and caring people" you have witnessed in your life or in the lives of those around you? Tell who these people are and exactly what they did that showed their kindness.

Violet's aunt died for her country even though she never wore a uniform or fired a bullet. Write about what values or people you would sacrifice your life for if you were pushed to do so.

O'Keefe (2000: 99, 141)

Expressivism encourages writers to explore their beliefs, engage with the ideas of others, and connect with readers. It assumes, however, a strong individualistic ethos which may discourage, and even disadvantage, students from cultures that place a different value on 'self expression'. As noted in Chapter 1, it is also difficult to extract from the approach any clear principles from which teachers can base their teaching or evaluate what 'good writing' looks like. It simply assumes that all writers have a similar innate creative potential and teachers can unlock this if their students' originality is allowed to flourish. Teachers merely have to set writing tasks on topics of potential interest to writers and which encourage self-discovery, which can be a tall order for teachers who do not themselves write creatively.

7.2.2   *Writing as a Cognitive Process*

While the process approach is similar to expressivism in emphasising the writer as an independent producer of texts, it goes further to advise teachers on what they can do to assist this. The various manifestations of this approach all recognise basic cognitive processes as central to writing activity and stress the need to develop students' abilities to plan, define a rhetorical problem, and propose and evaluate solutions. It thus extends the Expressivist approach to provide students with the resources to produce text modelled on the processes of expert writers.

The recursive, planned and goal-driven conception of composing proposed in this model has led to the growth of a raft of classroom practices which have become almost self-evident for many writing teachers. It is, in fact, difficult to exaggerate the impact of process ideas on both L1 and L2 writing classrooms. Teachers are encouraged to set pre-writing activities to generate ideas about content and structure, support brainstorming and outlining, require multiple drafts, give extensive feedback, facilitate peer responses and delay surface corrections until final editing. Process research has meant that cooperative writing, teacher conferences, problem-based tasks, journal-writing, group discussions and mixed portfolio assessments are now all commonplace in our methodological repertoire (e.g. Casanave, 2004; Leki, Cumming and Silva, 2008).

Concept 7.4   A Process Model of Writing Instruction

Potentially process writing classes involve the following steps, which can be recursive, repeated and simultaneous:

Selection of topic—by teacher and/or students
Prewriting—brainstorming, notetaking, outlining, journal writing, etc.
Composing—getting ideas down on paper
Response to draft—teacher/peers respond to ideas, organisation and style
Revising—reorganising, style, adjusting to readers, refining ideas
Response to revisions—teacher/peers respond to ideas, organisation and style
Proofreading and editing—checking and correcting form, layout, evidence, etc.
Evaluation—teacher evaluates progress
Publishing—by class circulation, presentation, blog, noticeboard, website, etc.
Follow-up tasks—to address weaknesses

The lack of any evidence for the success of process approaches in the classroom, or for any approach if it comes to it, is not really surprising as 'the approach' is actually many different approaches applied unevenly and in different ways. Nor should any method be expected to automatically produce good writers. The process of writing is a rich mix of elements which, together with cognition, include the writer's experiences and background, as well as a sense of self, of others, of situation and of purpose. There are, however, two serious reservations about this perspective. The first concerns the underlying individualistic emphasis of the methods, which have little to say to students about social aspects of either language use or language learning, and which may handicap ESL students from more collectivist cultures (Ramanathan and Atkinson, 1999a). The second relates to the problems associated with the fact that process courses offer general writing skills instruction (GWSI), what Kaufer and Young (1993) have called "writing with no particular content".

This approach underlies the 'composition' courses which almost all first-year students are required to take at U.S. universities. The U.S. seems to be alone in providing curricular space in higher education for formal writing instruction of this kind, and it has the potential benefits of making students more aware of the uses of written discourse in higher education and society, and for broadening access to new social and professional roles. It does, however, have widely recognised limitations, such as arbitrary content, a lack of intellectual rigour and limited effectiveness (e.g. Kitzhaber, 1960). More seriously, however, is the fact that such process writing courses tend to assume what Street (1995) calls the myth of autonomous literacy: that students can acquire writing skills independently of some specific human activity and then apply these skills to contexts as they need them. In contrast, we need to see literacy as always and everywhere bound up with the purposes, communities and contexts within which individuals write.

7.2.3 Writing as a Situated Act

As discussed in part 1.2.3, this approach, while focusing on the writer, recognises that writing is a social act which occurs in particular situations. It therefore gives more attention than process theories to the experiences and understandings of writers in the immediate contexts in which they write. However, while the social routines surrounding acts of writing have been studied in detail to see how contexts can both assist and constrain acts of writing, there is no explicit teaching method which organises writing around these understandings. It does, though, encourage teachers to see writing as involving far more than texts or grammatical forms, and look beyond expressive and cognitive writing strategies to consider how they can set up writing classrooms as sites for interactions where relationships, and the conventions which organise them, can best help their students to write. The teacher's role, then, is to exploit the reality of the classroom as a resource for teaching writing.

Classrooms have certain effects on learning to write in that the activities and relationships constructed within them relate to psychological change. Writing is a socially situated process of making meanings through texts, so that becoming a competent writer is not just a linguistic or cognitive process but a socio-cultural one, which requires learners to appropriate the meanings created in the contexts in which they operate (e.g. Kostouli, 2005). The particularly situated nature of writing means, for one thing, that the social group of the class is likely to interact with the situated personal histories of the individual learners within it. What Breen says about language learning in Quote 7.8 below can therefore be equally applied to learning to write.

Quote 7.8 **Breen on the Class as a Culture**

A language class—outwardly a gathering of people with an assumed common purpose—is an arena of subjective and intersubjective realities which are worked out, changed, and maintained. And these realities are not trivial background to the tasks of teaching and learning a language. They locate and define the new language itself as if it never existed before, and they continually specify and mould the activities of teaching and learning.

Breen (2001: 128)

Working on writing tasks and creating texts involves constant socio-cognitive construction and reinterpretation, and for Breen this means teachers have to recognise that learners have two important contributions to make to the process of learning, and of learning to write:

1. their prior definitions and experiences of writing, learning and working in classrooms;
2. the ability to be able to talk about and collectively explore and construct texts.

Classroom arrangements, particularly grouping practices and how students are asked to work together and with the tools (computers, websites, etc.) which mediate their relationships, become important considerations. These play an important role in influencing how students understand writing and the ways they develop their plans and intentions for communicating. By encouraging talk around texts and by structuring the support provided by teachers and peers, teachers can boost the confidence and motivation of students. At the same time, the use of evaluative and review practices which recognise individual and collective contributions and achievements can help build a sense of security and of writing in a community.

Essentially, however, this is just one aspect of context. An overemphasis on the culture of the classroom fails to account for the operation of wider communities and the beliefs and expectations of those who will read the texts written in the classroom. We turn to approaches which address this aspect in the final part of this chapter.

7.3   Reader-Oriented Approaches to Teaching

Reader-oriented approaches extend the idea of *context* beyond the classroom and how the composing situation is set up for writing to include consideration of what readers expect to find in a text, what they want from it, and how they are likely to use it. Reader awareness is a key aspect of this perspective but conceptions of audience vary, together with teaching practices, depending whether the audience is seen as a specific person, members of a community or the constraints of institutional power-holders.

7.3.1   *Writing as Social Interaction*

This perspective understands that coherence and meaning in writing are not accomplished by the writer alone but through the interaction of the writer and reader in concert. Writing always has a purpose, a context and an intended audience, and involves making choices about how best to get one's meanings over effectively to particular readers by writing in ways they will recognise and understand. The writer imagines the reader of his or her text and crafts it to engage them. A major implication of an interactionist approach for teachers, then, is that a cultivated sense of audience is crucial to the development of effective writing strategies, and that this can only be accomplished through an awareness of social context. An important aspect of the teacher's role is therefore to set writing tasks which encourage students to see their texts through another's eyes, and so anticipate reader's needs.

However, while accomplished writers are quite good at imagining their audiences, novices often find it difficult to anticipate what unfamiliar readers might want from a text and cannot flesh out a mental image of their readers in the same way as experienced writers. Students know that their teacher or supervisor is their main reader, and finding alternative audiences outside the writing class can be a headache for teachers. One solution, suggested by Patricia Hedge (2005), involves asking students to imagine the conversation that might replace a letter of application or request so that they visualise their audience and work out how the dialogue might have transpired had the interaction been verbal rather than written. This encourages students to think of the questions which 'the reader' might ask and so helps them to include all the relevant content and to order it in a helpful way. Alternatively, Schriver (1992) recommends asking writers to predict the problems which readers' might have with a text and then provide them with detailed reader responses, perhaps gathered from Think Aloud Protocols as readers read the text.

One potential source of trouble for writers is misjudging the knowledge and attitudes they share with readers. A useful task here is to ask students to consider the likely response of readers to the content of their text. How, for example, will readers of a student newspaper react to an article arguing for higher tuition fees? Will they be immediately sympathetic to the idea or need persuading? What arguments and rhetorical choices might best help them accept it? These kinds of issues also encourage talk around texts as students collaborate to consider their audience. Tribble (1997), for example, discusses this issue when considering a writing task which asks students to write a list of instructions on how to use a public telephone (or other piece of technology) on arriving in the U.S.

Quote 7.9   **Tribble on Thinking about the Reader**

The 'important American businessman' is an unfamiliar audience for students with little knowledge of the USA. Although he might be kept as an eventual reader, it may be more useful to assume other class members as immediate readers. For example the class might discuss what the American businessman would not know about the local technology, and draw up a needs profile which could be used at various stages of a writing process. The profile would make it possible to bring together the students' own knowledge of reader-writer relations in written instructions and their understanding of the gap between how things are done in their own country and how they are done elsewhere. This, in turn, would help with the planning and composing of the text.

Tribble (1997: 106)

A	B	C	D
What do I know about the topic?	What does my reader already know about it?	What does my reader not know?	What is my reader's attitude likely to be?
Customer ordered 5000 pairs of Nike shoes but only 500 were delivered.	As for A	What the company will do about it, e.g. apologise, refund the price, send more stock.	Customer is probably very annoyed. She will expect action or compensation

Figure 7.1 An audience awareness heuristic.

Another way of encouraging students to attend to shared knowledge can be achieved by offering them a simple checklist. Following a task originally suggested by White and Arndt (1991: 32), the example response to a letter of complaint in Fig 7.1 can help students think of their readers.

Focusing on the potential effects of language choices on readers can also be instructive for students. One example is the effect that hedges can have on readers of academic and professional texts. Hedges are items like *possible, might* and *perhaps*, and they are important in several registers, including academic writing, as they weaken the writer's commitment to statements. They present information tentatively, either because the writer is unsure of its truth or wants to convey respect for readers who may hold alternative views. As the following example from a student dissertation from my corpus shows, hedges are useful in displaying audience awareness and in weighing the degree of certainty to invest in a statement:

> The low average score in this study *might suggest* that the subjects are under pressure and this is also *possibly* true for most Hong Kong students who have to get a high grade in order to get into the university or to get a good job. Hong Kong students *may* be able to reduce their anxiety by noticing it in their learning. Their ignorance of affective strategies *may account for* why there are students who commit suicide since they cannot stand the pressure in learning.

Hedges are important to students as they draw attention to the fact that academic statements don't just communicate ideas, but also the writer's attitude to them and to readers. Hedges have roughly the same frequencies in academic research articles as past-tense verbs or passive voice (Hyland, 1998), yet they tend to present considerable problems for second-language students, who often make excessively strong claims (Hyland and Milton, 1997).

A different approach is suggested by Ann Johns (1997), who advocates that students should get out of the classroom and research the interests and expectations of real readers. These projects involve reaching out to potential readers of the texts students are learning to write in workplaces, universities, or other parts of the building, and interviewing them about their uses of texts and what they expect to find in them. Johns believes this can improve students' writing through a better understanding of the interaction between their purposes, the interests and values of real audiences, and the genres that are appropriate for specific contexts. This interest in real audiences as a context for writing has also stimulated discussions about the use of peer and teacher feedback (e.g. Ferris, 2003; Hyland and Hyland, 2006). Mittan (1989: 209), for example, argues that "the social context created by peer interaction is more realistic and therefore the feedback more powerful (than that provided by teachers alone)". It has also encouraged teachers to experiment with non-assessed student journal writing, where teachers can be real non-judgmental readers of their students' writing (e.g. Connor-Greene, 2000).

Most centrally, however, students need a clear context for writing, and the importance of the social-interactionist orientation for teachers is that it encourage a focus on context as a set of recognisable conventions in a text. It is through these that a piece of writing achieves its force.

7.3.2 Writing as Social Construction

There are various classroom approaches for realising social constructivist principles, but prominent among them are textually focused genre methodologies (see part 3.2). In many classrooms, students are learning the genres of occupational, professional or academic groups, and the writing teacher's role here is to help students discover how valued text forms and practices are socially constructed in response to the common purposes of these target communities. As noted in Chapter 1, most writing is done as members of communities of different kinds and being able to use their discourses demonstrates competence as an 'insider'.

Concept 7.5 Social Construction and EAP

Academic disciplines use language in different ways (Hyland, 2004a) and might therefore be seen as academic tribes (Becher and Trowler, 2001) with their own particular norms and practices. Through the use of these disciplinary conventions and practices, members construct academic knowledge, as they generate support, express collegiality, resolve difficulties, and negotiate disagreement through patterns of rhetorical choices which connect their texts with their disciplinary cultures. Persuasion, then, is accomplished with language. But it is language that demonstrates legitimacy. Writers must recognise and make choices from the rhetorical options available in their fields to appeal to readers from within the boundaries of their disciplines.

Here students attend to the texts they will most need to write beyond the classroom, so that genres become a talking point and focus for analysis to raise awareness of the interdependence of texts and the communities that use them. Genre-based writing instruction follows modern theories of learning in recognising the importance of *collaboration*, or peer interaction, and *scaffolding*, or teacher-supported learning. Together, these concepts assist learners through two notions of learning:

- shared consciousness—the idea that learners working together learn more effectively than individuals working separately;
- borrowed consciousness—the idea that learners working with knowledgeable others develop greater understanding of tasks and ideas.

Genre pedagogies thus draw on the ideas of Russian psychologist Vygotsky (1978) and the American educational psychologist Bruner (1990), who emphasised the role of interaction with peers and others who have more experience to move learners through "the zone of proximal development" from their existing level of performance to a level of "potential performance" where they are able to work without help.

The notion of scaffolding receives its most sophisticated expression in the *Teaching-Learning Cycle* (e.g. Feez, 1998) shown in Fig 7.2.

The cycle informs classroom activities by showing the process of learning a genre as a series of linked stages which provide the support needed to move learners towards understanding texts. These stages are:

1. setting the context—to reveal genre purposes and the settings in which the genre is commonly used

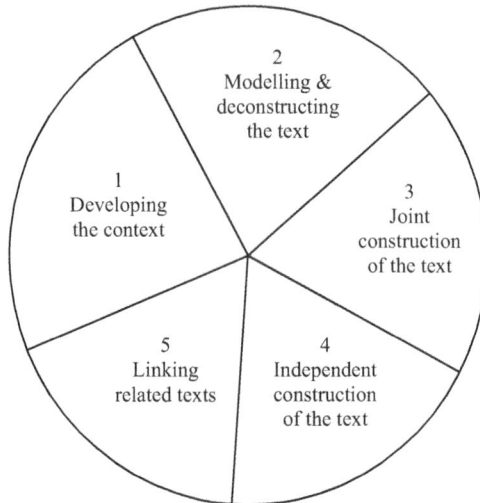

Figure 7.2 The teaching learning cycle.

2.   modelling—analysing the genre to reveal its stages and key features
3.   joint construction—guided, teacher-supported practice in the genre
4.   independent construction—independent writing monitored by the teacher
5.   comparing—relating what has been learnt to other genres and contexts

Each stage therefore seeks to achieve a different purpose, and as a result is associated with different types of classroom activities and different teacher-learner roles.

The cycle is intended to be used flexibly, allowing students to enter at any stage depending on their existing knowledge of the genre, so when a genre is being introduced for the first time, students will probably work through all the stages. It is also possible that participants may want to return to earlier stages of the cycle for revision purposes, or that teachers will decide to go through the cycle again. The model therefore allows vocabulary to be recycled and the skills already gained to be further developed by working through a new cycle at a more advanced level of expression of the genre (Hyland, 2004c).

Complementing genre approaches, rhetorical consciousness-raising has proved useful in assisting novice authors to create, comprehend and reflect on the ways texts work to address and construct discourse communities. Instead of building up a text from particular grammatical forms, this is a 'top down' approach which encourages writers to see grammatical features as "the on-line processing component of discourse and not the set of syntactic building blocks with which discourse is constructed" (Rutherford, 1987: 104). It therefore focuses on the ways meaning is constructed as part of the overall intentions of writers. While this kind of inquiry can take a variety of forms, including collaborative projects, comparing texts, modelling, text deconstruction and so on, it most simply involves training students to read rhetorically and to reflect on the practices they observe and use themselves. It means providing conditions whereby students are exposed to discourses from a variety of contexts and are encouraged to inquire into their own literate lives and the literacy practices of others.

One approach to consciousness-raising is to involve students in contrastive reflection, asking them to compare how features are used in different texts or contexts. For instance, students can compare the advice found in style guides and textbooks with the actual practices of academic writers, or how a feature such as hedging or self-mention is used in different genres or in the same genre in different disciplines (Hyland, 2008b). Rhetorical consciousness-raising always involves a focus on texts, and this can also be achieved by encouraging students to conduct mini-analyses of the genres they have to write or of their own writing. For example, teachers can ask students to identify where writers have chosen to use or avoid *I* and determining possible reasons for this. So by analysing texts, considering advice, and discussing uses, students can work towards a more informed understanding of language use. Ann Johns (1997) calls this a 'socioliterate' approach to teaching.

> **Quote 7.10**   **Johns on 'Socioliterate' Approaches to Teaching**
>
> In socioliterate views, literacies are acquired principally through exposure
> to discourses from a variety of social contexts. Through this exposure,
> individuals gradually develop theories of genre. Those who can suc-
> cessfully produce and process texts within certain genres are members
> of communities, for academic learning does not take place independent
> of these communities . . . What I am advocating, then, is an approach in
> which literacy classes become laboratories for the study of texts, roles,
> and contexts, for research into evolving student literacies and developing
> awareness and critique of communities and their textual contracts.
>
> Johns (1997: 14–19)

Rather than modelling the practices of experts, this approach offers students
a guiding framework for producing texts by raising their awareness of the connections between forms, purposes and roles in specific social contexts. The
danger of a constructionist perspective, of course, is that teachers may inadver-
tently represent particular conventions as normative, static and natural. There
is a risk that particular forms and practices will not only be seen as fixed and
'correct', but uncritically regarded as naturally superior forms of communication, blessed with the prestige of the social groups which routinely employ
them. This can only make the learning task harder for novice writers, since
they may view the indigenous literacies that they bring with them to the classroom as a deficit which has to be rectified and replaced. This brings us to the
final perspective in this chapter.

7.3.3   *Writing as Power and Ideology*

The question of how far politics plays a role in the day-to-day teaching of writing, particularly to second-language students of English, remains a controversial and emotive issue. On one side is the view that all education is ideologically
loaded, as it tacitly encourages acceptance of existing social arrangements and
prepares students to fit into subordinate roles in their courses and workplaces
(e.g. Canagarajah, 1999). On the other side is the view that writing teachers are
tasked with the pragmatic goal of developing the language and writing abilities
students need to prosper in their studies and be successful in their careers (e.g.
Santos, 1992). This pragmatic view ensures that action is informed by understanding (Allison, 1996), so that curricular decisions are underpinned by a sensitivity to the contexts of teaching and to the most urgent needs of learners.

Most teachers are probably aware that ideological issues lay behind their
work and recognise the institutional power that stands behind prestigious
genres. Equally, though, they see their job as empowering learners by initiating

them into the ways of making meanings that are socially valued by particular communities. Fewer teachers, however, systematically employ the principles of critical pedagogy in their teaching. The goal of this perspective, drawing inspiration from the works of Freire (2007) and CDA (discussed in part 1.3.3), is to help students become aware of how writing is grounded in social (and especially institutional) structures. By the close study of texts and their contexts, students might come to see the ideological assumptions which underlie the authority of the discourses they encounter in their everyday lives. More directly, CDA helps to reveal writing as relative to particular groups and contexts, and so encourages teachers to assist students in understanding more about their target communities. What appears as a dominant and superior form of writing can then be seen as simply another practice, one among many, and thus open like others to scrutiny and contestation. This has been called 'critical language awareness'.

Quote 7.11 Ivanic and Clark on Critical Language Awareness

(It aims to) empower learners by providing them with a critical analytical framework to help them reflect on their own language experiences and practices and on the language practices of others in the institutions of which they are part and the wider society in which they live.

Clark and Ivanic (1997: 217)

Critical theorists ask teachers to think about how their teaching may unreflectively accept existing conditions and reproduce them in their classes, advising them to question the extent to which their goals and activities are actually politically neutral. Benesch (2001), for example, encourages us to review our assumptions that students should simply go along with the demands of academic assignments, the behaviours expected in academic classes, and the hierarchical arrangements of academic institutions.

These ideas have been implemented in various ways in writing classes, and to give students the means to question and challenge existing power relationships within their institution and discipline. Fundamental to Benesch's position, for example, is *critical needs analysis*, or *rights analysis*. This transforms a core tenet of EAP and ESP writing instruction by rejecting their perceived emphasis on needs defined by stakeholders, such as employers and teachers, to start from the position that students typically "are entitled to more power than they have" (Benesch, 1996: 736). Similarly, the ethnographic exploration of readers discussed in part 3.1, for example, lends itself to students researching faculty practices through interviews to discover why subject tutors selected certain readings, textbooks, writing assignments or assessment procedures

(Johns, 1997). In addition, it is often possible for students to participate in the negotiation of classroom pedagogies to take greater control of the ways they learn (Breen and Littlejohn, 2000; Canagarajah, 2002), or for teachers to engage learners in a critical dialogue about topics or teaching (Benesch, 2001). The idea behind all these approaches is that students are not merely passive subjects to be shaped to meet the needs of the academy, but are empowered as potentially active participants.

The critical pedagogy movement, however, has had a relatively limited impact on English language education, in large part because it has failed to engage teachers and has largely avoided any serious critique of its own practices (Usher and Edwards, 1994). MacCallister (2016), for example, observes that without greater self-reflection, critical pedagogy risks assuming the kind of hegemonic position that it sets out to challenge. Instead, he suggests that a 'second wave' critical EAP should start by engaging with the local positions of students rather than adopting a universal critical narrative that risks imposing its ideas on the classroom. Grande (2004) and Pennycook (2010) similarly suggest that it is only by starting with local positions and negotiating common ground between the critical and the local that a genuinely progressive agenda can be developed.

More immediately, we can see that writing teachers are not the unthinking instruments of the status quo which some suggest. On the contrary, rather than simply brainwashing students into accepting the inevitable superiority of valued genres, providing learners with greater understanding of and access to them is a key aspect of demystifying such genres. Learning about genres, in fact, gives students the necessary basis for critical engagement with cultural and textual practices, providing them with ways of talking and thinking about language. This meta-language facilitates critical analysis by allowing students to discuss written texts in precise and explicit ways so the texts they need to write can be analysed, compared and criticised (Hammond and Macken-Horarik, 1999). Understanding how texts are socially constructed and ideologically shaped reveals the ways that they work to represent some interests and perspectives, and neglect others. This helps undermine a view of writing as a universal, naturalised and non-contestable way of participating in professional or academic communities, so that what appear as dominant and superior forms of writing can be seen as simply different practices, thereby opening them to scrutiny and challenge.

7.4   Conclusion

In this chapter I have tried to elaborate some of the ways that the understandings of writing discussed in Chapter 1 translate into understandings of teaching. The main job of writing teachers involves conceptualising, planning and delivering courses, and while this may seem to be mainly an application of professional knowledge gained through practical hands-on experience, classroom decisions are always informed by our theories and beliefs about what writing is and how people learn to write. A familiarity with what research and theory tell us about writing, and about the teaching of writing, can therefore help us to reflect on our assumptions and enable us to approach teaching methods with an informed and critical eye. The fact that teachers are professionals and not simply robots applying procedures also suggests that we consider the ethical dimensions of our practices and recognise that the learning experiences we offer our students can have political outcomes. The challenge here is in applying instruction and assessment procedures which are principled, effective and fair as we contribute our expertise to understand the social and communicative demands that our students face.

Further Reading

Benesch, S. (2001) *Critical English for academic purposes*. Mahwah, NJ: Erlbaum.
A clearly written discussion of critical pedagogy in English for academic purposes, covering theoretical issues and grounding these in the demands of real teaching contexts.

Ferris, D. and Hedgecock, J. (2005) *Teaching ESL composition*, 2nd edn. Mahwah, NJ: Lawrence Earlbaum.
A practical book for language teachers.

Hyland, K. (2004) *Genre and second language writers*. Ann Arbor: University of Michigan Press.
An overview of genre and how it can be used by teachers of EFL/ESL writing.

Johns, A. (1997) *Text, role and context*. Cambridge: Cambridge University Press.
An accessible and interesting discussion of a 'socioliterate' approach to writing teaching based on students' experiences and researches into academic texts.

Johns, A. (ed) (2002) *Genre in the classroom*. Mahwah, NJ: Lawrence Earlbaum.
This edited book represents the different traditions in genre and shows how they have been applied in the classroom.

8   Teaching Writing
Classes and Courses

This chapter will . . .

*   show how research contributes to teaching writing in a variety of English language courses;
*   examine the methodologies, materials, and theoretical premises, of these courses;
*   explore how each course draws on and reflects a major orientation to writing.

The research discussed in Section II has contributed to the development of classroom practices in numerous ways. Teachers are far better informed than in the past and so seek to ensure that students are provided with a range of writing and revising strategies, have the formal and rhetorical knowledge to encode content and relationships appropriately, and make lexical and grammatical choices which anticipate the views of their readers. But research offers no universal solutions to the challenges of classroom practice, which means teacher beliefs about language, about writing, about students and about learning all play crucial intervening roles. How we see these aspects of teaching and how we see ourselves as teachers mediate our teaching practices. We also work in a wide range of different contexts with different resources, class sizes and constraints on our freedom to innovate or choose; we work with students of different backgrounds, proficiencies and future goals; and we work in different institutions and countries with their own preferred teaching approaches and attitudes towards English.

Theory, research and context therefore shape instructional practices in important ways, and by reflecting on examples of how others have come to terms with these decisions, we can improve our own practice. This chapter provides some extended examples of how different conceptions of writing and learning have influenced teaching in real classrooms. Taking examples from New Zealand, Australia, Papua New Guinea, Hong Kong and England, I attempt to reveal the impact of research on five very different writing courses in very different contexts of teaching and learning.

8.1   Writ 101: A Modified Process Approach

This first case is a successful combination of process and rhetorical approaches to writing pedagogy[1] as discussed in parts 1.1.2 and 1.2. Designed to develop the academic writing skills of New Zealand undergraduates, the course was originally written by Janet Holst to "give process a classroom presence" (Holst, personal communication) and then revised by Derek Wallace and Robin Cohen to include rhetorical aspects of writing (Wallace, 2015). *Writ 101: Becoming an Effective Writer* demonstrates an explicit appreciation of writing as purposeful, social and recursive, as it progressively builds an awareness of genre and composing to assist students to:

1   Employ efficient and effective techniques for drafting and revising a range of written texts for different purposes and audiences.
2   Reflect on their writing development.
3   Respond effectively to, and evaluate, the writing of others.
4   Carry out and document research according to the conventions of academic writing.

(Writ 101 course outline)

The course thus resists both a narrow focus on form and an exclusive preoccupation with writing strategies to develop techniques for generating, revising and responding to a variety of texts and encouragement to consider readers. While it makes use of text structure and audience, it is also influenced by Flower's work on writing as problem-solving; Elbow's emphasis on prewriting, revision and peer response; and Murray's views on writing for learning. The pedagogical implications are that writers can be guided, through multiple drafting and revision, to adopt the practices of experts.

Concept 8.1   A Process View of Writing

- **Writing is problem-solving**: writers use invention strategies and planning to resolve the rhetorical problems that each writing task presents.
- **Writing is generative**: writers explore and discover ideas as they write.
- **Writing is recursive**: writers constantly review and modify their text as they write it.
- **Writing is collaborative**: writers benefit from focused feedback from a variety of sources.
- **Writing is developmental**: writers should be evaluated on their improvement and not just on their final products.

8.1.1   The Approach

Writ 101: *Becoming an Effective Writer* is an elective course which seeks to be both accessible and relevant to all majors, proficiencies and years. It begins by encouraging students to think about the rhetorical context of writing and proceeds through a series of research-related assignments to a final reflection on how their writing has developed during the course. Underlying the approach is encouragement for students to engage in a recursive process of planning, drafting, reviewing, evaluating and revising within a supportive environment which makes use of various feedback sources.

Quote 8.1   Aims and Philosophy of Writ 101

Aims of the Course

1. The first aim is to provide a *general foundation* for *any* kind of writing. How? By providing a framework for thinking about the important considerations:

    *   Who is the *writer*?
    *   What is the *purpose*?
    *   Who is the *reader* or readers?
    *   Therefore, what *type* (or *genre*) of text—report, essay, review, etc.?

    These factors are interrelated. The type of text (genre) will depend on the particular combination of the other elements. This framework helps us identify the *context* of writing.
2. The second aim is to provide specific instruction in writing at university.

Principles of instruction

The teaching philosophy of this course is that more effective and better quality writing occurs when writers:

1. Clarify the context of their writing task.
2. Obtain feedback from readers.
3. Repeatedly revise their work.

Wallace (2015: 5)

8.1.2   The Structure

The *Writ 101* course comprises a three-hour workshop each week for 12 weeks. It begins by focusing students on the rhetorical context of academic writing and the desirability of problem-setting compared with "factual finding out". A large part of this context involves finding and evaluating appropriate sources and encouraging students to reflect on their own literacy development and practices as writers. While introducing key textual features of cohesion, argument structure and signposting rhetorical relationships, the course also encourages students to practise invention, drafting and revising techniques.

The course begins by introducing students to a basic meta-language to talk about the different functions of writing, particularly *explaining* and *persuading,* and how genres make use of different "modes of writing" (or 'macro genres' in Systemic Functional terms). One way this is done is by asking students to bring a short text to class which they found either *enlightening*—" i.e. which explained something you hadn't understood properly before" or *persuasive*—" i.e. which changed or modified your view on some issue", or that captured their interest, and discuss what it was about *the way the text was written* which contributed to that effect. This helps students to talk about texts while guiding them towards understanding them. An example is the model provided in Table 8.1 as "one possible format for writing a research essay or report". The format on the right *parallels* the research process in the left-hand column, and the three main sections of introduction, report and discussion are associated with the mode or *macro genre* of narrative, exposition and argument.

Writ 101 focuses on providing instruction and feedback on how to organise a piece of writing to suit its purpose and is organised around four core assignments, each involving a different genre:

- a research proposal (mainly expository writing) of 600 words
- a critical review (emphasising argument writing) 600 words
- a research paper 1500 words
- a personal reflection 900 words

The first three assignments allow the student to progressively develop a response to a particular research question and the fourth requires them to reflect on how their writing has improved during the course. Students work on each of these assignments with their peers in the workshops. All assignments begin with some kind of group discussion of texts, analysis of their typical contexts, freewriting and practice, but they develop in different ways, focusing

Table 8.1 A research essay format.

Process of Inquiry	*Research Essay: Parallel Format*
Identify a question or problem	Title
Describe and explain the question/problem	Introduction (may involve *narrative*)
Why is the question or problem important?	Introduction
	Focusing statement
Research possible answers or solutions (*different perspectives*)	Report (*exposition*)
Compare and contrast different answers or solutions (*evaluation*) to arrive at a conclusion	Discussion (*argument*)
(preferred answer/solution)	Conclusion

on salient features of the genre and highlighting a particular aspect of the composing process.

The genres that drive the course are distinguished in terms of their different purposes and audience with the acronym RAFT (Role and Purpose, Audience, Focus, Tone) being strongly emphasised throughout. Quote 8.2 is an abridged version of this.

Quote 8.2   Writing in Different Genres: RAFT

The more fully we understand the complexities of any situation to which writing is an appropriate response, the more effective will be the text we write. The following categories are the most important considerations for understanding this *rhetorical context*—the term for a situation involving purposeful communication.

1. Role (or purpose)

What does the writer hope to achieve by writing? In this course we will be mainly concerned with the purposes, or functions, of *informing*, *explaining*, and *persuading*. These are the main functions of *transactional* writing such as is done at university and in the workplace—i.e. writing that involves an exchange of information or opinion.

2. Audience (or readers)

Questions that can help shape your writing for your audience:

• *How much do my readers already know about the topic or situation I am writing about?*
• *How much do my readers expect me to tell them, regardless of how much they know?*
• *Are my readers likely to agree with what I am writing? Or will they be hostile? Will they be open-minded, interested, or indifferent? If a mixture, how do I respond to that?*

3. Form (or Genre)

What type of text is appropriate in this situation? This refers to the particular linguistic style and organisation that is characteristic of a text: academic essay; report; article; short story. But the question also asks you to think about whether you need to *vary* that organisation or structure to suit a particular occasion.

4. Tone

How do you want to 'sound' in your text? Serious or humorous? Formal or informal? Passionate or laid back? This question of tone, or *register*, will have considerable impact on your choice of language. You will usually make this decision once the questions of purpose and audience have been answered. And probably after the question of form has been decided.

Wallace (2015: 9–10)

8.1.3   *Feedback and Assessment*

Students have the chance to revise the first three assignments in response to tutor and peer feedback. Each text receives commentary based on a rubric which focuses the reader on specific aspects of the genre in question, thereby raising both participants' awareness of important issues. The peer response sheet for the third assignment is shown in Table 8.2. Writers redraft their essays on the basis of this commentary and submit the revised version to their tutor along with an evaluation of how they have performed the task and what they have done in response to feedback. Final drafts should therefore show improvement and bear the influence of peer and tutor comments. The final assignment,

Table 8.2 Sample peer response sheet.

PEER RESPONSE SHEET: RESEARCH PAPER
Writer's name _____
Title of Draft: _____
Responder's name _____
What do you think is the strongest part of the text? Can you say why this is?
Were you confused at any point in the text? Do you have any suggestions about this?
Is there any part that would benefit from expansion or elaboration?
Is there any part that is irrelevant or over-explained?
What other suggestions do you have to help the writer develop the inquiry further?
Ask the writer what else he/she would like you to comment on.
• Writer's additional questions to be listed here.   • Peer Response
WRITER'S REFLECTION ON PEER RESPONSE

Wallace (2015: 99–100)

however, is edited and revised without written tutor feedback. While students are able to conference with their tutors, they have to develop, edit and revise the reflective paper alone.

8.1.4   Conclusions

Writ 101 is a popular and successful course which gives a clear pedagogical focus to process-writing research while incorporating ideas from genre theory and rhetorical analysis. It involves students in a great deal of writing practice as well as opportunities for reflection and feedback. As a result, students are given the opportunity to develop not only their writing skills but also a critical awareness of good writing and effective expression in several genres. The course places heavy burdens on tutors, however, as extensive feedback and conferencing are necessary if students are to benefit from the redrafting the course requires. These efforts obviously pay off, however, as the course is consistently over-subscribed and receives glowing recommendations from students.

8.2   Genre in South Australian Schools

Writing is central to children's intellectual, social and emotional development and plays a critical role in learning. In implementing the new Australian National Curriculum (ACARA, 2015), many states remain committed to a genre approach, particularly in the primary and English as an Additional Language (EAL) sectors. South Australia is one of these states (DECS, 2004). Informed by a Systemic Functional model of language (see page 148 and Concept 8.2) and by research into writing in schools (e.g. Martin, 1993; Feez, 2001), the syllabus encourages an explicit focus on the organisation of texts and the language writers need to achieve particular purposes.

Concept 8.2   A Functional Model of Writing

- Language is a system for communicating meaning.
- Meanings are organised as texts and have distinctive characteristics depending on their purposes.
- Texts are never individual; they always relate to a social context and other texts.
- Context is realised in texts through conventions of field (what), tenor (who) and mode (how).
- A knowledge of the resources for creating texts allows writers to write more effectively.
- All texts can be described in terms of both form and function, i.e. their organisation of elements for making meanings and the purposes that are being served with them.

8.2.1 The R-10 English Syllabus[2]

While the major national curriculum innovation mandates an explicit focus on knowledge about language in English (Derewianka, 2012a, 2012b), it is relatively silent about genre, which has been a central pedagogy in many Australian classrooms for 30 years. This follows from the work conducted at the University of Sydney in the early 1980s which sought to identify the genres found in primary (and later in secondary) schools by analysing the discourse and register features of samples of students' writing (e.g. Rothery, 1986; Christie, 2005). Many of these ideas are found in the South Australian school syllabuses. In addition to their centrality in the English syllabus, moreover, genres are also key to teaching and learning across the entire curriculum (DECD, 2013). Thus, the professional development module for teachers stresses the value of genre knowledge in presenting and representing content in both primary and secondary schools (see Quote 8.3).

Quote 8.3   Professional Development for Secondary Teachers on Genre

- A range of school genres can be identified in the Australian Curriculum and the South Australian Certificate of Education with each genre having a particular purpose
- Different learning areas use genres with particular structures and language features to construct specific learning area knowledge
- Some genres are more complex than others—e.g. a practical investigation report is more complex than a procedural text
- Each genre increases in complexity through the years of schooling—e.g. a sequential explanation should be taught earlier than a causal explanation
- Secondary school genres are commonly macro-genres, that is, combinations of various genres—e.g. an investigative report may require aspects of a procedural recount, a description, a discussion and an evaluation
- Teachers need to understand the language demands of their learning area genres, especially those used for assessment, in order to effectively scaffold students' language and literacy

DECD (2013: 3)

At the core of the English syllabus is a range of genres seen as fundamental to how students' should learn to interpret and compose texts—oral, written and multimodal—to communicate their different purposes to a variety of audiences. A basic distinction is made between literary genres, which explore and interpret human experience; factual genres, which present information or ideas in order to enlighten or persuade; and response genres, which require writers to interpret and react to another text. Table 8.3 lists the main genres and their purposes.

Table 8.3 Typical genres in education contexts (DESC, 2004: 101).

Category	Genre	Purpose
Story genres	Narratives and traditional stories	To entertain and instruct the reader about cultural values.
	Personal recount	To record chronologically past personal events to entertain readers.
Factual genres	Description	To describe some of the features of particular people, places or things.
	Information report • taxonomic • descriptive	To provide information about the world, often with visual material. A taxonomic report usually answers the question: What type? while a descriptive report will answer: What about?
	Practical report	To recount the method used to do something along with the results and conclusions.
	Recount • biographical • historical	To relate chronologically past events to inform readers. These events may concern a particular individual (biographical recounts) or events in a specific historical period (historical recounts).
	Historical account	To explain why events occurred during a particular historical period, adding the causes to an historical recount.
	Explanation • sequential • causal	To explain social and natural processes. Sequential explanations connect events in a process chronologically. Causal explanations both connect the events chronologically and causally.
	Expository genres	To present arguments on an issue.
	• argument analytical hortatory • discussion	An analytical argument seeks to persuade the reader/listener to agree with a particular viewpoint. An hortatory argument also tries to persuade the reader/listener to take some action. Discussions present the case for more than one point of view about an issue.
	Procedure	To instruct someone to make or do things.
Response genres	Personal response	To respond personally to a cultural work.
	Review	To assess the appeal and value of a cultural work, providing both information and evaluation.
	Interpretation	To interpret a cultural work; providing information from the work to support an interpretation.
	Critical response	To critique a cultural work through analysis and evidence to support the critique.

Accompanying documents offer a description of the social purpose, structure and principal grammatical features for each of these target genres. The features of *recounts*, for example, are described in Quote 8.4.

Quote 8.4 **Recount Genre**

Purpose/social function Variations within the genres

To retell events for the purpose of informing or entertaining a listener/reader.

- Personal recount (e.g. anecdote, diary entry)
- Factual recount (e.g. newspaper article, police report, biography, historical event)
- Imaginative recount (e.g. a day in the life of; I thought things like that only happened in nightmares . . .)

Structural features

- Commences with *orientation*—providing background information
- Contains a *sequence of events*—covering a specified period of time
- May involve *personal commentary* (optional) at any stage in the sequence of events
- Closes with re-orientation (optional)—usually a summary statement or comment (e.g. That really was a terrible day) or a relocation in space and time (e.g. . . . and then I woke up and realised it was all a dream; We were so glad to reach home).

Language features

- Past tense
- Human participants in theme as orientation to the message (*I, mum, they, the entertainers*)
- Time elements typically in theme to signal the unfolding phases (*It was the weekend, In 1066*)
- Evaluative language to express feelings and judgments of people and events

DESC (2004: 14)

8.2.2 Planning and Outcomes

English is organised into three inter-related strands in South Australia: texts and contexts (which includes genres), language (linked to appropriate genres) and strategies (for composing and interpreting texts). At each stage of students' progress through school, teachers are provided with an advisory framework in each area which describes possible growth points as learners move towards demonstrating curriculum outcomes. An explicit focus on grammar is central to this process as it enables students not only to understand how sentences are structured so that they are meaningful, clear and syntactically accurate, but also helps them to see the relationship between a text and its context and how language changes in different situations. The *Teaching Resource* booklet (DECS, 2014) advises teachers how they can build on students' prior knowledge by introducing increasingly difficult genres which are recycled as they progress. Table 8.4 shows starting points for teaching at three different levels to achieve target outcomes.

8.2.3   Classroom Practices

Various materials have been developed to support young learners towards understanding different genres in Australia (e.g. Gibbons, 2002; PETTA[3]). An important principle of such learning, however, is the idea that learners' development of unfamiliar genres should be carefully supported through interaction with peers and teachers and with clear modelling, as outlined in Quote 8.5 from Martin, Christie and Rothery (1987).

Table 8.4 Possible starting points for texts and contexts strand at three-year levels.

Year 1	Year 4	Year 7
• Begins to write for a purpose (i.e. use genres), recognising the audience for the writing: – recount – narrative – procedure.	• Constructs a range of texts, collaboratively and independently, for different audiences and purposes (including descriptions, recounts, procedures, narratives, poems, sequential explanations, reports).	• Composes a range of texts using text features (e.g. recount, narrative, procedure, report, exposition, explanation).
• Uses writing to convey meaning to others (e.g. lists, notes, stories).	• Writes about familiar topics and researched topics.	• Explores how texts are altered to suit different audiences, including letters written for different audiences.
• Uses pictures and labelled diagrams to add meaning or clarification to written texts.	• Writes for a variety of personal and more formal purposes (e.g. filling in forms, composing letters).	• Writes to explore local or global issues and topics (e.g. community facilities, conflict, politics).
• Develops an awareness of the purposes of genres.		• Writes showing awareness of a wider range of perspectives at the community, regional and state level.
• Shows an awareness of the steps required to publish work.		

Quote 8.5 **Genre Modelling in Schools**

1. *Introducing a genre*—modelling a genre implicitly through reading to or by the class
2. *Focusing on a genre*—modelling a genre explicitly by naming its stages
3. *Jointly negotiating a genre*—teacher and class jointly composing the genre under focus; the teacher guides the composition of the text through questions and comments that provide scaffolding for the stages of the genre
4. *Researching*—selecting material for reading; notemaking and summarising before writing
5. *Drafting*—a first attempt at individually constructing the genre under focus
6. *Consultation*—teacher–pupil talk, involving direct reference to the meanings of the text
7. *Publishing*—writing a final draft that may be published in class.

Martin et al. (1987: 68–9)

A good example of such support is suggested by Derewianka (1990) for introducing recounts to grade 2 children.

Quote 8.6 **Constructing a Form 2 Recount**

During the week some children from 4th class visited Alix's classroom and in small groups shared Recounts of what they had written of the school camp they had just been on. Over the next few days Alix read the children a number of different types of Recounts which she wrote out on butcher's paper and pinned around the room as models. She then suggested that they might like to write a Recount of the coming excursion.

On the day of the excursion, she took along the school's videocamera. . . . On their return to school, they shared their observations in the form of oral Recounts. . . . The video served as a memory jogger reminding them of details which might otherwise have gone unrecorded. At various points Alix put the video on 'pause' and constructed a flowchart of the stages of the excursion. . . . The flowchart gave the children a visual idea of the sequence, and served as a prompt for them when it came to constructing a class Recount of the excursion. Alix guided them in writing a text telling what happened during the outing and what they discovered at the various sites by asking questions like these:

Where did we go first?
What sort of plants did we find there?
What did they look like?

When they had finished, Alix suggested that they might start off by letting their readers know a bit of background information, like *who* took part in the excursion, *why*, *when* it happened. The session finished with a brief review of how the class had structured their Recount—an orientation followed by a series of events. The next day the children tried writing their own Recounts of the excursion for their families.

Derewianka (1990: 11–12)

8.2.4   Conclusions

When children begin their school lives, they face a major shift in their language use from a familiar, spontaneous mode of face-to-face conversation to the more structured patterns of writing. By distinguishing learning to use language from learning about language, and by providing careful scaffolding, the approach described here provides a way for children both to develop the language they need to construct genres and to reflect on how language is used to accomplish this. Genres thus form the foundation of learning to write. The success of the model for teaching which underlies it undoubtedly derives from its solid research base.

8.3   English for Clinical Pharmacy: A Specific EAP Course

English for Clinical Pharmacy is a third-year course offered to students in the Faculty of Medicine at Hong Kong University[4]. It represents what can be achieved when writing instructors and faculty experts collaborate to create a highly specific EAP course. It also illustrates the fact that in most university contexts, students are not attending academic writing classes in order to learn to "write', or even to write in some abstractly academic way; they are learning to write for purposes which lay outside the English class. For them, writing is a tool they need in order to participate in their disciplines and to demonstrate their learning to readers in those disciplines. Writing therefore contributes to the acquisition of an academic competence in both disciplinary knowledge and the ability to discuss it appropriately: it is 'Writing-to-Learn'.

Concept 8.3   Writing-to-Learn vs. Learning-to-Write

Most of the writing that matters to students at university occurs in subject disciplines. This kind of writing can often take a very different form to that which goes on in writing classes, evoking a distinction made by Manchón (2011) between Learning-to-Write (LW), where students are learning to express themselves in writing, and Writing-to-Learn (WL), where they are using writing to develop their expertise in a particular area—in this case, the content of the discipline. This is the way students learn to display their critical and analytic skills, their use of English for reasoning and persuasion, their grasp of subject matter issues, and their ability to shape an argument using the conventions of their field.

8.3.1   *Background and Overview*

The ability to construct disciplinary arguments is at the heart of conceptual understanding of a field and this means that students must learn to craft their writing in community-specific ways. Learners are required to think their way into their disciplines through writing. The *English for Clinical Pharmacy* course has therefore been designed with input from colleagues in the Department of Pharmacy and Pharmacology to develop students' communicative abilities to meet the demands of drug information delivery in pharmacy contexts. At the beginning of the course, there is a focus on introducing specific vocabulary and strategies for analysing and learning medical terms through morphological analysis of roots, prefixes and suffixes. The objectives of the course, however, focus on the effective communication of drug information to different audiences in different contexts, in oral and written form (see Table 8.5). Drug evaluation is a basic part of a pharmacist's career as many of the documents they write concern evaluating and recommending appropriate drugs. The course comprises 120 learning

Table 8.5 English for Clinical Pharmacy course assignments.

Assessment Task	Length / Timing	Weighting
Drug Enquiry Assignment (written)	approx. 2 pages	15%
Drug Profile Presentation (spoken)	5 mins per student	10%
Medical Terminology Test	40 mins	30%
Drug Evaluation Assignment (written)	1000–1200 words	30% (20% English/10% pharmacy)
Poster Presentation (written/spoken)	50 mins per student	15% (10% English/5% pharmacy)

hours: 36 hours in class, 44 hours in independent learning and 40 hours in preparing for assignments.

8.3.2   *Writing Assignments*

The *English for Clinical Pharmacy* course thus requires a high degree of involvement from students, both in and out of class, as they learn to adjust their language for different audiences using different genres. In the first assignment, for example, students have to search for and select relevant drug information from reliable sources and respond to enquiries about drugs from different stakeholders, indicating their sources. Figure 8.1 shows an example of the format of the exercise. Students are assessed on their use of genre conventions, content, language, structure and writing ethics in the assignment.

The second written assignment really drives the course and involves applying genre knowledge in writing a comparative drug evaluation, and synthesising and properly citing information and evidence from multiple sources in order to provide recommendations. Together with the follow-up poster presentation of the recommendation, it carries 45% of the marks for the course (half of these given by faculty colleagues). When the students start the course, they are each allocated a different drug chosen by the faculty based on what the students know at the end of their second year. Before starting this assignment, students have therefore already researched the drug and been assessed individually in both responding to drug enquiries and presenting a drug profile.

For the comparative drug evaluation, each student is paired with another student, and they share their research from the drug profile to write a comparative evaluation of the two drugs, which informs their recommendations on the use of these drugs in the context of a particular medical condition. Again, the pairings of the drugs is advised by faculty. The Pharmacy Department also advises on the writing task—a hospital bulletin article—as this is a common genre for clinical pharmacists working in a hospital. The drugs assigned are different for each group and the students need to conduct further research to make an informed comparison: sometimes one drug has replaced the other, while sometimes they can be used concomitantly; sometimes one drug will be older than the other, or they may have developed at the same time; sometimes the action of the drugs will be similar and sometimes very different. The students have to decide which aspects of the drugs are worth evaluating and comparing, and decide on an appropriate structure for the bulletin article that is relevant.

Students receive input on the hospital bulletin article by analysing two exemplars of the genre, looking at its key features. Each pair of students receives an article and identifies its moves/sections, comparing findings with another pair looking at the other text (Fig. 8.2). They then go on to study the language of comparison and likelihood as well as to link words and given/new structures before planning the structure of their own drug evaluation article.

CITY H☺SPITAL
Drug Information Services

Online Forum

Post your question here and it will be answered by our registered pharmacists:

Question:

I bought some cimetidine from the pharmacy to try and help my reflux problems. I have also been taking antacids and the pharmacist said something about not taking antacids and other medications at the same time and also something about not taking cimetidine for too long. Can you please remind me of these details?

Response:

Email

From: Dr. Ho Man Wei
To: (Student's name)
Cc:
Subject: Cimetidine

Dear (student's name),

My patient appears to have developed gynaecomastia and he believes that this is due to the cimetidine that I have prescribed him to treat his GORD symptoms. Could this be possible and if so, what alternatives would you suggest?

Best regards,
Dr. Ho
City Hospital
Hong Kong

Email: response

From: (Student's name)
To: Dr. Ho Man Wei
Cc:
Subject:

Figure 8.1 Drug enquiry assignment from *English for Clinical Pharmacy* course.

	Text 1	Text 2
Heading	✓	✓
Posing of a problem/significance of an issue		
Information about the drugs		
Information about the medical condition		
Reporting on studies		
Advice to healthcare professionals		
Summarising		
References		

1. What do you think are the functions of these moves? How do these functions relate to the purpose of the writing? e.g. *Heading—Tells the reader what the article is about.*
2. What have you noticed about the way that the two articles are organised and structured?
3. What have you noticed about how these moves/sections are sequenced? Do you see any logic in the sequencing?
4. Information about the drugs can be further sub-divided in these articles. How?

Figure 8.2 Drug evaluation genre task from *English for Clinical Pharmacy* course.

Before the final interactive poster session, where students have to discuss and answer questions on a poster summary of their article, each student is encouraged to reflect on the strengths and weaknesses of their writing. They receive tutor feedback on their assignment and then attend a ten-minute face-to-face appointment to ask and answer questions about their work and suggest what they need to do to improve it.

8.3.3   *Conclusion*

Drug evaluation is fundamental to a pharmacist's career as many of the documents they write are based on it. The project therefore provides an opportunity for learners to develop and practice valuable and highly discipline-specific research and academic writing skills. The involvement of pharmacy tutors in designing and co-assessing the course helps ensure motivation and authenticity, and the students appreciate the efforts made to support their learning. While collaboration with faculty experts can be a difficult and bruising experience, often involving rebuffs or attempts to subordinate the writing course to faculty imperatives, this case shows how useful to students a successful partnership can be.

8.4   Go for Gold—Writing for a Reason

Here I discuss a course that follows neither a process nor genre path, but which employs writing as part of an overall communicative process in an experiential learning context. Here writing is a *social practice*, incidental to wider communicative goals in a chain of texts and interactions. It is produced to accomplish specific purposes with real audiences and is based on research which sees writing as interaction (Nystrand, 1989). Go for Gold (GfG) also draws on educational research emphasising the value of collaborative learning (e.g. Bruffee, 1984) by providing students with an environment of mutual support within their 'zone of proximal development' (Vygotsky, 1962), the difference between what a learner can do alone and through cooperation with capable peers. This is, then, an ESP course based on learning by doing, requiring learners to respond actively and engage purposefully in authentic communication with others (Hyland and Hyland, 1992).

Quote 8.7   **Raymond Williams on Learner Engagement**

There is no way to help a learner to be disciplined, active and thoroughly engaged unless he perceives a problem to be a problem or whatever it is to be learned as worth learning, and unless he plays an active role in determining the process of solution. That is the plain unvarnished truth, and if it sounds like warmed over 'progressive education', it is nonetheless true for it.

Williams (1962)

Williams' brief statement linking learning with students' active involvement is a view echoed by writers who advocate process syllabuses (e.g. Breen and Littlejohn, 2000) and learner control (e.g. Pierce, 1995). Rather than focusing exclusively on the outcomes of learning, process syllabuses are based on the idea that learning derives from the interaction and negotiation which students engage in. Creating a simulated environment which encourages both speaking and writing, GfG establishes a balance between these two. It provides a structured framework of tasks, learning content, materials and broad outcomes, while allowing opportunities for learner reinterpretation and decision-making as they decide which methods and approaches they will use to achieve their goals. This potential for a variety of learner options means participants can reflect on the situations that confront them and respond strategically in writing to their audiences. Concept 8.4 summarises some advantages of this approach.

Concept 8.4   Advantages of Writing in a Simulation

- **Discoursal rehearsal:** helps learners establish ways of engaging in spoken and written interaction by simulating real-world events
- **Learning-to-write:** provides opportunities to employ genres under realistic conditions

- **Rhetorical consciousness-raising:** promotes understanding of reader needs and of writing as a means of achieving social and persuasive purposes
- **Motivated involvement:** provides students with reasons for writing based on their target needs and current interests
- **Cooperative engagement:** requires students to work with others to collect data, exchange information and make decisions
- **Learner control:** offers learners opportunities to determine their own routes and strategies to achieve the goals established by the simulation
- **Real feedback:** requires students to respond immediately and authentically to peers' texts, helping writers to judge the effectiveness of their communication and develop reader sensitivity

8.4.1   Background

Go for Gold is an ESP course for second-year business students at the English-medium Papua New Guinea (PNG) University of Technology. The students come from a wide variety of language backgrounds and speak English as a second or third language at upper-intermediate or advanced levels. The course simulates the awarding of a contract to mine one of the world's richest gold reserves on a small island off the PNG coast. It runs for 56 hours over a 14-week semester and involves the students taking roles and engaging in a series of linked and roughly graded communication tasks to gather information, make decisions, cooperate in problem-solving and produce various written and spoken genres. The language is purposeful and authentic as it addresses issues of immediate interest to the participants and their future professional needs. Not only is the exploitation of PNG's natural resources by giant multi-nationals a highly charged political issue, but also these students are an educated elite who typically rise rapidly to influential positions after graduation where good English skills are vital.

8.4.2   Course Structure

The GfG course is organised in three main stages: input, activity and feedback, as described in Concept 8.5.

Concept 8.5   Course Description

Input stage

Information input	Language input
Bid for Power video (BBC, 1983)	Bid for Power video
Public lecture	Focus on genres and language forms
Newspaper articles, reports, studies, etc	Role-information cards

Activity stage

1. Preparations

arranging and holding meetings
intragroup and intergroup discussions
individual and group data collection—both from each other and source
   materials

2. Presentations

ministers' policy statements and local politicians' statements of interest
government's specification report
companies' bid proposal reports
oral presentations of reports
announcement of decisions
reactions to decisions

Feedback stage

Activity evaluation	**Language evaluation**
discussion of the tasks	discussion of language use
journal writing	assessment sheet
	corrected written work
	discussion of presentation
	video replays

Hyland and Hyland (1992: 228)

The **input** stage prepares students for the roles and activities they will meet in the project. Relevant concepts, identities, genres and language forms are introduced through the business English video 'Bid for Power' (BBC, 1983) which raises parallel issues to the GfG scenario and presents relevant aspects of language in a natural context. Students are also instructed in formal oral presentations, business writing, research skills and group work. Relevant written genres are introduced through study of authentic documents with reports, minutes and memos closely examined and their rhetorical structure discussed. While learning about these genres, students are gathering background information on the mining project through a public lecture from a mining company representative and a range of policy documents, newspaper articles, company reports, feasibility studies, maps, census data and economic projections. Teachers are highly interventionist during this stage, particularly in modelling written genres and guiding writing practice, but once the activity is underway their main responsibility is to establish the conditions for communication, be available for consultation and monitor what goes on.

The **activities** require participants to select a role from a *political group*, consisting of ministers, a provincial premier and local village representatives; a *business group* made up of a number of competing consortia; and a small *consultant group* to advise the government. These different roles involve different perceptions of the modelled reality and require different information and genres. Some relationships involve cooperation and sharing information while others entail competition and secrecy. Students gradually adopt their roles as they collect the information they need to meet activity objectives, interacting with others and collecting data from the library. Then the focus shifts to more cooperative approaches with meetings between consortia, politicians and consultants. This phase involves a considerable amount of writing in terms of notes, formal letters and memos, and minutes of meetings, much of which serves to facilitate interaction.

The role information also helps structure the syllabus in terms of text outcomes. Those in the political group write reports, summaries and press statements on the government's views on mining, finance and environmental protection; the interests of the provincial government; and the demands for compensation and protection of the local community. Those in the business consortia write detailed bid proposals and the consultants write a project specification and a decision announcement. Writing depends on students resolving various problems concerning how best to develop the resource, raise capital, provide infrastructure and balance local, provincial and national interests. Thus, written texts are not simply project goals but provide information essential to other participants and lead to the final decision regarding which consortium will win the contract.

Concept 8.6   Writing in Go for Gold

Input stage: Notes from public lecture, video, and original sources
                              (reports, cuttings, etc.)
                              Target lexis and structure practice
                              Practice of focus genres

Activity stage: Memos and letters to other groups
                              Notes and minutes of meetings and discussions
                              Various reports, press statements and written
                              announcements.

Feedback is vital to the process of learning. Research shows it enables students to assess their performances, modify their behaviour and transfer their understandings (e.g. Hattie and Timperley, 2007), and in GfG this occurs both during and after the activity. During the simulation, learners receive constant peer feedback on the effectiveness of their communication as they respond in discussions, react to written material and question speakers after presentations. Because reports, memos and minutes contain important information for readers' own roles, they receive close scrutiny from an interested audience. Any vagueness or ambiguity is seized upon, and this encourages writers to present their ideas clearly. Following the activity, the teacher feedback reviews what was learned, helping students to interpret events and find connections which will make the experience transferable. Students also receive more conventional feedback in the form of detailed comments and conferencing on their writing.

8.4.3 Conclusions

Perhaps the main advantage of the GfG course is that content reality and task variety encourage the use of language for genuine communicative purposes and promote conditions of natural language use. In particular, the scale of the activity opens up considerable possibilities for interaction and avoids the potential artificiality of shorter activities which concentrate on specific areas of language, content or function. The course materials are those of the real world, and activities such as participating in discussions, reading documents and writing memos and reports all prepare students for work after graduation. Thus, writing is not seen as artificially detached from actual communicative needs; it is a crucial aspect of what it means to engage with others in tackling real problems. Students are exposed to a wide range of different linguistic material and produce a variety of outputs, both within groups and individually, and in so doing learn a lot about what it means to write for real purposes and audiences.

Course evaluations by students and the Business faculty have been positive, and teachers have been impressed with the improvement of students' confidence and writing skills. On the negative side, teachers have expressed doubt about the limited opportunities the course offers to correct errors and provide students with feedback on written work during the simulation itself. Accuracy is sacrificed to fluency, and teacher intervention through modelling or correction becomes intrusive and inappropriate. GfG also involves a number of esoteric genres, so while students will almost certainly need to write memos, minutes, letters and reports soon after they graduate, bid proposals and project specifications are unlikely to form part of their initial repertoire. But, in their struggle to construct them, writers both become conscious of the relationship between purpose and rhetorical function, and learn the importance of writing clear and persuasive prose.

Overall, GfG provides a rich learning environment which offers participants both a fruitful context for writing and an awareness of the relationships between purpose, audience and appropriate rhetorical structure.

8.5 Understanding Professional and Academic Texts

My final case study looks at a credit-bearing writing support course offered by a writing centre as part of a UK Foundation degree programme: 'Understanding professional and academic texts'. It mainly draws on ideas discussed in part 1.3 and reader-oriented work. Foundation Degrees were introduced into the UK Higher education award system in 2001 as part of a strategy to help widen participation, making higher education accessible to students who had not traditionally considered it an option, and to integrate academic and work-based learning.

Concept 8.7   UK Foundation Degrees

These two-year qualifications provide alternative routes into higher education and allow those already employed to undertake a degree programme to get ahead in their chosen career or to academically frame their industry experience whilst continuing to work. Courses cover a diverse range of subject areas, although almost half of all students study either education, business, or art and design. Courses often involve flexible teaching arrangements, including work-based, online and distance-learning modes, although most students study full time, juggling work, study and other responsibilities. It is common for Foundation degree holders to 'top-up' to a full Honours Degree with a further year of full-time study, and about half of all graduates do so. There were 72,000 students on Foundation degree programmes in 2007–08 and over 100,000 in 2012.

8.5.1   Course Aims

Understanding Professional and Academic Texts (UPAT)[5] is a first-year course for those working in educational contexts. It is offered by the Centre for Professional and Academic Literacies (CAPLITS) at the Institute of Education in London, and the students are typically working in teaching support roles such as teaching assistants, nursery and youth workers, and learning support assistants. They are taking the degree to gain relevant knowledge, understanding and skills to improve their performance in these education posts. The students generally attend part time and have few formal qualifications and no experience of higher education. The UPAT course is therefore a crucial component of students' initial experience of higher education and a key aspect of their ability to participate in it successfully. Essentially, it aims to facilitate their involvement in both their workplaces and the university through writing.

Quote 8.8   UPAT Learning Outcomes

As a result of participating in this module you will be able to:

(a) better understand the relationship between your work and academic contexts

(b) understand workplace texts in terms of how audience and purpose influence language
(c) construct appropriate frameworks in which to analyse and evaluate workplace texts
(d) conduct small-scale workplace investigation
(e) understand academic texts in terms of audience, purpose and language
(f) write academic essays of a standard required in your coursework

UPAT course document (2005)

A key aspect of the course is the integration and comparison of workplace and academic genres. This allows students to see how texts are socially situated and to understand the ways that writing is differently organised for different purposes and audiences. The course moves through a series of mini-research projects and writing tasks which encourage students to reflect on the ways that language works in professional and academic contexts, while at the same time developing the abilities to meet tutors' expectations of their assignments in other courses. These tasks are supported by regular readings by authors such as Pecorari and Shaw (2012) on intertextuality, Crème and Lea (2008) on assignment writing, and Gibbons (2009) on academic literacy learning, as well as educational authors on the work of teaching assistants and professional practice in education.

8.5.2   Course Structure

The UPAT course is structured in five units, each comprising two classes of two hours' duration. The first class is given in the morning and normally involves input of various kinds, such as a discussion of readings or a teacher-led interactive lecture. The second class follows in the same afternoon and is based around activities which arise from the input. It is ordered in this way:

A) *Sessions one and two—texts, observations and reflection.* These sessions provide students with the basic tools for looking at texts in an informed way, providing practice in the type of writing they will need for the work-based task later in the course.

- identifying key ideas and relationships in texts
- ethics in the collection of workplace data
- analysing work-based texts—e.g. policy documents, manuals instructions, etc.

B) *Sessions three and four—planning and structuring academic essays.* These sessions focus on the planning and presentation of academic writing, covering issues of formality, academic style, text organisation and referencing.

C) *Sessions five and six—criticality and argument.* These sessions explore the meaning of these key terms within the university and make explicit how students can incorporate them into their academic writing.

D) *Sessions seven and eight—using sources.* These sessions look at evaluating sources and how students can bring information into their academic writing from both academic texts and the research data they collect in their workplace projects. They involve referencing conventions, summary writing and creating a bibliography.

E) *Sessions nine and ten—proofreading and editing.* These last sessions focus on editing for clarity, focusing on grammar, spelling and punctuation, as well as how students can create proofreading check sheets and make use of peer-editing groups.

The fact that these students have never studied in a college or university before, and less than a third stayed at school beyond the minimum required leaving age, means that they are at a disadvantage in academic environments. They are unfamiliar with the expectations of academic settings and generally lack confidence in their writing and communication skills. As a result, this course carefully scaffolds their learning, so that aspects of writing and knowing about writing unfold following a structured pattern of development.

8.5.3   *Tasks and Assessment*

While the UPAT course is relatively short and involves what is often a considerable amount of new input for students, it seeks to be supportive through input and activities which draw on students' everyday situations, which increase in difficulty only gradually, and which build assessment into classroom activities. It also offers significant opportunities for learner collaboration within a teacher-scaffolded context. In particular, students are asked to discuss texts, plan activities and carry out small projects, either in groups or individually, after dialogue with others. It therefore draws on educational theory (Vygotsky, 1962) and research which suggests that learning is improved through collaboration and negotiation (Dooly, 2008). Cooperative peer response to writing is seen to be important for exposing students to real readers (Min, 2006), for building their confidence as writers and for encouraging them to make active writing decisions rather than slipping into a passive kind of unthinking model-following.

Assessment for the course consists of a work-based portfolio (50%) and a 1500–2000 word academic essay (50%). The portfolio requires three workplace observations that incorporate reflection (each reflection is about 800 words) and three work-based texts with a 400-word critical analysis of each. The tasks are based on the idea that writing is improved when students see the relevance of what they are asked to do. As a result, they begin with the kinds of texts students are familiar with in their workplace contexts and then move towards the more esoteric academic genre of the essay assignment expected by their other subject tutors. Some examples of the portfolio tasks are given in Quote 8.9.

Quote 8.9   **Example Tasks**

Task one for Work-based Portfolio

Design an observation sheet in which to investigate your role in the workplace. You may want to contrast your role with someone else in your workplace. This observation sheet should be in the form of a table (example given). Include the headings—Activity, your role, main tasks—and do the same for someone else. Conduct your observation (checking the boxes) and then **reflect** on the observation sheet (incorporating your reading), what you found (choose a maximum of three activities) and yourself. The following is an example for a Teaching Assistant. . . .

Task two for Work-based Portfolio

Observe people working together in an activity and describe in detail: the context, who is involved and what was generally said / what happened. Reflect on this activity (you could include commentary on whether you thought this activity was successful, typical, anything unusual etc.) and try to incorporate your reading into your reflection.

. . .

Task four for Work-based Portfolio

Collect three work-based texts for analysis (e.g. emails, reports, notices, etc.). Make sure that the texts are of a sufficient length and contain a sufficient amount of detail. These three texts should also be quite different from each other. In your analysis of the texts, comment on the intended audience, the language used, and the purpose (indirect and direct) of the text. Do not forget to give sufficient context for your analysis.

UPAT course document (2005)

In addition to the portfolio material, students have to write a longer piece of work, selecting one from three essay topics which are constructed to dovetail with the work-based study tasks mentioned above. These are:

a) To what extent is an academic text different from a professional text?
b) Discuss what you view to be the main ethical concerns regarding observation in the workplace.

c)   Discuss the implications of the differences between your role and the role of someone else close to you in your workplace.

Support for the essay task is provided not only in the classes, but in the analysis of exemplar essays by previous students on similar topics and by the suggestions included in essay advice packs. These include essay plans, useful phrases, suggested readings and ideas for issues to address in the essay. So, for example, students choosing to write on topic b) concerning ethical observation are advised that they might consider including information on children's rights, getting permission, anonymity and confidentiality, the observer's paradox and the intrusiveness of different recording media.

8.5.4   Conclusion

While not linked explicitly to a particular theory of writing or body of research, UPAT nevertheless draws together a number of educational principles and research findings on academic writing. In particular, it recognises the value of 'starting where the students are' by considering their writing proficiencies, learning backgrounds and workplace experiences, and of asking 'why are these students learning to write?' by embedding instruction in their immediate and future writing needs as defined by academic and professional exigencies. As Johns (1997) points out, learners acquire a socio-literate competence through exposure to particular genres in specific contexts. They develop the skills to participate in particular communities by understanding how genres work in those communities, and the course discussed here helps scaffold such exposure through introduction, practice and discussion of the texts and writing practices they find in their workplaces and which they need in their studies.

Notes

1. I am grateful to Derek Wallace of Victoria University of Wellington, and before him Janet Holst, for providing me with information and materials for *Writ 101*. The coursebook *Becoming an Effective Writer* (Wallace, 2015) is available from the Bookshop, Victoria University, Wellington, New Zealand.
2. The full teaching resource booklet is available at http://www.sacsa.sa.edu.au/ATT/% 7BF51C47E3-B6F3–4765–83C3–0E27FF5DD952%7D/R-10_English.pdf
3. Primary teaching resources can be found at PETTA: http://www.petaa.edu.au/imis_ prod/teaching-resources.
4. The course was developed by Lai Kun Tse, Jane Stokes and Laura Wakeland of the Centre for Applied English Studies (CAES) with advice from faculty colleagues.
5. I would like to thank Stephen Hill of CAPLITS for making his materials and commentaries on them available to me.

Further Reading

Bowring, M., Carter, R., Goddard, A., Reah, A. and Sanger, K. (2013) *Working with texts*, 3rd edn. London: Routledge.

A good introduction to language analysis to support students' understanding of language variety and purpose.

Derewianka, B. (1990) *Exploring how texts work*. Newtown, NSW: Primary English Teachers Association.

Imaginative and teacher-friendly ideas for teaching primary school written genres.

Elbow, P. (1998) *Writing with power: techniques for mastering the writing process*, 2nd edn. Oxford: Oxford University Press.

A classic handbook for writers.

Gibbons, P. (2009) *English learners, academic literacy and thinking*. Portsmouth, NH: Heinemann.

Plenty of classroom examples to show how disadvantaged and EFL students can benefit from a challenging, inquiry-based curriculum.

Nunan, D. (2005) *Task based language teaching*. Cambridge: Cambridge University Press.

A comprehensive appraisal of the field, including planning, designing and using tasks in language classes.

9 Teaching Writing
Materials and Practices

This chapter will . . .

- discuss how teaching applications such as textbooks, computer software, classroom instruction and assessment methods draw on writing research;
- examine how new technologies can contribute to teaching and learning writing;
- illustrate how current research has influenced teaching using genre, corpora, academic vocabulary, portfolios and writing frames.

9.1 Research Writing: A Series of Advanced Writing Guides

Swales and Feak's (2009–11) series of writing guides for graduate students and junior scholars is grounded in current conceptions of academic discourse analysis. The guides are revised and expanded editions of *English in Today's Research World* and bundled as four volumes[1], dealing respectively with the writing of abstracts, literature reviews, introductions and support genres. The books effectively draw on current academic genre research to describe how particular aspects of the real communicative world work and translate these into learning applications.

Concept 9.1 A Genre Orientation to EAP Writing Teaching

- Academic writing needs to be acceptable to target communities.
- Academic writing reflects variations in disciplinary traditions and conventions.
- Research genres reveal the influence of cross-cultural variation.
- Academic writing requires writers to make continuous rhetorical decisions.
- Student materials should be based on analyses' of target discourse samples.
- Analyses and teaching are descriptive and interpretive rather than prescriptive and didactic.

- Descriptions should offer a functional account of discourse features.
- Teaching should raise awareness of the rhetorical and linguistic constraints and opportunities involved in using different genres.

9.1.1 The Approach

The texts follow a task-based approach to develop in novice writers both a sensitivity to the language used in different academic genres and insights into the conventions of their target disciplines. This is principally accomplished through consciousness-raising by encouraging readers to analyse the features of text extracts.

Quote 9.1 **Swales on the Approach of the Series**

There are several assumptions and principles that undergird the teaching materials. First, that there is value in a genre-based approach, especially one that sees academic communications as being comprised of a loose network of interlocking genres. Second, we take it as given that we are more concerned with producing better academic writers than with simply producing better academic texts. In other words we aim to provide our participants with skills and strategies that will generalize beyond the narrow temporal domains of our actual courses. This in turn means that we place considerable emphasis on rhetorical consciousness-raising and linguistic awareness. One activity that increases this level of linguistic meta-cognition is to have the participants themselves engage in their own discourse analysis.

Swales (1999)

The activities encourage students to apply their often considerable research and analytical skills to texts, developing an exploratory attitude towards rhetorical practices. There is also an emphasis on exploiting the disciplinary heterogeneity of many advanced writing classes to foster a comparative approach which reveals the social, relativistic nature of academic writing discussed in part 1.3.2. Students can learn from each other and from the tasks by discussing the published research findings provided in the text and sharing their own rhetorical experiences. The different rhetorical strategies and social practices of different communities thus become part of the teaching material. Teachers' notes and commentary are available for free download. In terms of content, the series addresses key genres of research writing and the main features of those related genres, covering the conference poster, career-oriented genres such as proposals and CVS as well as conventional parts of the dissertation. In all cases, grammar and lexis are subordinated to the rhetorical features of these genres, so that tense and reporting verbs appear in the volume on literature reviews, for example, and how to express agreement and disagreement appears in the book on Introductions.

9.1.2   *Some Extracts from the Materials*

The third book in the series is titled *Creating Contexts* and is concerned with writing introductions. While it uses the CARS model (see Quote 7.4 in Chapter 7 of this volume), it also looks at other introductions graduate students may be required to write, such as those in course papers, critiques, proposals and dissertations. It contains a series of tasks and reflection activities designed to heighten users' awareness of writing as a disciplinary practice, as a process of thinking and composing in the context of a wider text, and as a strategy for presenting research in the most engaging way. A good example of how these tasks make use of the research literature is Task 4 from the book shown in Quote 9.2 which summarises some of the cross-genre research.

Quote 9.2   **Opening Introductions**

Here are some possible types of first sentences or openings to an intro-duction. Mark with a check those that you think would be appropriate in your field for a course paper and/or a research article for publication or a proposal (consider either a dissertation proposal or a small grant proposal to fund travel to a conference, or another research proposal).

	Course Paper	Proposal	Publication or report
1. surprising idea or statistics, particularly those highlighting a problem or unusual finding			
2. a comment on the scope or focus of past or current research			
3. a story about real people and their experience (or even one focusing on yourself)			
4. common knowledge in your field			
5. a definition			
6. a question that engages the reader			
7. an opinion regarding research findings			

8. a reference to a single study, a quote, or a leading scholar
9. a comment on research directions or orientations
10. a statement indicating the purpose of the paper

Can you think of any other ways to open?

Now look at these openings from published papers. Working from this list, label the opening according to the ten types given. Do any of these make you curious about the paper content? Which, if any, suggest that the student author is engaged in the topic?

Feak and Swales (2011: 13)

This kind of contrastive reflection is useful for raising students' awareness of rhetorical strategies in academic writing in English and how these might differ across genres. While the points may seem initially to be roughly interchangeable to students, they obviously have different pragmatic and rhetorical effects and offer different possibilities for text organisation. Other tasks are devoted more explicitly to language itself and draw on text analysis research. In each case, forms are clearly connected with the functions they perform in academic genres, such as the example in Quote 9.3 from the first volume on abstracts. Here Swales and Feak briefly discuss Hyland and Tse's (2005) research on the role of *evaluative that* in abstracts to discuss findings. Students are then encouraged to reflect on the use of this structure to highlight key findings and simultaneously signal the strength of the claim through the choice of reporting verb from strong (e.g. *prove*) to weak (e.g. *suggest*).

Quote 9.3 **Main Results and *that* Clauses in Traditional Abstracts**

Convert five of these noun phrases into appropriate *that* clauses. Some of the later ones are not so easy to convert! Here is an example:
The results offer clear evidence of the reality of global warming.
The results offer clear evidence that global warming is a reality

1. Results confirm the influence of year of study and academic discipline influence student information choices.

2.   The evidence shows a primary associated between the word elderly and discourses of care and disability.
3.   The analysis indicates the dependence of the peak pressure of shock waves on the deformation speed of the overlays.
4.   The findings generally support the idea of a profitable introduction of structured abstracts into research journals.
5.   Our investigations indicate the greater probability of a future decline in U.S. home construction.
6.   Numerical results are presented as a demonstration of the efficiency of the algorithms from two points of view: mesh quality and computational effort.
7.   Results show the R-value of transparent composites panels over that of current glazing systems.
8.   I argue in favour of a constructivist theory of truth in opposition to other theories.

As you probably noticed, the *that* clause variants give a somewhat greater emphasis to the findings than their noun-phrase equivalents.

Swales and Feak (2009: 19)

9.1.3   Conclusions

The booklets in this series recognise that the communicative demands of research writing are both a major component of professional expertise and a serious challenge to students. Although biased towards an American tradition of writing and post-graduate study, they represent an excellent example of how research in a particular area of writing can be exploited for pedagogical purposes. The books establish writing for the purpose of communicating research and invite readers to explore the conventions of their fields for themselves. The view they take of writing thus places texts at the centre of pedagogic practice.

9.2   Corpora-Assisted Writing Instruction

Corpora, or electronic collections of naturally occurring texts, have been at the forefront of two of the most significant changes in language teaching in recent years. On the one hand, they have provided teachers and materials designers with new ways of understanding how language is patterned and used, and on the other they have given students the means to take a more active and reflective part in their learning. New descriptions of language based on phraseology and patterning have informed syllabus design, dictionaries, reference grammars, teaching materials and assessment. In the classroom itself, corpora have contributed to the shift from teaching as imparting knowledge, to teaching as mediating learning, by providing a way for students to explore authentic examples of language.

Concept 9.2   Corpus Analysis

A corpus is a collection of naturally occurring, computer-readable texts, often comprising many millions of words, which is considered more or less representative of a particular domain of language use. While it does not contain any new theories about language, it can offer fresh insights on familiar, but perhaps unnoticed, features of language use, replacing intuition with evidence. Using text retrieval and concordancing software, analysts (or students) can isolate, count and see patterns in lexical and grammatical features from large numbers of texts to better understand the ways language is used in a particular genre, register or community.

9.2.1   Corpora and Writing Instruction

The application of corpora in writing instruction dates back to the work of Tim Johns (1991) and the textbook by Tribble and Jones (1990). Their value lies most centrally in replacing instruction with discovery and moving the study of language away from correctness to typicality, as recently extolled by Flowerdew (2012), McCarthy and McCarten (2012) and Hyland (2015b). Leech lists the advantages in Quote 9.4.

Quote 9.4   Leech on the Advantages of Concordancing for Teaching

1. *Automatic searching, sorting, scoring.* The computer has immense speed and accuracy in carrying out certain low-level tasks, and can therefore deliver data in a form valuable to the human learner. Concordances and frequency lists are obvious examples.
2. *Promoting a learner-centred approach.* The computer brings flexibility of time and place, and adaptability to the student's need and motivation.
3. *Open-ended supply of language data.* The computer thus encourages an exploratory or discovery approach to learning.
4. *Enabling the learning process to be tailored.* The computer can customize the learning task to the individual's needs and wishes, rather than simply providing a standard set of examples or data.

Leech (1997: 10–11)

Corpora are analysed using text analysis software such as the freely available *AntConc*[2] (Anthony, 2014) to display frequency, phraseology and collocation. Frequency lists are useful for identifying the most commonly occurring words and phrases in target texts, such as *'a result of the'* and *'this suggest that'* in academic writing (Hyland, 2008a). In addition to frequency, such programmes create a concordance, bringing together all instances of a search word in its local co-text. So typing in a search word or phrase collects lines from all the texts in a corpus with the search item at the centre of the screen. These lines give instances of language *use* when read horizontally and evidence of *system* when read vertically. This makes it possible for the user to see regularities that might otherwise be missed, making it possible, for example, for students to decode frequently confused adjectives such as *interested* and *interesting*, with the former overwhelmingly preceding *in* (*someone is interested in something*) and the latter almost always used before a noun (*an interesting thing*) (Hunston, 2002: 10). Figure 9.1 shows an *AntConc* concordance indicating the productivity of the grammatical *is verb + ing* structure in writing. Here the wildcard * character has been used to summon up any word which fills that slot and so reveal the value of this structure regardless of any particular lexical items which fill it.

A further capability of a concordance programme is revealing collocations: the statistical probability of words to co-occur. Thus it may be useful for learners to know that *utterly* occurs before *different* but not before *similar*, or that the immediate left collocates of *of* in academic writing are mainly nouns and comprise a narrow range of terms (*form of, terms of, case of, effect of*, etc.) (Scott and Tribble, 2006: 100). Figure 9.2 shows the most common clusters for '*conclu**' sorted by the word on the left in a corpus of M.A. dissertations, showing that 'to conclude' occurs both more frequently and in a greater range of texts than alternatives. By clicking on the patterns, users can pull up concordance lines to show examples of actual use.

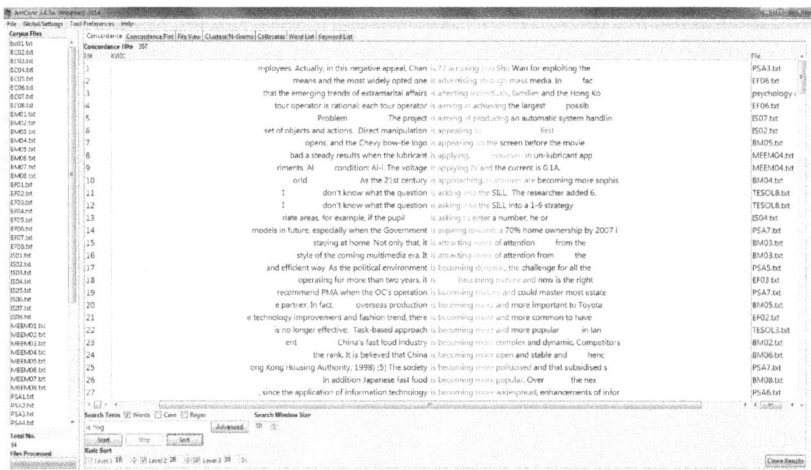

Figure 9.1 Antconc concordance for "is *ing" in student essay corpus.

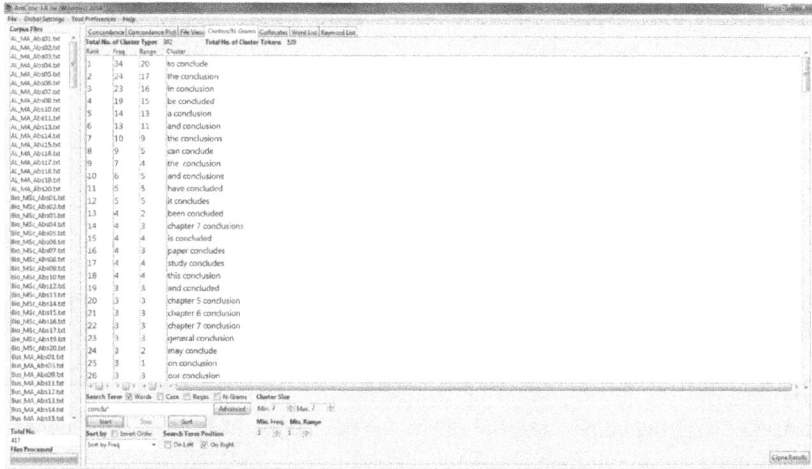

Figure 9.2 Cluster patterns for 'conclu*' in 120 M.A. dissertations.

9.2.2 Direct and Indirect Applications of Corpora

In discussing corpora in teaching, Romer (2010) distinguishes between *indirect applications*, where research findings feed into syllabuses, references works and teaching materials, and *direct applications*, which refer to more hands-on involvement by teachers and learners working with corpora in classrooms.

Indirectly, corpora have provided the theoretical and phraseological bases for dictionaries such as the *Oxford Dictionary of English* (2010). They have also brought innovations to grammars like the *Cambridge Grammar of English* (Carter and McCarthy, 2006), and textbooks such as the *Touchstone* series (McCarthy, McCarten and Sandiford, 2006), both of which are based on the huge Cambridge and Nottingham Corpus of Discourse in English (CANCODE) corpus. More generally, corpora have informed teaching by showing that words tend to occur not randomly or only in conformity with grammatical rules, but in preferred sequences. This is Sinclair's 'idiom principle' (Sinclair, 1991) which is that every word is used in a common phraseology. He argues that corpus evidence shows that meanings (and often constraints on sequence) are attached to whole phrases rather than as a unit with lexical fillers completing available grammatical slots (e.g. *that's a good idea; you see what I mean*). This view informs the lexical syllabus (Willis, 1990) and has assisted student writers by encouraging them to construct texts in chunks rather than word-by-word.

While teachers can use corpora in this way in their own teaching materials, a more effective pedagogy is to train students to explore corpora themselves. This more *direct* approach encourages inductive learning and raises students' awareness of patterns in writing by becoming 'detectives' to discover facts about language use through analysing authentic corpus examples. Such data driven learning (DDL) (Johns, 1991) typically involves teachers setting up activities which encourage students to notice salient features through the recurrent phrases they find in concordance lines. This direct learner access suggests two further approaches (Aston, 1997). First, corpora can be treated as *reference tools* to be consulted for examples when problems arise while writing, such as discovering the correct preposition to use with a particular verb or how *since* and *for* differ, for example. Alternatively, they can be used as *research tools* to be investigated to gain greater awareness of language use, such as whether *but* or *however* is more common in academic writing. *AntConc,* for example, allows users to search for two or more words at the same time and shows *but* to be almost twice as common in this corpus of 240 research articles (1800 cases compared with 3200). Figure 9.3 shows a screen of concordance lines for these words. Again, clicking on a line brings up the context.

But although independent use can stimulate enquiry, promote independent learning and reveal unfamiliar or typical uses to students, it is an analytical process involving considerable skill and, on their own, students are not always sure what they should look for (Yoon and Hirvella, 2004). Nor is this problem relieved by the complexity of many corpus query tools available (Krishnamurthy and Kosem, 2007). Hunston (2002: 171) therefore suggests it may only be suitable for advanced learners who are "filling in gaps in their knowledge rather than laying down the foundations". Despite this, studies of student attitudes and behaviour towards corpora as a second-language writing tool have shown that students see the approach as beneficial to the development of their writing skill and increased confidence (e.g. Yoon and Hirvella, 2004).

9.2.3   Learner Corpora and D-I-Y Corpora

Until recently, pedagogical materials and tasks have been largely based on native corpora rather than learner corpora, although the latter are now

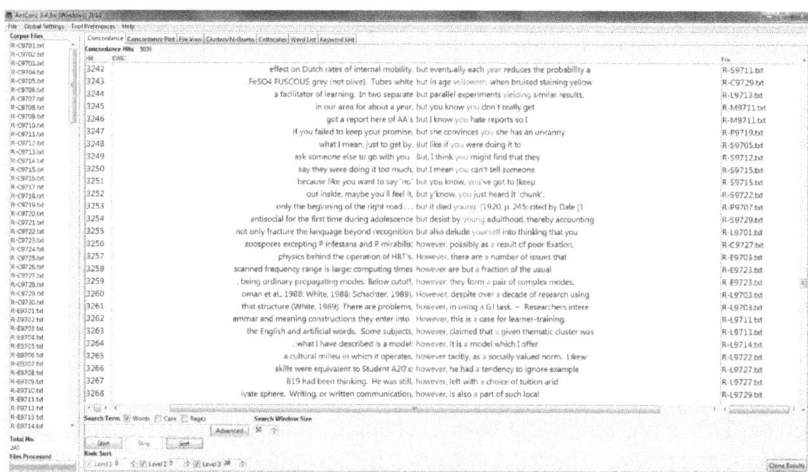

Figure 9.3 A concordance for *but* and *however* using *AntConc* and a corpus of articles.

becoming more widely available for classroom use (e.g. Granger, 2003; Gilquin, Granger and Paquot, 2007). Such corpora have been used to identify typical difficulties of learners at certain proficiency levels or native languages, and thus provide a way for identifying frequently occurring mistakes in learner language. Various explanations are given for errors in learner corpora, including the effects of L1 transfer, the use of coping strategies, transfer from speech patterns, and interlanguage development (e.g. Barlow, 2005). The extent to which native English speaker (NES) norms should form the basis for comparison has generated considerable debate, although Granger (2009) argues that, even where comparisons are not made explicitly with NES corpora, such norms often lay just below the surface in many studies of L2 writing.

Another, more recent, innovation has been where teachers extend the training they give students in using corpus tools by encouraging them to first build, and then analyse, their own individual, discipline-specific corpora (Lee and Swales, 2006; Charles, 2012, 2015). Such do-it-yourself (D-I-Y) corpora not only have the advantages of encouraging language analysis and consciousness-raising, but also benefit students by addressing their specialist needs. The corpus can address disciplinary requirements and conventions in situations where it may be impossible for the tutor to respond in detail to all individual demands (Charles, 2012). An outline of a course using a D-I-Y corpus approach is presented in Quote 9.5.

Quote 9.5 Lee and Swales on a Writing Course Using D-I-Y Corpora

Participants were given access to specialized corpora of academic writing and speaking, instructed in the tools of the trade (web- and PC-based concordancers) and gradually inducted into the skills needed to best exploit the data and the tools for directed learning as well as self-learning. After the induction period, participants began to compile two additional written corpora: one of their own writing (term papers, dissertation drafts, unedited journal drafts) and one of 'expert writing', culled from electronic versions of published papers in their own field or sub-field. Students were thus able to make comparisons between their own writing and those of more established writers in their field. At the end of the course, participants presented reports of their discoveries with some discussion of how they felt their rhetorical consciousness was raised and reflected on what further use they might be making of corpus linguistics techniques in their future careers.

Lee and Swales (2006: 56)

Charles (2012, 2015) describes a similar course where heterogeneous classes of graduate students were given instruction in how to turn ten PDF research articles into plain-text format using the 'save as text' option, and in the use of the concordance, word list, collocates and cluster tools from *AntConc* (Anthony, 2014). They then used these tools to analyse the use of personal pronouns, linking adverbs, reporting forms, citation patterns and subordination and coordination in the texts. End-of-course questionnaires showed 92% of the 50 respondents stated that it was easy to build their own corpus and 90% agreed that its use helped them improve their writing. While some students criticised the small size of the corpus they had built, a follow-up survey showed that 68% had continued to use the corpus tools after the course, 20% at least once a day. This suggests that, for many of these students at least, having access to material of direct relevance to their own writing needs proved to be an important source of information and resource for learning.

9.2.4   Conclusions

As studies by Starfield (2004) and Yoon (2008) show, corpus use enables students to take more responsibility for their own writing and to become more independent learners. Corpora overcome the limitations of many CALL programmes, which are often autocratically didactic, and existing print materials, which cannot supply the quantity of authentic examples required for inductive learning. The major limitation is classroom corpora approaches are based on a procedural model of learning rather than a more familiar declarative model, and so challenge students' perceptions about how writing should be taught. But while a corpus approach may be daunting for students familiar with more directed learning, it offers considerable advantages to the development of effective and independent writers.

9.3   Writing Teaching and Academic Word Lists

The idea of an academic vocabulary has a long history in university writing instruction. Variously known as "sub-technical vocabulary" (Yang, 1986), "semi-technical vocabulary" (Farrell, 1990), or "specialized non-technical lexis" (Cohen, Glasman, Rosenbaum-Cohen, Ferrara and Fine, 1988), the term refers to items which are reasonably frequent in a wide range of academic genres but are relatively uncommon in other kinds of texts (Coxhead and Nation, 2001). Academic vocabulary knowledge is recognised as an indispensable component of academic abilities (e.g. Nagy and Townsend, 2012) and may be the most important discriminator in major gate-keeping tests such as TOEFL, SATS and IELTS (Gardner and Davies, 2014).

Concept 9.3   An Academic Vocabulary

The notion that some words occur more frequently in academic texts than in other domains is generally accepted and corresponds with a view that teaching should be based on the specific language features and communicative skills of target groups. This lexis is said to comprise a repertoire of specialised academic words which falls between an every-day general service vocabulary and a technical vocabulary which differs by subject area. However, whether it is useful for learners to possess a *general* academic vocabulary is more contentious, as it may involve considerable learning effort with little return.

9.3.1 Academic Word List (AWL)

The compilation of vocabulary lists from the most frequently occurring words in academic texts has been one of the major contributions of corpora to teaching academic writing. Such lists are useful in establishing vocabulary learning goals, assessing vocabulary knowledge, analysing text difficulty, creating materials and establishing expectations for writing assignments (Nation and Webb, 2011). Xue and Nation's (1984) university word list (UWL) was a significant departure from early word lists compiled by hand and based on small samples, but the first truly representative, corpus-based list was Cox-head's (2000) academic word list (AWL)[3]. Derived from a corpus of 3.5 million words of written academic texts, the AWL sought to identify the most frequent and wide-ranging words outside the first 2,000 most commonly occurring words of English. The 570 word families which make up the AWL account for around 10% of the total words in academic texts but only 1.4% of the total words in a fiction collection of the same size, suggesting that the list contains predominantly academic words.

The AWL has contributed to published materials (e.g. O'Regan, 2003; Schmitt and Schmitt, 2005) and is widely used by teachers. However, there are serious problems with the AWL, not least that it actually contains many words in the highest-frequency lists of the general British National Corpus (BNC) (Schmitt and Schmitt, 2012) while having a very uneven coverage across disciplines (Hyland and Tse, 2007). Some items are only frequent overall because of their concentration in one or two fields, and almost all the families have irregular distributions across science, social science and engineering.

Another problem with the AWL is that it is based on word families, i.e. a stem or headword plus all inflections and derivations from it. Thus, the stem *concept* has nine affixes that can be added to it (*conception, conceptual, conceptualise*, etc.) and *use* has 28 different meanings. While Bauer and Nation (1993) argue that it is relatively easy to comprehend regularly inflected members of a family if learners know the base word and have word-building strategies, members of some word families may not share the same core meaning (Nagy and Townsend, 2012). So the meaning of the headword *react* (respond), for example, differs enormously from reactionary (strongly opposed to change) or reactor (a device for generating nuclear energy). These meaning differences are accentuated further as members of word families cross over academic disciplines, so social science students are far more likely to meet *consist* as meaning 'to stay the same' and scientists to find it as meaning 'composed of', while 'volume' is a book for social scientists and a measure of mass for scientists (Hyland and Tse, 2007).

9.3.2   Academic Vocabulary List (AVL)

A more recent attempt to construct a core academic word list is the Academic Vocabulary List (Gardner and Davies, 2014) which is derived from the 120-million-word academic sub-corpus of the 425-million-word Corpus of Contemporary American English (COCA)[4] (Davies, 2012). This not only draws on a much larger corpus and is based on lemmas (the dictionary or citation form of a word) rather than word families, but also employs a more robust set of criteria to identify academic words. The list was generated using frequency and dispersion statistics which separate words which appear in the vast majority of the various academic disciplines in the corpus (academic 'core words') from those that appear with roughly equal frequency across all major registers of COCA (general high-frequency words) and from those that appear in a narrow range of academic disciplines (technical words). The most frequent words in the list are shown in Quote 9.6.

Quote 9.6   **Top 50 Words in the AVL with Parts of Speech**

1. study.n	18. change.n	35. role.n
2. group.n	19. table.n	36. difference.n
3. system.n	20. policy.n	37. analysis.n
4. social.adj	21. university.n	38. practice.n
5. provide.v	22. model.n	39. society.n
6. however.adv	23. experience.n	40. thus.adv
7. research.n	24. activity.n	41. control.n
8. level.n	25. human.adj	42. form.n
9. result.n	26. history.n	43. report.v
10. include.v	27. develop.v	44. rate.n
11. important.adj	28. suggest.v	45. significant.adj
12. process.n	29. economic.adj	46. figure.n
13. use.n	30. low.adj	47. factor.n
14. development.n	31. relationship.n	48. interest.n
15. data.n	32. both.adv	49. culture.n
16. information.n	33. value.n	50. need.n
17. effect.n	34. require.v	

Gardner and Davies (2014: 317)

Gardner and Davies (2014) show that the AVL discriminates between academic and other texts while covering over 14% of the academic sections of both COCA and the British National Corpus (33 million words). Particularly useful for teachers and students, moreover, is a related web-based interface that can be used by students to learn AVL words and to identify and interact with these in any text entered in the search window[5]. There are two main parts to this site: one showing frequency information and the other lexical characteristics of an inputted text.

The first application allows users to browse through the AVL and see frequency information for selected items by discipline. In addition, all words and phrases in the text window are searchable so that various kinds of useful information about them can be called up, including (i) synonyms, (ii) definitions, (iii) relative frequency across nine academic disciplines, (iv) the top collocates of the word to gain useful insights into meaning, usage, and phrasal possibilities, and (v) up to 200 sample concordance lines. Figure 9.4 shows a typical screenshot with the AVL items in the top right box with frequency across disciplines, a concordance on the selected word *research* and a histogram indicating the relative frequency of this word across disciplines.

The second screen option allows users to input an entire text such as a journal article, or an academic essay that a student has written, to get detailed information about the words and phrases in it. It first highlights and colour codes all the academic and 'technical' words in the text and creates lists of these words that students can use offline. The entries, moreover, are listed in order of frequency to help focus students on words that they will actually see in the real world rather than their word families. Then students can click through the words in the text to see a detailed characterisation of them,

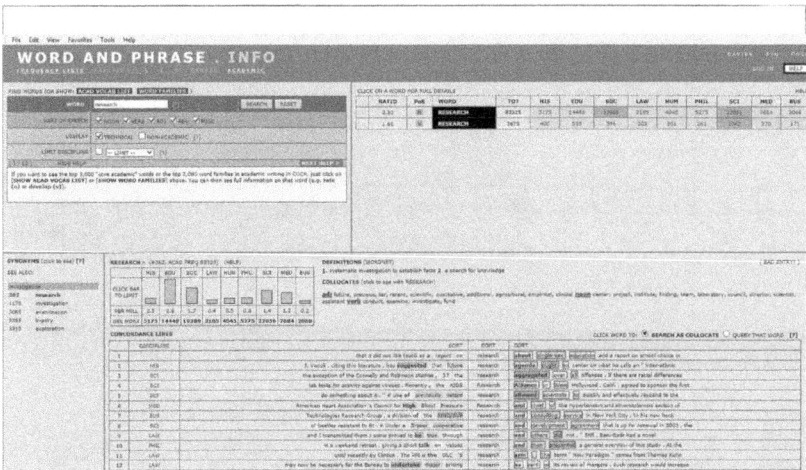

Figure 9.4 The 'Word and Phrase' site showing frequency information for the selected word *research*.

showing their definition together with collocates, re-sortable concordance lines, and the frequency of the word in different fields in COCA. Finally, writers can search on selected phrases in their text to show related phrases in COCA to see which seem most 'natural' or likely in different disciplines. Therefore, if a student clicks on the words *wrong claim* in the text he or she has entered, it will suggest alternate ways to express this (e.g. *unsubstantiated claim*, *unproven claim*) together with the frequency of those phrases overall in COCA and by discipline. Figure 9.5 shows the text analysis interface of the 'Word and Phrase' site.

9.3.3   Conclusions

The search for a common core of academic words to assist students with university reading and writing assignments has been a continuing quest in corpus research, and with the AVL it has reached its most sophisticated and useful point to date. Gardner and Davies' interface provides an excellent resource for students to check the meanings of words and common academic collocations as they write and edit their texts. The fact that students can look up words by part of speech is an enormous advance over the 'word families' approach, helping them to see, for example, that a highly frequent word like *process* occurs largely as a noun in science fields as a result of nominalisation where writers are more likely to transform experiences into abstractions. It remains unclear, however, how far a single inventory can represent the vocabulary of particular disciplines and be valuable to all students irrespective of their field of study. For this reason, together with attempts such as the AVL to identify a common core vocabulary, there has been a move toward more specialised AWLs in such

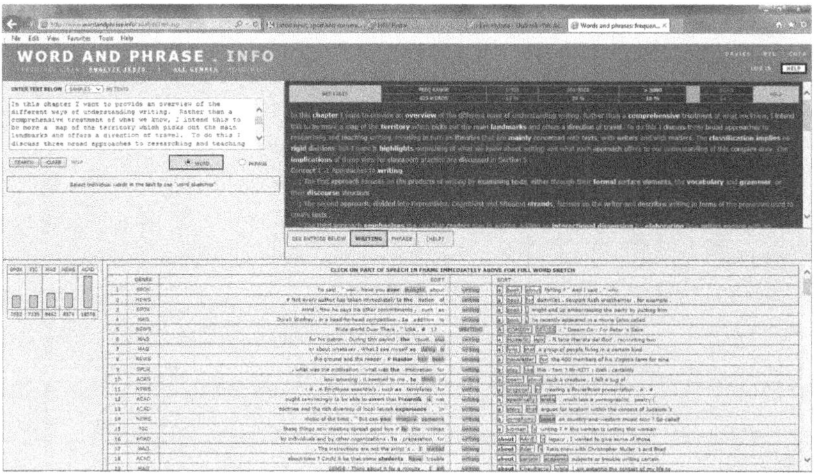

Figure 9.5 Text analysis interface of the 'Word and Phrase' site.

fields as agriculture (Martinez, Beck and Panza, 2009), medicine (Wang, Liang and Ge, 2008) and finance (Ha, 2015).

9.4 Scaffolding School Literacy: Writing Frames

Instructional scaffolding means providing students with sufficient supports to promote learning, particularly when new concepts and skills are first being introduced (see part 7.3.2). These supports are gradually removed as students develop familiarity with the task and acquire new cognitive, affective and psychomotor learning skills and knowledge. In writing instruction, *scaffolding* is closely related to the idea that learners develop greater understanding by working with more knowledgeable others.

Concept 9.4   Scaffolding

Bruner's metaphorical term 'scaffolding' has come to be used for interactional support, often in the form of adult–child dialogue. Scaffolding refers to the gradual withdrawal of adult control and support as a function of children's increasing mastery of a given task. Bruner (1978: 19) refers to it as "the steps taken to reduce the degrees of freedom in carrying out some tasks so that the child can concentrate on the difficult skills he or she is acquiring". It is thus a special form of help which moves learners towards new skills, concepts and understandings.

This model originates with Vygotsky (1978), who suggested that interaction with more skilled and experienced others assists learners to move through "the zone of proximal development" from their existing level of performance to a level of "potential performance", or what they are able to do without assistance. Children first experience a particular cognitive activity in collaboration with experts. The child is firstly a spectator, as the majority of the cognitive work is done by the parent or teacher; then, as the child develops greater capabilities in the task, the expert passes ever greater responsibility to the learner while still acting as a guide and assisting at problematic points. Eventually, the child assumes full responsibility for the task and the expert takes the role of a supportive audience. Using this 'apprenticeship' approach to teaching, children participate at a little beyond their current level so that the task continually provides sufficient challenge to be interesting; they are constantly 'stretched' in their language development but never have to perform an unfamiliar task (Gibbons, 2002).

9.4.1   Writing Frames

The kinds of tasks teachers select for students to engage with play a key role in offering a cline of support from closely controlled activities to autonomous extended writing (see part 7.1). The use of writing frames is one way that teachers have attempted to scaffold children's early attempts to understand and write a new genre.

Concept 9.5   Writing Frames

Writing frames consist of outlines, which can be used to scaffold learner's writing by setting out a sequence of cohesive ties to which the writer supplies the content. Each outline consists of different words or key phrases, depending on the particular genre which is being scaffolded. Writing frames guide learners through a writing activity by giving them a structure within which they can concentrate on communicating what they want to say, rather than getting lost in the form. They can be created for a range of genres and different stages of the writing process, such as planning or drafting.

Writing frames (Lewis and Wray, 1997; Wray and Lewis, 1997) are flexible and provisional forms of scaffolding to help young children develop a sense of genre when introducing them to non-fictional writing. Often children have considerable difficulty in recognising the appropriate genre they need for their purposes and fall back on familiar *narrative* and *recount* genres when they may need an *argument* or *report*. The tradition of getting learners to write about 'real experiences' clearly invites a personal telling, but it does not provide learners with the rhetorical resources to deal with more formal and abstract genres which they will meet in other areas of the school curriculum.

A frame is simply a skeletal outline to scaffold and prompt students' writing, providing a genre template which enables them to start, connect and develop their texts appropriately while concentrating on what they want to say. Frames provide a structure for writing which can be revised to suit different circumstances, taking different forms depending on the genre, the purpose of the writing, and the proficiency of the students. Essentially, however, they mirror the kinds of supportive oral guidance that teachers frequently offer children, providing the prompting missing between a writer and a blank sheet of paper.

Concept 9.6   Advantages of Writing Frames

- provide a varied vocabulary of connectives and sentence beginnings to extend learners' experience beyond 'and then'
- offer students a structure through the cohesive ties of the text and so help them maintain the sense of what they are writing

- challenge children by involving them in a close examination of the features of text
- model a wide range of techniques for responding to literature or their experience
- require learners to review and revise their responses after a guided reading of a text
- encourage learners to think about what they have learnt by reordering information rather than just copying out text
- improve self-esteem and motivation by helping learners achieve some success at writing
- avoid the discouragement of starting with a blank sheet of paper

9.4.2 Using Frames

Normally, frames are introduced only after extensive reading, teacher modeling, and explicit discussion of the forms needed for a particular kind of text. They are also seen as more effective if located in meaningful experiences and used to help learners produce writing they want to produce, rather than in de-contextualised skills-cantered lessons. The best use of a writing frame is therefore when learners have a purpose for undertaking some writing, like needing a new genre, or when they are stuck in a particular mode of writing, such as the repeated use of 'and then' when writing an account. Wray and Lewis (1997) show how frames can be useful for planning to write a discussion genre (Fig. 9.6).

Frames are, however, perhaps more usually employed in drafting (Fig. 9.7), providing students with both a skeletal outline of the genre and the connectives needed to logically develop their ideas.

The issue we are discussing is	*School uniform*

Arguments For	Arguments Against
1. it is smart 2. Represents the college 3. Parents because of washing 4. people might turn up to school in hundreds of kinds of clothes 5. expensive jewelry may get stolen 6. rich children could end up in fancy clothes	1. school uniform can be expensive 2. Make you feel the same as everyone else 3. people without much money can wear whatever they want 4. We won't get into so much trouble if we aren't wearing a jumper or something like that

My Conclusion

I think we should wear whatever we want but not being too outrageous and it is suitable to wear!

Figure 9.6 A writing frame for planning a discussion (from Wray and Lewis, 1997: 126).

There is a lot of discussion about whether   *Smoking should be allowed in public buildings*

The people who agree with this idea claim that   *people have rights and should be allowed to enjoy themselves*

They also argue that   *there are too many laws stopping people to do what they like*

A further point they make is   *Smoking is an addiction and people cannot stop easily*

However there are also strong arguments against this point of view.   *Most of our class* believe that   *people shouldn't be allowed to smoke anywhere they like.*

They say that   *smoking is dangerous even for people who do not smoke*

Furthermore they claim that   *it is a bad influence to children and creates pollution and litter.*

After looking at the different points of view and the evidence for them I think   *smoking should be banned in public*   **because**   *it is dangerous and dirty.*

Figure 9.7 A writing frame for first draft of a discussion (from Wray and Lewis, 1997: 128–9).

The frame therefore encourages students to think before they write, provides appropriate connectives, supports their efforts to achieve coherence, and scaffolds the generic form. Wray and Lewis suggest that following drafting, the students' frames can provide the basis for teacher–pupil conferencing or peer editing before the final version is written out.

9.4.3   Conclusions

Writing frames are useful to writing teachers in primary and secondary schools who can devise their own frames by drawing on their knowledge of the genres they are teaching and the particular abilities and needs of their students. They have been shown to encourage pupils both to develop and to express their procedural understanding in science (Warwick, Stephenson, Webster and Bourne, 2003; Webb, Williams and Meiring, 2008), helping young learners to gain familiarity with a new text type and experience ways of using language to express their purposes effectively. Students will need to use them less and less as their confidence in writing and their competence in writing target genres grows.

9.5   Check My Words: Technology and Autonomy

Learning technologies have a long association with autonomy, particularly in the area of computers in self-access, as they provide learners with opportunities to self-direct their own learning (e.g. Benson, 2013). Less celebrated, however, are automated feedback tools which encourage student writers to look up words and language patterns as they write and so become less dependent on their teachers' support. But while researchers now recognise that acquisition is optimised when learners are attending to both meaning and form (Ellis, 2006), teachers often feel demoralised by what seem ineffective efforts to correct sentence-level errors (see part 3.4). In response to these issues, Milton

(2010) has developed a suite of resources—*Check My Words*[6] and *Mark My Words*[7]—to provide students and tutors with the means to improve writing by referring to advice and resources during the writing process.

Driven both by the rapid advance of educational technologies and growth of MOOCs and distance courses, students now often find themselves reading feedback on their electronically submitted essays which has been produced by an unseen tutor or by the computer itself (see part 3.6). Sophisticated software is now available that is capable of scanning student texts and generating immediate evaluative comments on them, targeting grammatical errors, content and structure (e.g. Ware and Warschauer, 2006). The *Criterion e-rater* (Burstein, 2003), for example, scans a student text and provides real-time feedback on grammar, usage, style and organisation. But these automatic feedback programmes have been criticised for being unreliable (Krishnamurthy, 2005) and based on poor pedagogic principles (Perelman, 2013). Equally, such programmes only deliver formative assessment and so contribute to students' continuing dependence on expert response. A very different approach is *Check My Words* which offers a discovery-based approach, supporting novice writers as they write.

9.5.1   Check My Words *Programme*

> **Quote 9.7**   **Milton on *Check My Words***
>
> The approach provides students with the means to check and improve their language by referring to copious, authentic, and comprehensible resources during the writing process. This access, combined with resource-rich feedback from their teachers, can greatly increase the amount of positive and negative evidence available to students. Many researchers believe such evidence promotes acquisition, and if this approach can help students become more confident, responsible, and independent in selecting forms and patterns that are accurate and appropriate, it can also help relieve teachers of the need to act as proofreading slaves.
>
> Milton (2006: 125)

Check My Words is an add-on toolbar for Microsoft Word that helps learners of English to write more accurately and fluently (Fig. 9.8). The bar links writers to various online resources such as 'Word Neighbours', which brings

Figure 9.8 Check My Words toolbar.

up collocations of the target word, dictionaries, example sentences, word family information, grammar information, and a 'My Words' list of personal or assigned words to use, together with a list of lexical bundles common in academic writing. Additionally, students can get comments on the grammar of any word in their text by clicking the mouse on it.

Two of these tools are illustrated in Figure 9.9. Here a student has activated the 'highlight' button on the toolbar which has searched for, and highlighted, potential errors in the text, marking these in blue and common errors in red. The two pop-up screens overlaying the essay are in response to clicking the 'similar meanings' and 'check' buttons on the word 'facilitate'. This has thrown up a list of synonyms and antonyms and an information box on grammatical usage which allows the writer to review other members of the word family to see if he or she is using the correct form and to look up common grammatical errors.

The potential-errors list hyperlinks students to the *English Grammar Guide* (EGG) where they can find explanations for the most common grammatical errors made by second-language writers of English. Figure 9.10 shows the EGG main screen together with information called up by clicking on *which* in an essay, giving advice on its use and common difficulties for learners.

Other buttons in the toolbar allow writers to get definitions and translations of words, to hear stretches of text spoken aloud, and to get example sentences

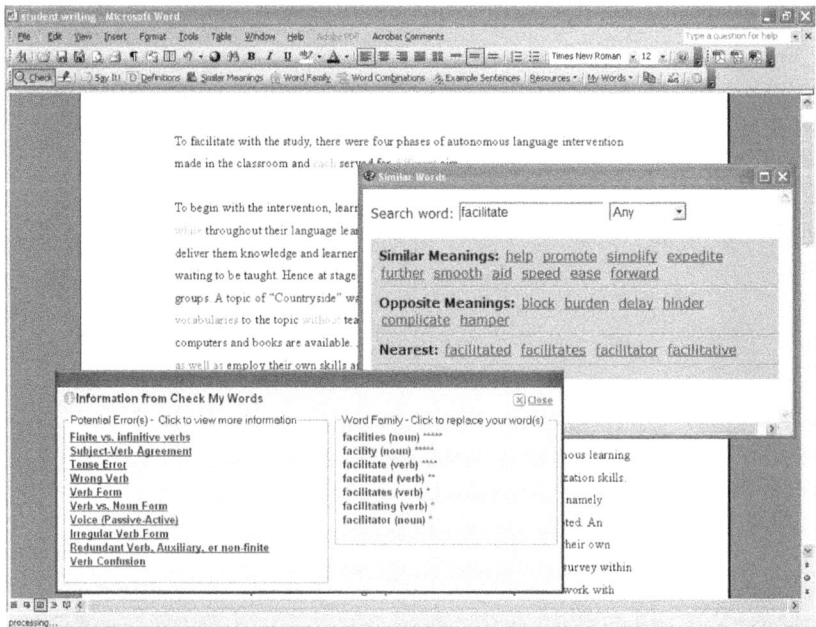

Figure 9.9 Checking the word 'facilitate' in *Check My Words*.

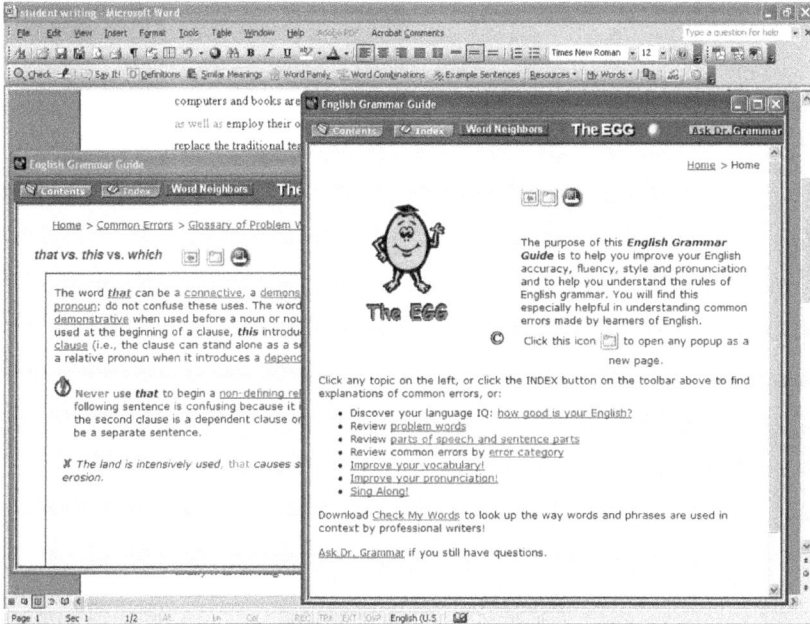

Figure 9.10 The *English Grammar Guide*.

which can help them select the appropriate phrasing. The 'resources' button pulls down a list of potentially useful websites and gives access to *Word Neighbours*, which displays the words that are most frequently used before or after a target word in a selected genre. *Check My Words* can access about 50 million words in 20 different genres; it makes such searches easy via a dialogue box which allows users to display up to four words on either side of the target word, choose whether to include all forms of the word, get a summary of collocations, and, if needed, see all sentences containing the target expression. Figure 9.11 is a screen showing the frequency of immediate right collocates of 'carry' and clustered by word class. This assists the writer to see the appropriate phrasal verb combination 'carry out', with the option to view real examples.

9.5.2 Mark My Words *Programme*

Mark My Words is the companion programme to *Check My Words*, allowing tutors to provide detailed feedback on student texts by using the same online resources. This not only allows the tutor to give detailed feedback without correcting the student's language, but also encourages students to use *Check My Words* itself.

Again, this programme installs as a word processor toolbar (Fig. 9.12) so that the teacher simply highlights a word or structure in a student text and

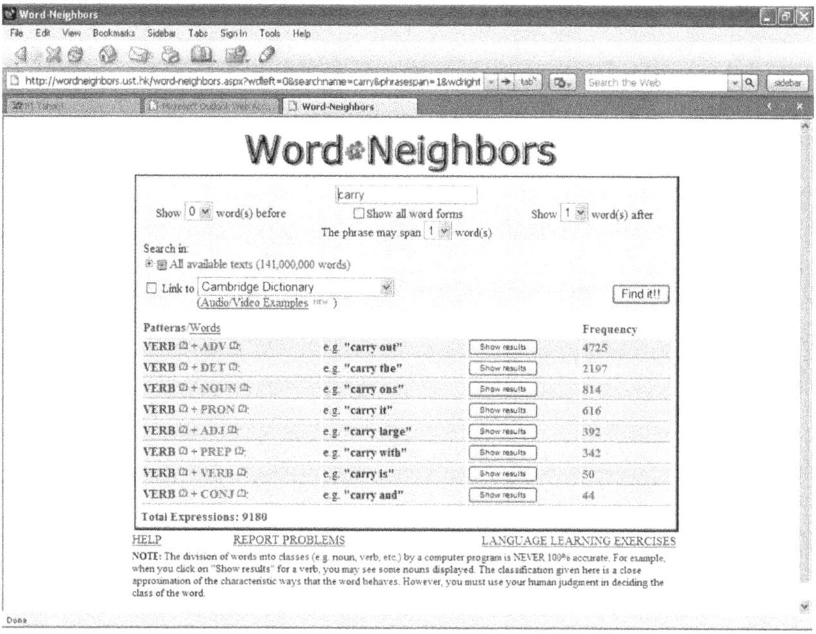

Figure 9.11 Word Neighbours concordance examples for facilitate.

Figure 9.12 Mark My Words toolbar in MS Word.

clicks the 'mark' button to indicate the lexical or grammatical error indicated. Teachers are aided here by the 'comments' button which allows them to insert brief pre-written (and customizable) comments linked to detailed web-based explanations, interactive tutorials, concordancers, references and so on. In addition, the software automatically identifies and inserts comments on a sub-set of common grammatical and lexical errors.

> **Quote 9.8   Milton on *Mark My Words***
>
> I designed Mark My Words to help teachers insert customizable comments in any language in a student's electronic document and to link the comments to the same online resources that are available to students. The commenting toolbar lists approximately 200 recurrent lexico-grammatical and style errors common in the writings of Chinese speakers, with suggested links to resources. Crucially, teachers who must respond

> to a wide range of sentence-level errors do not need to scroll through this long list. The programme can identify word classes and lexical patterns and automatically shortlist suggested comments.

Milton (2006: 130)

Figure 9.13 is a screen shot of a student essay with drop-down options from the 'comment' button and a number of comment bubbles created by the programme and posted by the tutor into the text. These include links to relevant resources, such as *Word Neighbours*.

After comments have been inserted in a student's assignment, the teacher can generate a summary for each student or assignment, including running totals for the semester, by clicking the 'grid' button. This log provides a record of comments given to particular students and groups of students from one assignment, semester, course and instructor to another. In this way, instructors can maintain a database of frequent errors, track student progress, identify learnability problems, and remind individual students of previous comments.

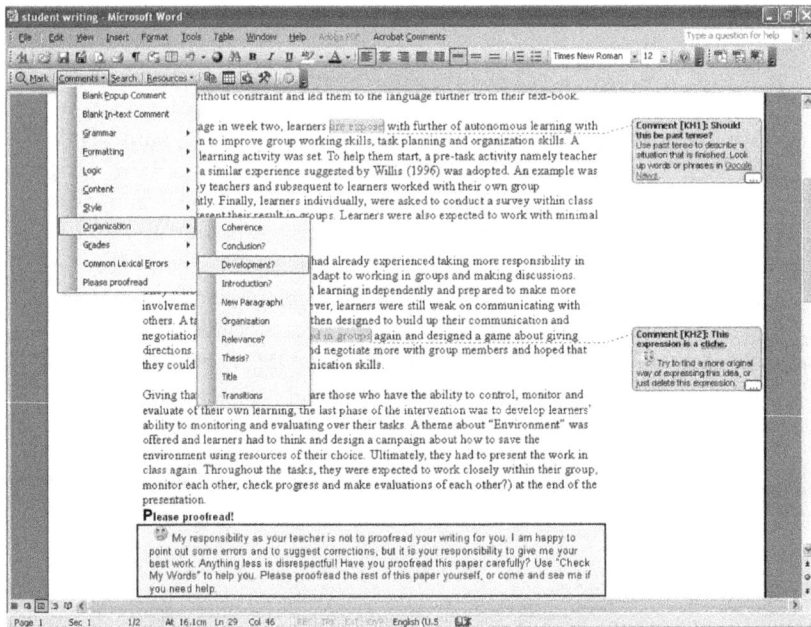

Figure 9.13 Drop-down comments menu and tutor-posted comments from choices available.

9.5.3   Conclusions

The *Check My Words* and *Mark My Words* programmes build on current research on feedback and autonomy and on automated grammar-checking software which facilitates writing through point-of-need assistance and specific teacher response. This combination seems to overcome some of the limitations of existing error-flagging mechanisms by making the writer responsible for judgements of correctness with the aid of advice and authentic data. To be successful, however, such an approach has to be integrated into the curriculum and potential resistance overcome. Students are not always comfortable revising without explicit reformulation of their errors, and teachers may be uneasy about using new methods and correcting online. Server logs, which track student revisions, and surveys of teachers using the programmes, however, suggest that students eventually use the resources effectively and that rates of successful revisions increase (Milton, 2006). Such resources may therefore be a step towards the development of autonomous writing skills (Hyland, 2013b).

9.6   Writing Portfolios: Pedagogy and Assessment

In this final illustration I focus on the evaluation of writing performance through the use of portfolios, looking at some examples and highlighting central issues.

Concept 9.7   Writing Portfolios

Portfolios are multiple-writing samples, written over time, purposefully selected from various genres to best represent a student's abilities, progress and most successful texts in a particular context. They can include drafts, reflections, readings and teacher or peer responses as well as a variety of finished texts. Most are assembled by students in a folder and comprise four to six core items in categories determined by curriculum designers to reflect the goals of their programme. There are two types of portfolio. *Showcase portfolios* contain only the student's best work while *process types* include both drafts and final products. In both types, the act of assembling texts over time encourages students to observe changes and discover something about the entries and their learning.

9.6.1   Some Advantages

The purpose of a writing portfolio is to demonstrate a writer's improvement and achievements, giving the instructor a view of a student's writing that focuses more on the complete body of work than on individual assignments and encouraging students to reflect on their work and measure their progress (Kirszner and Mandell, 2012). The use of writing portfolios is a response to the problems of traditional multiple-choice tests and, later, of holistically scored single-essay tests (Brown and Hudson, 1998). Yancey (1999) points out that the first approach stressed *reliability* by consistently measuring writing through standardisation and rater-proofing statistical correlations. The use of essay tests, by contrast, addressed the importance of *validity*, stressing the need to base judgements on actual writing. Behind portfolios is the idea that multiple samples will increase validity and at the same time make evaluation more congruent with teaching programmes. Some of the main advantages discussed in the literature are summarised in Concept 9.8.

Concept 9.8   Potential Pros of Writing Portfolios

- **Integrative:** combines curriculum and assessment to make evaluation developmental, continuous and fairer by reflecting writing progress over time, genres and contexts
- **Valid:** closely related to what is taught and what students can do
- **Meaningful:** students often see their portfolio as a record of work and progress
- **Motivating:** students have a range of challenging writing experiences in a range of genres and can see similarities and differences between these
- **Process-oriented:** focuses learners on multi-drafting, feedback, collaboration, revision, etc.
- **Coherent:** assignments build on each other rather than being an unrelated set of texts
- **Flexible:** teachers can adopt different selection criteria, evaluation methods and response practices over time, targeting their responses to different features of writing
- **Reflexive:** students can evaluate their improvement and critically consider their weaknesses, so encouraging greater responsibility and independence in writing
- **Formative:** by delaying grading until the end of the course, teachers can provide constructive feedback without the need for early, potentially discouraging, evaluation

---

Portfolios therefore help integrate instruction with assessment, representing a coherent model of organising writing processes and products for ongoing reflection, dialogue and evaluation. A growing literature advocates the use of portfolios as a way of strengthening learning by exposing students to a variety of genres, encouraging them to reflect on their writing processes and promoting greater responsibility for writing (Purves, Quattrini and Sullivan, 1995). They are said to enhance learning by increasing teacher and student involvement in the writing-testing process and by engaging students in a variety of tasks. Finally, they can potentially give teachers a more central coaching role by providing more data on individual progress (Brown and Hudson, 1998).

9.6.2 Two Example Portfolios

Concept 9.9 is a portfolio used by a group of English teachers for a class of advanced EFL students studying for a public school-leaving examination in Singapore. The portfolio includes five core entries and reflection questions.

Concept 9.9   A Portfolio for a High School Class in Singapore

1. **A timed essay.** Students select one timed essay (argumentative, expository or reflective). Reflection questions include: What was your interpretation of the question? How did you decide when dividing your paragraphs? What was your main problem and how did you solve it?

2. **A research-based library project.** Students submit all materials leading to the final paper. What timing and other goals did you set? What difficulties did you find? What did you learn?

3. **A summary.** Students select one summary of a reading for inclusion. Why did you select this particular summary? How is it organised? Why is it organised like this? What are the basic elements of all the summaries you have written?

4. **A writer's choice.** A 'wild card' in the L1 or L2 that has been important to the student. What is this? When and where did you write it? Why did you choose it? What does it say about you as a literate person?

5. **An overall reflection of the portfolio.** A general reflection integrating the entries. What were the goals of this class? Describe each entry and why it was important for achieving these goals.

Johns (1997: 140–41)

This structure is obviously highly flexible and shows that portfolios can have value even in a curriculum constrained by a public exam. A second example (Concept 9.10) is from Carleton College, a leading U.S. liberal arts college, which requires all its undergraduates to submit a portfolio of their writing halfway through their four years of study to ensure they can write competently in a range of genres[8]. This involves between three and five papers from college courses of between 10 and 30 pages, plus a reflective essay in which writers argue for their accomplishments in the portfolio criteria, using their papers as evidence.

Concept 9.10   Portfolio Instructions from a U.S. College

1. Papers from at least three different departments or programmes. Do not submit more than one paper from a single course—variety shows your breadth as a writer;
2. At least one paper that reports on something you have observed (e.g. field notes for science or social science courses, a laboratory report, a description of art, a play, or music, etc.);
3. At least one paper that demonstrates your ability to analyse complex information (e.g. numeric data, multiple texts, multiple observations, etc.);
4. At least one paper that provides interpretation (of data, a text, a performance, etc.);
5. At least one paper that demonstrates your ability to identify and effectively use appropriate sources (other than the primary text for the assignment), properly documented;
6. At least one paper that shows your ability to articulate and support a thesis-driven argument;
7. Evidence that you can effectively control Standard American English in multiple curricular settings.

Student reflections are a key element of both these examples and a major strength of portfolios as they encourage a meta-cognitive awareness among students of their strategies, attitudes, writing experiences and the texts themselves. Such reflections make visible what students see in their work, in their development, and what they value about writing. This information can therefore both guide instruction and enhance learning through students' self-awareness of what they have done and what they can do. This emphasis on the portfolio as a teaching tool thus provides opportunities for feedback, conferencing and awareness-raising, which can be extended to classmates by publishing portfolios on the web. The growth of e-portfolios in recent years, often as graduation requirements or as evidence of performance in job applications, underlines the continuing value of this form of assessment (e.g. JISC, 2008; Zimmerman, 2012).

9.6.3   *Some Problems with Portfolios*

While Elbow and Belanoff (1991) question whether it is appropriate to grade portfolios, this is often a necessary evil for teachers. Although portfolios provide more evidence for assessment, its multiple entries complicate the process because of the need to ensure reliability across raters and rating occasions, and because of the heterogeneous nature of what is assessed. Standardising a single score to express a student's ability from a variety of genres, tasks, drafts and different disciplines can be extremely difficult. To address the problems with reliability, some schools have added a timed essay test to the portfolio assessment. Concept 9.11 lists some of the assessment problems.

Concept 9.11   Potential Cons of Writing Portfolios

- **Logistic:** can produce a daunting amount of work for teachers
- **Design:** needs to ensure grading criteria are clearly understood by all teachers
- **Reliability:** needs to ensure raters are trained and standardised grading processes adhered to across raters, genres, portfolios and courses
- **Product variation:** problem of fairly assigning a single grade to a mixed text collection
- **Task variation:** some tasks may be more interesting, and therefore elicit better writing, so teachers may be evaluating the task rather than students' performance on it
- **Authenticity:** lack of close teacher supervision may mean some students plagiarise or get considerable external help

---

Hamp-Lyons and Condon (2000) point out that for a portfolio programme to be fully accountable, it must have explicable, shared and consistent criteria which teachers fully understand and regularly review. In practice, portfolios are often scored holistically, requiring raters to respond to a sample as a whole, rather than focusing on a single dimension. Scoring criteria are a crucial part of the pedagogic context as they can be fed into the course as principles of good writing. This guide, however, provides no basis for using assessment information in instruction, making it difficult to support process pedagogies. More critically, it is doubtful whether a single holistic score can be reliably assigned to a complex collection of materials as raters are likely to weigh one text against another rather than get an impression of the whole (Hamp-Lyons and Condon, 1993). Quote 9.9 is the holistic scoring rubric for the Carleton College portfolio mentioned in Concept 9.10.

Quote 9.9   **Scoring Guide for Writing Portfolio**

Carleton College Writing Portfolio Scoring Sheet

Student name: Student ID#:

Reader #:   Date scored:

Score (**circle one**):   Needs Work   Pass   Exemplary

	Demonstrates Partially	Demonstrates adequately	Demonstrates fully
The rhetorical strategy and diction should be appropriate for the audience and purpose.			
If argument is a part of the rhetorical strategy, it should contain a thesis and develop that thesis with coherence, logic, and evidence.			
Whatever the purpose, writing should be as clear, concise, and interesting as possible.			
Narration, description, and reporting should contribute to analysis and synthesis.			
Writing should be edited to address surface error, including irregularities in grammar, syntax, diction, and punctuation.			

Carleton College portfolio assignment and grading rubric

9.6.4   *Conclusions*

While there are clear advantages to using portfolios for both teachers and students, the approach may not actually be a better assessment tool than, say, a timed essay. Portfolios do not necessarily bring greater accuracy to assessment, but they do promote a greater awareness of what good writing might be and how it might be best achieved. The advantages lie principally in that the validity, and value, of assessment is increased if it is situated in teaching and learning practices. By basing assessment on a clearer understanding of what it is we value in writing, we enhance learning by firmly creating a link between research and teaching as an ongoing, integrated and reflective practice.

Notes

1. The books are: Vol. 1, Swales, J.M. and Feak, C. (2009), *Abstracts and the writing of abstracts*; Vol. 2, Feak, C. and Swales, J.M. (2009), *Telling a research story: writing a literature review*; Vol. 3, Feak, C. and Swales, J.M. (2011), *Creating contexts: writing introductions across genres* ; and Vol. 4, Swales, J.M. and Feak, C. (2011), *Navigating academia: writing supporting genres*.
2. *AntConc* is freely available from: http://www.laurenceanthony.net/software.html.
3. The headwords of families in the AWL, together with the items grouped by sub-list, are available from the Massey University website at: http://language.massey.ac.nz/staff/awl/headwords.shtml.
4. COCA is a freely available corpus of 450 million words from spoken, fiction, popular magazines, newspapers and academic texts with an interface which allows searches for words, parts of speech, collocates etc. It can be found at http://corpus.byu.edu/coca.
5. The AVL online resource can be found at www.wordandphrase.info/academic.
6. The toolbar for *Check My Words version 1.9.7* can be downloaded free from http://mws.ust.hk/cmw/.There is also a tutorial screen at the site and information about the suite of programmes.
7. *Mark My Words* can be downloaded free of charge from http://mywords.ust.hk/mmw/.
8. Details of the Carleton College portfolio assignment and grading rubric can be found at https://apps.carleton.edu/campus/writingprogram/carletonwritingprogram/.

Further Reading

Aijmer, K. (ed) (2010) *Corpora and language teaching.* Amsterdam: John Benjamins.
   A useful text that deals with all aspects of using corpora in classrooms.
Ferris, D. and Hedgcock, J. (2014) *Teaching L2 composition: purpose, process, practice*, 3rd edn. Mahwah, NJ: Lawrence Erlbaum.
   Presents practical applications of research for L2 writing teachers, including portfolios.
Hamp-Lyons, L. and W. Condon (2000) *Assessing the portfolio: principles for practice, theory, and research.* Cresskill, NJ: Hampton Press.
   Clear and informative discussion of writing portfolios in a variety of contexts.
Hyland, K. (2003) *Second language writing.* New York: Cambridge University Press.
   An introduction based on current research to teaching writing to EFL/ESL students.
Lewis M. and Wray, D. (1997) *Writing frames.* Reading: NCLL.
   Offers theoretical support for using writing frames together with photo-copiable frames and planning grids to support pupils in writing a range of genres.

Section IV

References and Resources

10   Significant Areas and Key Texts

This chapter will . . .

*   offer a series of thumbnail sketches of the main fields in writing;
*   briefly outline the ways that writing is understood in these areas;
*   suggest a selection of key texts for further reading in these fields.

10.1   Literacy

The field of literacy studies has, in recent years, been concerned with the use of writing as a situated social practice, as discussed in part 2.2. Work in the New Literacy Studies (NLS) has shown that writing is a complex human activity, always located in particular times and places and indicative of wider social forces and relationships. This perspective therefore draws on many of the same sources as contemporary writing research, such as critical theory and social constructionism, shares a similar interest in detailing the activities and talk that surround writing, and employs similar ethnographic approaches to research. However, contemporary literacy theory also complements writing research in applied linguistics and language teaching. The study of everyday practices has expanded both our understanding of literacy, by making connections between research data of literacy-in-use and social theory, and our understanding of writing, by showing how it is positioned in relation to social institutions and dominant ideologies.

In other words, by focusing on the study of writing in peoples' everyday lives, literacy studies have moved writing research away from academic, media, literary and other published texts to embrace what people do when they read and write, the contexts that surround these activities, and how they understand them.

Key Readings: Literacy

Barton, D. (2007) *Literacy*, 2nd edn. Oxford: Blackwell.
Barton, D. and Hamilton, M. (2012) *Local literacies: reading and writing in one community.* 2nd edn. London: Routledge.

Barton, D., Hamilton, M. and Ivanic, R. (eds) (2000) *Situated literacies: reading and writing in context*. London: Routledge.

Barton, D., Ivanic, R., Appleby, Y., Hodge, R. and Tusting, K. (2007) *Literacy, lives and learning*. London: Routledge.

Baynham, M. and Prinsloo, M. (2009) *The future of literacy studies*. London: Palgrave MacMillan.

Blommaert, J. (2008) *Grassroots literacy: writing, identity and voice in central Africa*. London: Routledge.

Lea, M. and Street, B. (1998) Student writing in higher education: an academic literacies approach. *Studies in Higher Education,* 23(2): 157–72.

Grainger, T. (ed) (2004) *The Routledge Falmer reader in language and literacy*. London: Routledge.

Street, B. (1995) *Social literacies: critical approaches to literacy in development, ethnography and education*. Harlow: Longman.

Street, B. and Lefstein, A. (2008) *Literacy: an advanced resource book*. London: Routledge.

10.2   Rhetoric

Rhetoric is essentially the role of discourse toward some end: how language can be used to persuade, convince or elicit support. In the west it originated with Aristotle, Cicero and Quintilian, and describes the ways that writers (and speakers) attempt to engage their audiences, gain assent for their views, or establish the credibility of a reported event through the organisation and style of their discourses. While other rhetorical traditions, particularly African and Indian, have influenced the features of political and religious spoken rhetoric in English, many of the analytic and presentation skills of traditional rhetoric are still taught and extensively used in writing in a range of fields.

Classical rhetoric was organised into a series of categories which describe the composition and delivery of a text, namely: *invention, arrangement, style, memory* and *delivery*, with each further subdivided to elaborate the different strategies that can be used. Modern rhetorical analysis has largely tended to focus on the subdivision of *invention* and particularly the appeals of non-evidential, or 'artificial', proof. These are *logos*, the appeal to reason, *pathos*, the appeal to the passions or emotions, and *ethos*, the appeal to the character and authority of the writer.

The rhetorical study of written discourse today flourishes in a range of analytical approaches, particularly critical linguistics, sociolinguistics and genre studies, and seeks to elucidate the interaction of a text with its context to see how it responds to, reinforces or alters the understanding of an audience. Rhetorical genre studies, in particular, have been influential in North America, seeing genre as the exigency, or purpose, of the writer, rather than the features of the writer as defining texts and how genres realise social actions (see parts 1.2.2 and 3.2). Rhetorical theory also reaches beyond politics and advertising into genres which were not previously considered rhetorical such as academic, technical and business texts. The rhetorical appeals underlying newspaper, fund-raising, and commercial discourses, for example, have been explored using discourse and corpus research. The list below includes classic texts and coursebooks which are widely used to teach rhetoric.

Key Readings: Rhetoric

Bizzell, P. (2005) *Rhetorical agendas: political, ethical, spiritual.* London: Routledge.

Faigley, L. and Selzer, J. (2010) *A little argument,* 2nd edn. New York: Longman.

Faigley, L. (2016) *Writing: a guide for college and beyond,* 4th edn. New York: Longman.

Freedman, A. and Medway, P. (eds) (1994) *Genre and the new rhetoric.* London: Taylor & Francis.

Foss, K. (2004) *Rhetorical criticism: exploration and practice,* 3rd edn. Prospect Heights, IL: Waveland.

Foss, K., Foss, S. and Trapp, R. (2002) *Readings in contemporary rhetoric.* Prospect Heights, IL: Waveland Press.

Lindemann, E. and Anderson, D. (1987) *A rhetoric for writing teachers.* New York: Oxford University Press.

McGroskey, J.C. (2005) *Introduction to rhetorical communication.* Boston: Allyn & Bacon.

Roberts, R. and Good, J. (eds) (1993) *The recovery of rhetoric.* Charlottesville, VA: University of Virginia Press.

Sloane, T. (ed) (2001) *Encyclopaedia of rhetoric.* New York: Oxford University Press.

Soliday, M. (2011) *Everyday genres: writing assignments across the disciplines.* Carbondale, IL: NCTE/CCCC and Southern Illinois University Press.

10.3   Scientific and Technical Writing

Resources in this area comprise both practical primers to assist students and novice researchers to produce technical papers and reports, and academic studies which seek to illuminate the features of these discourses. While the former mainly confine themselves to advice about the nature of scientific writing, the latter recognise the importance of writing for a community, and that successful writing depends on the writer's projection of a shared context. Writers write for communities of peers existing at a particular time and place, and texts embody the ways that knowledge is constructed, negotiated and made persuasive for those communities. In other words, they tend to take a social constructivist view which sees language choices as helping to create a view of the world, constructing what we can know.

Research has, for instance, examined the practices of a particular lab or research programme, the negotiations involved in the referee process, the regularity of patterns in academic texts, and the ways these features have changed over time in response to changes in the social context of science. These research issues and methods closely overlap and intersect with the interests of applied linguistics, particularly with ESP and CDA.

Key Readings: Scientific and Technical Writing

Atkinson, D. (1999) *Scientific discourse in sociohistorical context: the philosophical transactions of the Royal Society of London, 1675–1975.* Mahwah, NJ: Erlbaum.

Day, R. and Sakaduski, N. (2011) *Scientific English: a guide for scientists and other professionals,* 3rd edn. Santa Barbara, CA: Greenwood.

Glasman-Deal, H. (2010) *Science research writing for non-native speakers of English.* London: Imperial College Press.

Gross, A. (2006) *Starring the text: the place of rhetoric in science studies.* Carbondale, IL: Southern Illinois University Press.

Halliday, M.A.K. (2006) The language of science. In J. Webster (ed), *The collected works of MAK Halliday,* vol. 5. London: Continuum.

Latour, B. and Woolgar, S. (1986) *Laboratory life: the construction of scientific facts.* Princeton, NJ: Princeton University Press.

Martin, J. and Halliday, M.A.K. (1993) *Writing science: literacy and discursive power.* London: Routledge.

Myers, G. (1990) *Writing biology: texts in the social construction of scientific knowledge.* Madison, WI: University of Wisconsin Press.

Penrose, A.M. and Katz, S.B. (2010) *Writing in the sciences: exploring conventions of scientific discourse,* 3rd edn. London: Longman.

Scanlon, E., Hill, R. and Junker, K. (eds) (1999) *Communicating science: professional contexts.* London: Routledge.

10.4   Professional and Business Writing

Training courses which focus on the specialised communication needs of engineers, business people, lawyers, therapists, technicians and other professional groups have burgeoned in recent years. Language is now recognised as one of the most important tools of the workplace and a marker of professional expertise, particularly in English, as it becomes the accepted medium for cross-language transactions. The value of effective writing to these professionals is obviously crucial, and courses, textbooks and reference materials have addressed both writing skills and the components of texts such as manuals, technical reports, memos, proposals and a variety of report genres. Only recently, however, have these materials come to be informed by writing research.

This applied research has drawn on a range of approaches, including text linguistics, discourse analysis, corpus studies, social constructionism and critical linguistics, and has played an important part in developing both linguistic theories and methods for analysing writing more generally. Studies of professional texts have been important, for example, in sharpening our understanding of genre analysis and the ways social interactions are negotiated in writing, as well as providing insights into bureaucratic obfuscation, promotional discourses and the connections between texts and graphics. There is every reason to believe that research into professional communication will continue to deepen our knowledge of many aspects of written communication in the future.

Key Readings: Business and Professional Writing

Bamford, J. and Bondi, M. (eds) (2006) *Managing interaction in professional discourse*. Rome: Officina Edizioni.

Bazerman, C. and Paradis, J. (1991) *Textual dynamics of the professions.* Madison, WI: University of Wisconsin Press.

Bargiela-Chiappini, F. (2009) *The handbook of business discourse*. Edinburgh: Edinburgh University Press.

Bargiela-Chiappini, F. and Nickerson, G. (eds) (1999) *Writing business: genres, media and discourses.* Harlow: Longman.

Bhatia, V.K. (2004) *Worlds of written discourse: A genre-based view.* London: Continuum.

Bhatia, V., Candlin, C. and Engberg, J. (eds) (2008) *Legal discourse across cultural systems.* Hong Kong: HKU Press.

Breeze, R. (2013) *Corporate discourse.* London: Bloomsbury.

Candlin, C. (2002) *Research and practice in professional discourse.* Hong Kong: City University of Hong Kong Press.

Christie, F. and Martin, J.R. (eds) (1997) *Genre and institutions: social processes in the workplace and school.* London: Cassell.

Gunnarsson, B.-L. (2009) *Professional discourse.* London: Continuum.

Gunnarsson, B.-L., Linell, P. and Nordberg, B. (eds) (1997) *The construction of professional discourse.* Harlow: Longman.

Koester, A. (2010) *Workplace discourse.* London: Continuum.

Orna-Montesinos, C. (2012) *Constructing professional discourse: a multiperspective approach to domain-specific discourses.* Newcastle: Cambridge Scholars Press.

Palmer-Silveira, J-C., Ruiz-Garrido and Fortanet-Gomez, I. (eds) (2006) *Intercultural and international business communication.* Bern: Peter Lang.

10.5 Academic Writing

Not long ago there was a widespread view that writing was peripheral to the more serious aspects of academic life—doing research, studying subjects and teaching students. Today it is widely recognised that universities are ABOUT writing and that specialist forms of academic literacy are at the heart of everything that goes on in them: central to constructing knowledge, educating students and to negotiating a professional academic career. Seeing literacy as embedded in the beliefs and practices of individual disciplines, instead of a generic skill that students have failed to develop at school, helps explain the difficulties both students and academics have in controlling the conventions of disciplinary discourses.

There is also a growing awareness that students have to take on new roles and engage with knowledge in new ways when they enter university, and in particular this involves writing and reading unfamiliar genres. Interest in academic writing has also extended backwards to writing in schools, in postgraduate contexts, and writing for publication. English for Academic Purposes aims at capturing thick descriptions of academic language use at all age and proficiency levels, incorporating and often going beyond immediate communicative contexts to understand the demands placed by academic contexts on communicative behaviours and the nature of disciplinary knowledge itself.

Key Readings: Academic Writing

Benesch, S. (2001) *Critical English for academic purposes.* Mahwah, NJ: Erlbaum.

Becher, T. and Trowler, P. (2001) *Academic tribes and territories.* Buckingham: Open University Press.

Brodkey, L. (1987) *Academic writing as social practice.* Philadelphia: Temple University Press.

Charles, M., Pecorari, D. and Hunston, S. (2009) *Academic writing: at the interface of corpus and discourse.* London: Continuum.

Christie, F. and Martin, J. (2007) *Language, knowledge and pedagogy.* London: Continuum.

Flowerdew, J. and Peacock, M. (eds) (2001) *Research perspectives on English for academic purposes.* Cambridge: Cambridge University Press.

Halliday, M.A.K. (2009) Language and education. In J. Webster (ed), *The collected works of MAK Halliday*, vol. 9. London: Continuum.

Hyland, K. (2004) *Disciplinary discourses: social interactions in academic writing.* Ann Arbor, MI: University of Michigan Press.

Hyland, K. (2006) *English for academic purposes: an advanced resource book.* London: Routledge.

Hyland, K. (2009) *Academic discourse.* London: Continuum.

Hyland, K. (2012) *Disciplinary identities.* Cambridge: Cambridge University Press.

Hyland, K. (2015) *Academic publishing: issues and challenges in the construction of knowledge.* Oxford: Oxford University Press.

Hyland, K. and Shaw, P. (2016) *Routledge handbook of English for academic purposes.* London: Routledge.

Johns, A.M. (1997) *Text, role and context: developing academic literacies.* Cambridge: Cambridge University Press.

Lea, M. and Steirer, B. (eds) (2000) *Student writing in higher education: new contexts.* Buckingham: Open University Press.

Lillis, T. (2001) *Student writing: access, regulation, desire.* London: Routledge.

Prior, P. (1998) *Writing/disciplinarity.* Mahwah, NJ: Earlbaum.

Swales, J. (2004) *Research genres.* Cambridge: Cambridge University Press.

Wingate, U. (2015) *Academic literacy and student diversity.* Bristol: Multilingual Matters.

10.6   Journalism and Print Media

Research on written media texts has always interested linguists and has tended to have a generally applied or critical focus. Efforts have been mainly devoted either to teaching or to elaborating how these texts use language to shape and reflect political and sociocultural forms in society.

The considerable influence that print media exercises in contemporary society is a powerful driver of interest in the forms which news, entertainment and advertisements take. In addition, the easy accessibility of these texts has long made them popular with writing teachers as sources for topics and models for writing, while the growth of courses specialising in writing for the media in recent years has increased the attention given to the rhetorical features of media texts. Research has identified a highly aggressive, audience-oriented style across a range of genres. Competing in a market crowded with information and stimulation, media writing is characterised by attention-getting and promotion devices, sometimes involving literary-like creativity, but almost always based on the inverted-triangle principle which draws the reader from a general statement or idea into the message of the text. Whether a headline and lead paragraph, an advertising graphic, or a sports report, media genres appear to rely heavily on a similar formula, often described as AIDCA (Attention, Interest, Desire, Conviction, Action).

The second broad area of linguistic research into media texts emphasises a concern with issues of power and ideology and the ways that (principally) news media work to construct particular representations of the world. This research has examined text structure, topic organisation, vocabulary, production practices and audience comprehension, and has largely been conducted under a CDA banner. A number of authors have noted the modified narrative structure of media texts and the ways that their 'news-driven' organisation may distort source information. Trends towards 'commodification' and 'conversationalisation' in news reporting (i.e. shifts to market models and linguistic informality) are examples of intertextuality seen in other forms of public discourse. This growing research not only helps us to understand what media language is like and what it reveals about the media, but it also tells us a lot about writing more generally. In addition, the analytical methods employed in this research are increasingly, and usefully, applied to other texts.

Key Readings: Mass Media

Bell, A. (1994) *Language in the news*. Oxford: Blackwell.

Bell, A. and Garrett, P. (eds) (1998) *Approaches to media discourse.* Oxford: Blackwell.

Bednarek, M. and Caple, H. (2012) *News discourse*. London: Continuum.

Conboy, M. (2006) *Tabloid Britain*. London: Routledge.

Cramer, P. (2011) *Controversy as news discourse*. New York: Springer.

Fairclough, N. (1995) *Media discourse*. London: Edward Arnold.

Fairclough, N. (2000) *New Labour new language*. London: Routledge.

Fowler, R. (1991) *Language in the news: discourse and ideology in the press.* London: Routledge.

Myers, G.A. (1994) *Words in ads*. London: Edward Arnold.

Reah, D. (2002) *The language of newspapers*, 2nd edn. London: Routledge.

Richardson, J. (2006) *Analysing newspapers: an approach from critical discourse analysis*. London: Palgrave MacMillan.

Scollon, R. (1998) *Mediated discourse as social interaction: a study of news discourse*. Harlow: Longman.

Thornborrow, J. (2009) *Media discourse*. London: Continuum.

van Dijk, T. (1988) *News as discourse*. London: Routledge.

van Dijk, T. (1991) *Racism and the press*. London: Routledge.

10.7   First-Language Writing

The field of first-language writing has informed much of what we know about texts and composition and has provided a theoretical basis for pedagogy and research. Research has followed a number of clear paths. Educational psychologists have sought to elaborate the stages which children pass through in learning to write, and to suggest some of the reasons why this can be problematic for some learners. This research has often employed case studies to follow individual children or focused on the learning experiences of groups of learners. The most interesting lines of study have explored the educational contexts for learning and have drawn on Vygotskian theories of language development.

More sociolinguistically-oriented research has examined educational disadvantage and the ways that school expectations can conflict with the home environments of learners. These studies have adopted ethnographic approaches to identify the various cultural and social features which can place learners' writing development at risk, pointing to the crucial role of literacy experiences, positive attitudes and meaningful teaching in acquiring writing skills. Two other areas of research have also been central to L1 writing. These are the studies conducted by cognitive psychologists into writing processes and by functional linguists into the genres written by school children. I have discussed this research, and some of the materials and teaching programmes that have emerged from them, in Chapters 1 and 3.

The growth of composition studies as an area of professional emphasis has drawn on, extended and sharpened our methods and theoretical perspectives, and been responsible for a tremendous transformation of both writing teaching and research. It has changed the teaching of writing from an intuitive, trial-and-error process to a dynamic, interactive and context-sensitive intellectual activity. As teachers, we are now more aware of the value of a thorough theoretical, social and pedagogical understanding of writing in our classrooms. We are also aware of the contribution that research can make to this understanding. The knowledge we have gained from these advances in L1 composition has had a considerable impact on virtually all the related fields sketched here.

Key Readings: First-Language Writing

Bazerman, C. (2009) *Handbook of research on writing: history, society, school, individual, text.* New York: Routledge.

Cope, B. and Kalantzis, M. (1993) *The powers of literacy: a genre approach to teaching writing.* Pittsburgh, PA: University of Pittsburgh Press.

Candlin, C.N. and Hyland, K. (eds) (1999) *Writing: texts, processes and practices.* Harlow: Longman.

Delpit, L. (1995) *Other people's children: cultural conflict in the classroom.* New York: The New Press.

Grigorenko, E., Mambrino, E. and Preiss, D. (2012) *Writing: a mosaic of new perspectives.* New York: Taylor & Francis.

Gimenez, J. (2010) *Narrative discourse.* London: Continuum.

Grabbe, W. and Kaplan, R. (1996) *The theory and practice of writing.* Harlow: Longman.

MacArthur, C., Graham, S. and Fitzgerald, J. (2008) *Handbook of writing research.* New York: Guildford Press.

Hasan, R. and Williams, G. (eds) (1996) *Literacy in society.* Harlow: Longman.

Kress, G. (1994) *Learning to write*, 2nd edn. London: Routledge.

Kress, G. (1997) *Before writing: rethinking paths to literacy.* London: Routledge.

Martin, J.R. (1989) *Factual writing: exploring and challenging social reality.* Oxford: Oxford University Press.

Schleppegrell, M. and Colombi, M. (eds) (2002) *Developing advanced literacy in first and second languages.* Mahwah, NJ: Earlbaum.

10.8   Second-Language Writing Instruction

Second-language teaching has been both a significant driving force and a major consumer of writing research in recent years, ensuring that research contributes to practice. While a great deal has been learnt about writing from studying how native speakers acquire composing skills, the emergence of L2 writing as a sub-discipline has opened new theoretical perspectives, research methods and pedagogical strategies. Particularly instructive has been the work on the differences between L1 and L2 writing practices, the significance of cultural background to writing, and the nature of L2 texts.

This research has suggested broad similarities between L1 and L2 writers. It seems that while writers proficient in their L1 are able to transfer strategies across to the L2 and display skills similar to those of L1 writers, writers inexperienced in their L1 are likely to suffer similar problems to their native-speaker counterparts. These weaker writers often lack direction and tend to focus on mechanical accuracy to the detriment of organisation, ideas and audience. Research also suggests, however, that it is unwise to overemphasise these similarities. As discussed in Chapter 1, the contrastive rhetoric literature indicates that L2 writers are likely to operate with very different schemata to first-language writers and have very different conceptions of rhetorical patterns. In addition to alerting teachers to these possible difficulties, research has identified key features of target discourses and the problems L2 writers typically have in controlling these in their own texts.

This research, based on the empirical findings from a range of different theoretical standpoints and methodological approaches, has significantly influenced our assumptions and practices. It has fed into classrooms and greatly assisted composition teachers better to address the specific, and highly distinct, rhetorical, linguistic and strategic needs of L2 writing students.

Key Readings: Second-Language Writing Instruction

Belcher, D. and Braine, G. (eds) (1994) *Academic writing in a second language: essays on research and pedagogy.* Norwood, NJ: Ablex.

Canagarajah, S. (2002) *Critical academic writing and multilingual students.* Ann Arbor, MI: University of Michigan Press.

Casanave, C. (2004) *Controversies in second language writing.* Ann Arbor, MI: University of Michigan Press.

Connor, U. (2011) *Intercultural rhetoric in the writing classroom.* Ann Arbor, MI: University of Michigan Press.

Ferris, D. and Hedgecock, J.S. (2014) *Teaching ESL composition: purpose, process and practice*, 3rd edn. Mahwah, NJ: Lawrence Erlbaum.

Hinkel, E. (2013) *Teaching academic ESL writing: practical techniques in vocabulary and grammar.* New York: Routledge.

Hyland, K. (2003) *Second language writing.* Cambridge: Cambridge University Press.

Hyland, K. (2004) *Genre and second language writing.* Ann Arbor, MI: University of Michigan Press.

Hyland, K. and Hyland, F. (eds) (2006) *Feedback in second language writing: contexts and issues.* New York: Cambridge University Press.

Kroll, B. (ed) (2001) *Exploring the dynamics of second language writing.* Cambridge: Cambridge University Press.

Manchón, R.M. (ed) (2011) *Learning-to-write and writing-to-learn in an additional language.* Amsterdam: John Benjamins.

Silva, T. and Matsuda, P.K. (eds) (2011) *Landmark essays on second language writing.* New York: Routledge.

10.9   Pragmatics and Writing

Pragmatics is a broad approach to discourse that studies the use of context to make inferences about meaning. In other words, the focus of pragmatics is on both the processes of communication and its products, including how language relates to its contexts and its consequences for that context. Historically, pragmatics originated in the philosophy of language and concerned itself with isolated utterances, but its contemporary linguistic importance lies in its approach to the analysis of discourse; although, unfortunately, this has mainly been restricted to conversation and other spoken forms. The relevance of pragmatics to writing, however, lies in the ways particular text features can be seen as signalling contextual presuppositions, or shared meanings, which provide an interpretive framework for understanding written discourse.

While researchers in pragmatics have not generally been active in studying writing, many of its central concepts have been applied to written texts. The goal has been to understand better the ways that writers interact with readers by drawing on and manipulating common ground and cultural understandings. Pragmatic processes such as speech acts, relevance, cooperation, reference and politeness provide ways to analyse how writers seek to encode their messages for a particular audience, and how readers make inferences when seeking to recover a writer's intended meaning. Speech-act theory, for example, has contributed the idea that linguistic communication involves not only surface forms but the ways these forms work to gain the reader's recognition of the writer's intention in the context of the discourse. Thus, in persuasive writing a writer not only wants his or her words to be understood (an illocutionary effect in speech-act terms), but also to be accepted (a perlocutionary effect, or reader action). This might be accomplished by various features such as hedges, boosters, attitudinal lexis and so on, which can mark consideration for the reader or appeal to common cultural understandings based on a shared professional or personal relationship.

Pragmatics thus points to the possible analysis of recurring patterns of specific text features, supported by discourse-based interviews with users of these texts, to identify the ways that writers engage with their readers by constructing a shared reality. But while such a programme promises to reveal a great deal about the notions of context and inference in writing, much of this value remains largely potential and awaits further research.

Key Readings: Pragmatics

Archer, D., Aijmer, K. and Wichman, A, (2012) *Pragmatics: an advanced resource book for students.* London: Routledge.

Blakemore, D. (1992) *Understanding utterances: an introduction to pragmatics.* Oxford: Blackwell.

Cutting, K. (2002) *Pragmatics and discourse.* London: Routledge.

Grundy, P. (2013) *Doing pragmatics*, 3rd edition. London: Routledge.

Horn, L.R and Ward, G. (eds) (2005) *The Handbook of Pragmatics.* Oxford: Blackwell.

Levinson, S. (1993) *Pragmatics.* Cambridge: Cambridge University Press.

Mey, J. (2001) *Pragmatics: an introduction*, 2nd edn. Oxford: Oxford University Press.

Thomas, J. (1995) *Meaning in interaction: an introduction to pragmatics.* Harlow: Longman.

Verschueren, J. (1999) *Understanding pragmatics.* London: Arnold.

Yule, G. and Widdowson, H.G. (1996) *Pragmatics.* Oxford: Oxford University Press.

10.10   Translation Studies

Translation research concerns the problems involved in transferring meaning from one culture to another. Obviously not all cultures interpret situations in the same way; perceptions can differ enormously, and words carry connotations which do not have exact equivalence in another language. Translation scholars are therefore occupied with many of the same concerns which interest writing researchers in other areas. Despite this, however, translation is often an invisible practice, and has tended to exist on the periphery of intellectual activity in applied linguistics.

Translation is the rewriting of an original text, and as such raises issues of subjectivity, ideological manipulation, cultural distortion, and the fossilisation of interpretation. More positively, however, this kind of writing can introduce new concepts, new genres, new meanings and new forms of expression, leading to innovation and change. Translation studies is, therefore, like other areas of writing, a field in which both theory and reflection on cultural, methodological and social issues are vital. Because of this, a number of questions central to writing more generally have emerged, including the nature of context and situationality, the role of interpretation in cross-cultural communication, the challenge of rendering idiomaticity and the part played by audience. Of particular importance has been the debate over 'equivalence' and the move away from absolute fidelity to a source text, to the production of a target text. This has increased the translator's role as a professional author and paved the way for greater creativity and interpretation.

Translation has also expanded beyond its established literary and technical areas. Both machine translation (MT) and computer-assisted translation (CAT) represent rapidly expanding domains of practice and flourishing research areas. Translators themselves have grown in importance in an ever-widening variety of communities, workplaces and languages. So, while notions of accuracy and correctness remain as measures of quality in assessing translated texts, translation studies are nevertheless deeply involved in the debates about meaning and communication which consume researchers and teachers in other areas of writing practice.

Key Readings: Translation

Baker, M. and Saldanha, G. (2009) *Routledge encyclopedia of translation studies*, 2nd edn. London: Routledge.

Bassnett, S. (2013) *Translation studies*, 4th edn. London: Routledge.

Bell, R.T. (1991) *Translation and translating: theory and practice*. Harlow: Longman.

Boase-Beier, J. (2011) *A critical introduction to translation studies*. London: Continuum.

Gentzler, E. (1993) *Contemporary translation theories.* London: Routledge.

Hatim, B. (1997) *Communication across cultures: translation theory and contrastive text linguistics*. Exeter: University of Exeter Press.

Hatim, B. and Munday, J. (2004) *Translation: an advanced resource book.* London: Routledge.

Kruger, A., Wallmach, K. and Munday, J. (2011) *Corpus-based translation studies: research and applications.* London: Bloomsbury.

Munday, J. (2012) *Introducing translation studies: theories and applications*, 3rd edn. London: Routledge.

Ricoeur, P. (2006) *On translation.* London: Routledge.

Schiffner, C. (ed.) (1999) *Translation and norms.* Clevedon: Multilingual Matters.

Venuti, L. (2012) *The translation studies reader*, 3rd edn. London: Routledge.

10.11 Literary Studies

Literary studies is an immensely important area of writing which covers a vast terrain. Studied as a product, literary texts are seen as aesthetic artefacts amenable to a range of critical theories or as models of writing to be emulated. Seen as a resource, they are valuable tools for the teaching of writing in both L1 and L2 contexts.

For the first 60 years of the twentieth century, reading and analysis of literature were the main principles motivating writing instruction. Native speakers were required to read short stories, plays, poems and novels, understand them, and then write about them, with little explicit instruction of how to do this. Instruction focused on knowledge about the texts themselves and the fixed, pre-given meanings they contained. This notion that a body of authoritative literary texts can provide models for good writing remains alive today in courses and texts on creative writing. The best of these take the student through the composing process from creative imagination to fixing a text on paper. They deal with both the mind observing, recalling and searching for ways to vividly recount experience, and with the engagement of the reader with the text through conscious editing and the shaping of interpretation. The practice of writing about literature employs the theories and resources of a range of approaches, from new criticism via feminism and cultural studies to deconstruction, and they are important to the work of discourse analysts and text linguists.

Literary texts have also been seen as a resource for focusing on language and developing both language and writing skills in L1 and L2 classrooms. Originally this mainly involved stylistic analyses, drawing on concepts such as 'foregrounding', the way that writers often use language which draws attention to itself in order to surprise the reader into a fresh appreciation of the topic. Stylistics draws heavily on linguistics, particularly pragmatics and discourse analysis, and provides a productive means of both raising learners' conscious awareness of how language is used, and a foundation for interpretation based on the text itself which can be transferred to other contexts and genres. More generally, however, teaching has sought to integrate language and literature by encouraging learners to actively construct and interpret texts rather than simply respond to an existing canon. In these ways, contemporary research and teaching practices have responded to current ideas and approaches in other areas of writing theory and pedagogy. The books listed here largely take a broadly stylistic or applied linguistic perspective towards the topic.

Key Readings: Literary Studies

Brumfit, C. and Carter, R. (1986) *Literature and language teaching.* Oxford: OUP.

Carter, R. and Stockwell, P. (eds) (2008) *The language and literature reader.* London: Routledge.

Carter, R. (1997) *Investigating English discourse: language, literacy and literature.* London: Routledge.

Carter, R. and Simpson, P. (eds) (1995) *Language, discourse and literature: an introductory reader in discourse stylistics.* London: Routledge.

Culler, J. (2011) *Literary theory: a very short introduction.* Oxford: OUP.

Jeffries, L. and McIntyre (2010) *Stylistics.* Cambridge: CUP.

Kirszner, L. and Mandell, S. (2011) *Literature: reading, reacting, writing,* 8th edn. Florence, KY: Wadsworth Publishing.

Leech, G. and Short, M. (2007) *Style in fiction: a linguistic introduction to English fictional prose.* London: Pearson Longman.

Lynn, S. (2010) *Texts and contexts: writing about literature with critical theory,* 6th edn. Harlow: Longman.

Nash, W. (1998) *Language and creative illusion: the writing game.* Harlow: Longman.

Roberts, E.V. & Zweig, R. (2011) *Literature: an introduction to reading and writing,* 10th edn. New Jersey: Prentice Hall.

Short, M. (1996) *Exploring the language of poems, plays and prose.* Harlow: Longman.

Simpson, P. (1997) *Language through literature.* London: Routledge.

Simpson, P. (2004) *Stylistics: a resource book for students.* London: Routledge.

Toolan, M. (1998) *Language in literature: an introduction to stylistics.* London: Routledge.

Verdonk, P. (2002) *Oxford introductions to language study: stylistics.* Oxford: Oxford University Press.

10.12   Texts, Tweets, Blogs and Wikis

While considerable emphasis has been devoted to the technological advances of these electronic channels, the language employed by writers of these genres have only recently begun to attract the attention of linguists and writing teachers. This interest not only focuses on aspects of the language such as grammar, spelling and innovative lexis, but also on discourse and the way language is used to accomplish interactions between people.

A *blog* is essentially a frequently updated web page with new entries placed above older ones. They are unlike personal home pages because they are regularly updated, and they are unlike diaries because they are built around links to other sites and blogs. They can contain text, pictures, sounds and video. A *wiki*, on the other hand, involves many authors collaborating on one text on a web page. Unlike a paper encyclopedia, a wiki is designed to enable anyone to contribute or modify its content using a simplified markup language. In contrast to the personal stance of blogs, wikis are impersonal, prompting Myers (2010: 2) to comment that: 'A wiki is a device for putting people together, and a blog is a device for setting them apart as individuals'.

The linguistic study of blogs, web sites and wikis is, like the genres themselves, very recent, but it allows analysts to say something about the writing and not just the content. This is interesting because they have emerged as distinctive kinds of text with characteristic ways of commenting, arguing, interacting and making sense. Analysis of the language can therefore reveal something of how language helps users to interact and construct social identities and communities. Most blogs, for example, show a careful informality, strong stance, tolerance of views and creative linking, while wikis display a creative construction of facts, multiply assembled, and sometimes vandalised, which offer immediate access to information for users. While the latter can be corrupted by the biases of its writers, it is the mix of cooperation, conflict and obstructiveness among writers and what they produce which provides interest to writing researchers.

Key Readings: Texts, Tweets, Blogs and Wikis

Barton, D. and Lee, C. (2013) *Language online: investigating digital texts and practices*. London: Routledge.

Bloch, J. (2008) *Technologies in the second language composition classroom*. Ann Arbor, MI: University of Michigan Press.

Blood, R. (2002) *The weblog handbook: practical advice on creating and maintaining your blog*. Cambridge, MA, Perseus.

Boardman, M. (2005) *The Language of Websites*. London, Routledge.

Bruns, A. (2008) *Blogs, Wikipedia, Second Life, and beyond*. New York: Peter Lang.

Bruns, A. and Jacobs, J. (eds) (2006) *The uses of blogs*. New York: Peter Lang.

Jones, R. and Hafner, C. (2012) *Understanding digital literacies: a practical introduction*. London: Routledge.

Keren, M. (2006) *Blogosphere: the new political arena*. Lanham, MD: Lexington Books.

Lankshear, C. and Knobel, M. (2006) *New Literacies: Everyday Practices and Classroom Learning*. Milton Keynes, Open University Press.

Myers, G. (2009) *The discourse of blogs and wikis*. London: Continuum.

Lamy, M.-N. and Hampel, R. (2007) *Online communication in language learning and teaching*. London: Palgrave.

Page, R. (2012) *Stories and social media: identities and interaction*. London: Routledge.

Page, R. (2014) *Researching language and social media: a student guide*. London: Routledge.

Tagg, C. (2012) *The discourse of text messaging*. London: Continuum.

Zappavigna, M. (2012) *Discourse of Twitter and social media*. London: Continuum.

10.13   Writing and Multimodal Texts

For many linguists, the analysis and teaching of writing cannot be restricted to linguistic forms of representation alone but must encompass all meaningful semiotic activity. While language plays a central role in written interaction, images are often a key aspect of many genres and have largely displaced text in arenas such as advertising and many web genres. There has certainly been a shift in our systems of representation away from the purely verbal to the visual in a whole range of informative, persuasive and entertainment texts in recent years. The trend has extended into textbooks and teaching materials, and students are now often required to produce essays or reports which include visual elements such as graphs, photographs and diagrams.

As I discussed briefly in part 2.3, researchers are interested in this area because text and images configure the world in different ways, with consequent shifts in authority, in forms of meaning, and in forms of engagement with both content and readers. Most dramatically, this can require very different semiotic work from the 'reader' as contemporary electronic texts often offer a range of entry points to the 'page' and different reading paths through it when compared with print texts. At the same time, the reader is more actively involved in filling the relatively 'empty' words with meaning. Multimodal analyses seek to describe these differences in various contexts and discover the potentials and limitations (or 'affordances') for making meaning which attach to different modes. Kress (2003), for example, suggests that writing and image are governed by different logics: writing by time and image by space. So in writing, meaning is attached to 'being first' and 'being last' in a sentence, while in a visual, centering and positioning something above gives it greater significance. The expansion of genres using new technologies hasten and intensify different potentials for communication, interaction and representation, and simultaneously encourages writing teachers to understand these changes and bring them into their classrooms.

Key Readings: Writing and Multimodal Texts

Archer, A. and Newfield, D. (eds) (2014) *Multimodal approaches to research and pedagogy*. New York: Routledge.

Böck, M. and Pachler, N. (eds) (2013) *Multimodality and social semiosis: communication, meaning-making, and learning in the work of Gunther Kress*. New York: Routledge.

Jewitt, C. (ed) *The Routledge handbook of multimodal analysis*, 2nd edn. London: Routledge.

Kress, G. (2003) *Literacy in the new media age*. London: Routledge.

Kress, G. (2010) *Multimodality: a social semiotic approach to contemporary communication*. London: Routledge.

Kress, G. and van Leeuwan, T. (2006) *Reading images: the grammar of visual design*, 2nd edn. London: Routledge.

Norris, S. (2004) *Analysing multimodal interaction: A methodological framework*. New York: Routledge.

O'Halloran, K.L. (2008) *Mathematical discourse: language, symbolism and visual images.* London and New York: Continuum.

O'Halloran, K.L. (2009) *Multimodal approach to classroom discourse*. London: Equinox.

O'Halloran, K.L. and Smith, B.A. (eds) 2011 *Multimodal studies: exploring issues and domains*. New York and London: Routledge.

Royce, T. and Bowcher, W. (eds) (2007) *New directions in the analysis of multimodal discourse.* Mahwah, NJ: Earlbaum.

Selfe, C.L. (ed) (2007) *Multimodal composition: resources for teachers.* Kresskill, NJ: Hampton Press.

Unsworth, L. (ed) (2009) *Multimodal semiotics: functional analysis in contexts of education.* London: Continuum.

10.14 Writing and Forensic Linguistics

Forensic linguistics deals with written and spoken texts that are involved in legal or criminal proceedings. Including everything from high-profile plagiarism cases, falsified confessions, hoaxes and ransom demands to suicide notes, hate mail and trademark copying, the field has developed rapidly in the past 15 years. Forensic linguistics is now of considerable use to law enforcement and criminal justice professionals in investigations, and linguists are called to appear as expert witnesses in courtrooms. There is even now an International Association of Forensic Linguists (http://www.iafl.org/).

Forensic linguistics has evolved from authorship studies and disputes over biblical and Shakespearian texts in the late 18th centuries. Statistical and computational linguistics, and then corpus linguistics, has helped support the idea that every text carries the 'linguistic fingerprint' or 'stylistic profile' of its writer, distinguishing it from the writing of others. Frequency and collocational differences, misspellings and preferences for particular forms of expression, grammar, lexis, punctuation or formatting can indicate particular patterns of choices and help reveal the writer of a given text. One high-profile example of the work of forensic linguistics was the overturning of Derek Bentley's conviction for murder in 1998. Professor Malcolm Coulthard was able to show that Bentley's statement to police, allegedly transcribed verbatim from a spoken monologue, actually contained features which suggested question and answer interactions and so indicated police co-authorship. In particular, his analysis compared the frequency of the word 'then', which was far more common in the confession than in a corpus of witness statements, and the particularly high frequency of *I then* rather than *then I*, which is fairly rare in general English usage outside of police statements.

Analyses such as these go beyond the courtroom to questions of plagiarism in educational settings (see part 3.4) and can help students and researchers to see individual diversity in the common patterns of various written genres.

Key Readings: Writing and Forensic Linguistics

Coulthard, M. and Johnson, A. (2007) *An introduction to forensic linguistics: language in evidence.* London: Routledge.

Coulthard, M. and Johnson, A. (2013) *The Routledge handbook of forensic linguistics.* London: Routledge.

Gibbons, J. (2003) *Forensic linguistics: An introduction to language in the justice system.* Oxford: Blackwell.

Hanlein, H. (1998) *Studies in authorship recognition: a corpus-based approach.* Frankfort: Peter Lang.

Olsson, J. (2004) *Forensic linguistics: an introduction to language, crime and the law.* London: Continuum.

Olsson, J. and Luchjenbroers, J. (2013) *Forensic linguistics*, 3rd edn. London: Bloomsbury.

Olsson, J. (2012) *Wordcrime: solving crime through forensic linguistics.* London: Continuum.

Shuy, R.W. (2005) *Creating language crimes: how law enforcement uses (and misuses) language.* Oxford: Oxford University Press.

Shuy, R.W. (2006) *Linguistics in the courtroom: a practical guide.* Oxford: Oxford University Press.

10.15   Creative Writing

Finally, an area of writing which, while more closely associated with reading for most of us, is taken up by many people from all backgrounds and walks of life: creative writing. The burgeoning market for would-be authors is fueled by the artistic impulse and the rags-to-riches success of authors such as J.K. Rowling. We can see this as any writing, fiction or non-fiction, that occurs outside of everyday professional, journalistic, academic and technical forms of writing. Most typically we think of novels, short stories and poems in this category, but it can also include screenwriting and playwriting, which are texts to be performed, and creative non-fiction such as personal and journalistic essays.

Creative writing is now seen as an independent academic discipline and taught both at undergraduate and post-graduate levels at some universities, leading to Bachelor or Masters of Fine Arts degrees. Unlike its academic writing courses that teach students the rhetorical conventions and discourse expectations of disciplinary communities, creative writing attempts to focus on students' self-expression. Creative writing students typically decide to focus on either fiction or poetry, although screenwriting and playwriting courses are also available in some programmes. Input normally involves critical appraisal of literature and the development of writing techniques such as editing, idea generation and overcoming writer's block. Courses normally follow a workshop format where students develop skills through process techniques of drafting and rewriting and submitting their original work for peer critique. Students also work outside their classes by participating in writing-based activities such as publishing clubs, university literary magazines or newspapers, and writing contests. Because many of these courses are run in the U.S., texts available in the area of creative writing tend to be American and address the needs of students on these courses.

Key Readings: Creative Writing

Anderson, L. and Neale, D. (2009) *Writing fiction.* London: Routledge.

Neale, D. (ed) (2009) A *creative writing handbook: developing dramatic technique, individual style and voice.* London: A&C Black.

Bell, J. and Magrs, P. (eds) (2001) *The creative writing coursebook: forty authors share advice and exercises for fiction and poetry.* Basingstoke: MacMillan.

Bernays, A. and Painter, P. (1991) *What if? Writing exercises for fiction writers.* London: Collins.

Burt-Thomas, W. (2010) *The everything creative writing book: all you need to know to write a novel, play, short story, screenplay, poem, articles or blogs.* Avon, MA: Adams Media.

Kiteley, B. (2005) *3 am epiphany.* Cincinnati, OH: Writers Digest Books.

Mueller, L. and Reynolds, J. (1990) *Creative writing: forms and techniques.* Lincolnwood, IL: National Textbook Co.

Nadell, J., Langan, J. and Comodromos, E. (2010) *The Longman writer: rhetoric, reader, research guide, and handbook,* 8th edn. New York: Longman.

New York Writers Workshop (2006) *Portable MFA in creative writing.* Cincinnati, OH: Writers Digest Books.

Scott, J. (2014) *Creative writing and stylistics: creative and critical approaches.* London: Palgrave.

Vogler, C. (2007) *The writers journey: mythic structure for writers,* 3rd edn. Studio City, CA: Michael Wiese.

Williams, B.A. (2006) *Writing wide: exercises in creative writing.* Kandiyohi, MN: Filbert Publishing.

11   Key Sources on Writing

This chapter will . . .

- catalogue some of the main sources of information relevant to teachers and researchers of writing;
- list the main books, journals, conferences and professional associations with an interest in writing;
- refer to a number of Internet writing sites, bulletin boards and email discussion groups.

The huge reach, scope and productivity of the field of writing, together with tight space constraints in this book, mean that I can offer only a very limited, and idiosyncratic, collection of resources. I hope, however, that this provides a starting point from which readers might explore some of these very rich areas in much greater detail. Because many sources cover a range of topics, I have organised the list by the type of source: books, journals, professional bodies, conferences, email lists and bulletin boards, Internet sites, and databases.

11.1   Books on Writing

The main texts in specific areas of writing have been appended as key readings at the ends of chapters and a good overview of the field should include reference to them. There is no shortage of textbooks about writing. These range from collections of grammar tasks to those representing serious scholarship which increases our understanding of the subject. Lists 11.1 and 11.2 suggest some books which together would represent a good library on writing. List 11.3 contains a number of books useful for teachers of writing, and List 11.4 contains some textbooks and learning materials for students.

List 11. 1   Some Classic Books on Writing

Belcher, D. and Connor, U. (2001) *Reflections on multiliterate lives*. Clevedon, UK: Multilingual Matters.

Casanave, C. (2004) *Controversies in second language writing*. Ann Arbor, MI: University of Michigan Press.

Clark, R. and Ivanic, R. (1997) *The politics of writing*. London: Routledge.

Fairclough, N. (2004) *Analyzing discourse*. London: Routledge.

Grainger, T. (ed) (2004) *The Routledge Falmer reader in language and literacy*. Oxford: Routledge.

Hinkel, E. (2002) *Second language writers' text: linguistic and rhetorical features*. Mahwah, NJ: Lawrence Erlbaum.

Johns, A.M. (1997) *Text, role and context*. Cambridge: Cambridge University Press.

Kroll, B. (ed) (2003) *Exploring the dynamics of second language writing*. Cambridge: Cambridge University Press.

Silva, T. and Matsuda, P. (eds) (2001) *Landmark essays on ESL writing*. Mahwah, NJ: Lawrence Earlbaum.

Swales, J. (1990) *Genre analysis: English in academic and research settings*. Cambridge: Cambridge University Press.

Swales, J. (1998) *Other floors, other voices: a textography of a small university building*. Hillsdale, NJ: Lawrence Erlbaum.

List 11.2 More Recent Books on Writing

Charles, M., Pecorri, D. and Hunston, S. (2009) *Academic writing: at the interface of corpus and discourse*. London: Continuum.

Hyland, K. (ed) (2016) *Academic writing: critical readings*. London: Bloomsbury. Three-volume set.

Manchon, R. (ed) (2011) *Learning-to-write and writing-to-learn in an additional language*. Amsterdam: John Benjamins.

Manchon, R. and Matsuda, P. (eds) (2016) *Handbook of second and foreign language writing*. Berlin: Mouton de Gruyter.

Nesi, H. and Gardner, S. (2012) *Genres across the disciplines: student writing in higher education*. Cambridge: Cambridge University Press.

Tang, R. (2012) *Academic writing in a second or foreign language. Issues and challenges facing ESL/EFL academic writers in higher education contexts*. London: Continuum.

Tardy, C. (2009) *Building genre knowledge*. West Lafayette, IN: Parlour Press.

List 11.3 Books for Teachers of Writing

Elbow, P. (1998) *Writing with power: techniques for mastering the writing process*. Oxford: Oxford University Press.

Devitt, A. M.J. Reiff and Bawarshi, A. (2004) *Scenes of writing: strategies for composing with genres*. New York: Longman.

Ferris, D. and Hedgcock, J. (2013) *Teaching L2 composition: purpose, process, and practice*, 3rd edn. New York: Routledge.

Hyland, K. (2003) *Second language writing*. New York: Cambridge University Press.

Hyland, K. (2004) *Genre and second language writers*. Ann Arbor, MI: University of Michigan Press.
Johns, A.M. (ed) (2002) *Genre and the classroom*. Mahwah, NJ: Erlbaum.

List 11. 4   Exceptional Textbooks

(Writing for publication)
Feak, C. and Swales, J.M. (2009) *Telling a research story: writing a literature review*. Ann Arbor, MI: University of Michigan Press.
Feak, C. and Swales, J.M. (2011) *Creating contexts: writing introductions across genres*. Ann Arbor, MI: University of Michigan Press.
Swales, J.M. and Feak, C. (2009) *Abstracts and the writing of abstracts*. Ann Arbor, MI: University of Michigan Press.
(Post-graduate) Swales, J. and Feak, C. (2013) *Academic writing for graduate students: essential tasks and skills*, 3rd edn. Ann Arbor, MI: University of Michigan Press.
(Undergraduate) Crème, P. and Lea, M. (2008) *Writing at university*, 3rd edn. Maidenhead: McGraw-Hill.
(High-intermediate) Oshima, A. and Hogue, A. (2006) *Writing academic English*, 4th edn. Harlow: Pearson.
(High-intermediate) Mulvaney, M.K. and Jolliffe, D.A. (2004) *Academic writing: genres, samples, and resources*. Harlow: Pearson.
(High beginners) Hogue, A. (2007) *First steps in academic writing*, 2nd edn. Harlow: Pearson.

11.2   Journals

This part lists the main writing periodicals, both print and online, together with journals in related areas that carry relevant articles. Web site addresses often provide a description of the journal, submissions guides, names of editorial board members, contents and so on, and I have supplied these where they exist. Be warned that the Internet is in constant flux and that sites regularly change, move or disappear entirely. A list of the web site addresses of major educational publishers can be found at Acqweb's directory of publishers and vendors at: http://www.acqweb.org/pubr.html. A list of journals in the field of language and literature can be found on the JStor site at http://www.jstor.org/action/showJournals?browseType=discipline&contentType=journals&discipline=43693407.

List 11.5   Core Writing Journals

Assessing Writing www.elsevier.com/locate/asw (interdisciplinary journal for writing teaching and assessment issues)

College Composition and Communication http://www1.ncte.org/store/journals/ 105392.htm (composition studies from a broadly humanistic perspective. For U.S. college writing teachers)

Composition Studies http://www.compositionstudies.tcu.edu/ (all aspects of composition and rhetoric, particularly in relation to U.S. universities)

Computers and Composition http://www.journals.elsevier.com/computers-and-composition/ (all aspects of computers in writing teaching: software, LANs, ethics, effects, etc.)

Discourse, Context and Media http://www.journals.elsevier.com/discourse-context-and-media/ (addresses all forms of discourse theory, data and methods— from detailed linguistic or interactional analyses to studies of representation, knowledge and ideology)

Journal of Academic Writing http://e-learning.coventry.ac.uk/ojs/index.php/joaw (peer-reviewed journal that focuses on the teaching, tutoring, researching, administration and development of academic writing in higher education in Europe)

Journal of Advanced Composition http://www.jacweb.org/ (theoretical articles on topics related to rhetoric, writing, literacy and politics of education)

Journal of Basic Writing http://www.asu.edu/clas/english/composition/cbw/ jbw.html (theory, research and teaching of basic writers)

Journal of Technical Writing and Communication http://www.baywood.com/ journals/previewjournals.asp?id=0047–2816 (functional writing in a range of technical, scientific and professional environments)

Journal of Second Language Writing www.elsevier.com/locate/jslw AND http:// www.jslw.org/ (the leading journal of theoretically grounded research into L2 writing issues)

Pre-Text http://www.pre-text.com (journal of rhetorical theory)

Rhetoric Review (journal of rhetorical theory and practice with a philosophical orientation)

Text and Talk http://www.degruyter.de/journals/text/detail.cfm (interdisciplinary forum for discourse studies)

Written Communication http://wcx.sagepub.com/ (the leading journal in the field of research, theory and application of writing; cutting-edge issues from linguistics, composition, sociology, psychology and cognitive sciences)

Written Language and Literacy http://www.benjamins.com/cgibin/t_series view.cgi?series=WL%26L (journal of writing systems and the institutionalised use of written language)

Writing Lab Newsletter http://writinglabnewsletter.org/ (monthly journal on one-to-one writing teaching issues)

List 11.6 Online Writing Journals

Academic Writing archived copies available from *Across the Disciplines*. See URL for *Across the Disciplines* below.

Across the Disciplines http://wac.colostate.edu/atd/archives.cfm?showat darchives=aw (refereed journal concerned with all aspects of writing across the curriculum)

The Internet Writing Journal http://www.internetwritingjournal.com/ (refereed journal which includes articles, interviews and reviews of creative writing in print)

Kairos http://kairos.technorhetoric.net/ (refereed electronic journal for teachers and researchers of all kinds of Internet-based writing and dealing with rhetoric, technology, and pedagogy)

List 11.7 Related Journals (Regularly Carry Papers on Writing)

Ampersand http://www.journals.elsevier.com/ampersand/

Applied Linguistics http://www3.oup.co.uk/applij/

English for Specific Purposes http://www.journals.elsevier.com/english-for-specific-purposes/

Discourse and Society http://www.sagepub.co.uk/journalsProdDesc.nav?prodId=Journal200873

Discourse Studies http://dis.sagepub.com/

International Journal of Applied Linguistics http://www.blackwellpublishing.com/journal.asp?ref=0802–6106

International Review of Applied Linguistics in Language Teaching http://www.degruyter.de/journals/iral/

Journal of Applied Linguistics http://www.equinoxjournals.com/ojs/index.php/JAL

Journal of Business Communication http://job.sagepub.com/

Journal of English for Academic Purposes http://www.journals.elsevier.com/journal-of-english-for-academic-purposes/

Linguistics and Education http://www.journals.elsevier.com/linguistics-and-education/

Modern Language Journal http://mlj.miis.edu//

System http://www.journals.elsevier.com/system/

TESOL Quarterly www.tesol.org/tq

11.3 Professional Associations

Given the variety of writing activities, and the lonely activity that writing tends to be, it is not surprising that there is a large and various number of writers' associations. Such associations provide different services and activities depending on their focus, from organising annual conferences and message boards for teachers and academics, to helping members find literary agents and arranging meetings with editors and publishers. Some are free and others have subscription charges; some have local memberships and others are large national bodies. A list of writers' associations for creative writers and editors can be found at: http://freelancewrite.about.com/od/writingcommunities/a/List-Of-Writers-Associations.htm

Lists 11.8 and 11.9 contain some associations, but they are only indicative of the numerous associations and groups that exist.

List 11.8   Associations Specifically Devoted to Writing

Alliance for Computers and Writing (ACW) A U.S.-based body committed to supporting teachers at all levels of instruction in the use of computers in writing instruction by providing a forum for sharing ideas and information. http://english.ttu.edu/acw/

American Medical Writers' Association The leading professional organisation for medical communicators. www.amwa.org/

Association of Writers and Writing Programs Seeks to foster literary talent and achievement, to advance the art of writing as essential to a good education, and to serve the makers, teachers, students and readers of contemporary writing. http://www.awpwriter.org/

European Association for the Teaching of Academic Writing (EATAW) A scholarly forum to bring together those interested in the teaching, tutoring, research, administration and development of academic writing in higher education in Europe. Membership is free and open to individuals from all over the world. http://www.eataw.eu/

European Society for Translation Studies (EST) An international society of translation and interpreting scholars devoted to translation studies. http://www.est-translationstudies.org/

European Writing Centers Association Devoted to exchanging ideas and establishing an infrastructure for writing centers across Europe. http://www.writingcenters.eu/

International Writing Centers Association (IWCA) Open to those interested in writing centers and the teaching and tutoring of writing. The IWCA is committed to strengthening the field of writing center studies. https://iwcamembers.org/

National Association of Independent Writers and Editors (NAIWE) An association for writers and editors who make a living from their work. http://naiwe.com/

National Association of Science Writers A body which fosters the dissemination of accurate information regarding science to the public. Members include science writers, editors and science-writing educators and students. http://www.nasw.org/

National Association of Writers' Groups A group that brings together creative writers from across the UK and, in some cases, across the globe. http://www.nawg.co.uk/

Society for Technical Communication An organisation dedicated to advancing the arts and sciences of technical communication. It is the largest organisation of its type in the world with 14,000 members which include technical writers and editors, documentation specialists, technical illustrators, instructional designers, academics, information architects, web designers and developers, and translators. http://www.stc.org/

List 11.9   Associations with an Interest in Writing Issues

American Association of Applied Linguistics (AAAL) http://www.aaal.org/

Association for Business Communication (ABC) An international organisation devoted to advancing business communication research and teaching. http://www.businesscommunication.org/

Association Internationale de Linguistique Appliquée (AILA) The International Association of Applied linguistics has several interest groups or Research Networks (ReNs) focused on special topic areas, some of which concern writing. http://www.aila.info/

British Association of Applied Linguistics (BAAL) http://www.baal.org.uk/

British Association of Lecturers of English for Academic Purposes (BALEAP) BALEAP supports the professional development of those involved in EAP through an accreditation scheme, professional issues meetings, and a biennial conference. https://www.baleap.org/home/

International Association for Teachers of English as a Foreign Language (IATEFL) http://www.iatefl.org

International Association of Business Communicators. http://www.iabc.com/

Japanese Association of Language Teachers (JALT) http://www.jalt.org/

Teachers of English to Speakers of Other Languages (TESOL) www.tesol.org/9.4

11.4   Writing Conferences

Conferences are important events for writers and writing teachers as they provide a venue for networking and sharing ideas with like-minded others. There are only a handful of international conferences devoted to writing, but many language conferences include presentations on writing. List 11.10 includes both conferences and sites where conferences are promoted. More details are available from the web sites.

List 11.10   Conferences and Meetings

Association for Business Communication (ABC) An organisation that hosts an annual conference on business communication in the U.S. and lists others on its web site. http://www.businesscommunication.org/

Association of Writers and Writing Programs Annual Conference One of the biggest literary gatherings in North America with 5,000 attendees and 400 publishers. http://www.awpwriter.org/conference/index.php

College Composition and Communication The world's largest professional organisation for researching and teaching composition, from writing to new media. http://www.ncte.org/ccc

Conal Conference Alerts http://www.conferencealerts.com/topic-listing?topic=Language

BAAL Conference diary http://www.baal.org.uk/mo_ling_confs.html

Internet TESL Journal's conference list http://iteslj.org/links/TESL/Conferences/

Linguists list conference list Lists up to 500 current teaching and linguistics conferences and calls for papers. http://linguistlist.org/callconf/browse-current. cfm?type=Conf

Symposium on Second Language Writing A biannual international conference for teachers and researchers who work with second- and foreign-language writers. http://sslw.asu.edu/

Right writing conference list Calendar of creative writing conferences and advice on the best ones. http://www.right-writing.com/conferences.html

Roy's resources Lists of conferences worldwide for linguistics, translators and teachers of languages. http://www.royfc.com/confer.html

TESOL conference list A list that includes conferences for teachers of English to speakers of other languages. http://www.tesol.org/attend-and-learn/calendar-of-events

Wikipedia list of creative writing conferences http://en.wikipedia.org/wiki/List_of_writers'_conferences

Writers Workshop Events list: http://www.writersworkshop.co.uk/events.html

11.5   Email Lists and Blogs

Online bulletin boards, blogs and electronic mailing lists are now important means of exchanging ideas and reaching out to those with like-minded interests. An **electronic mailing list** allows for widespread distribution of emails to many recipients simultaneously. Many educational and other professional organisations host such mailing lists, either to simply announce news and information to members, but more usually as discussion lists to which any member may post. On a discussion list, a subscriber is able to initiate and send messages to all the other subscribers, who may answer in a similar way, facilitating discussion and exchanges.

Blogs are online discussion sites consisting of posts, displayed in reverse chronological order, on a particular issue. Blogs are usually the work of a single individual, but professionally edited 'multi-author blogs' (MABs) have developed, with posts written by large numbers of authors. Twitter and other 'microblogging' systems means MABs and single-author blogs can be integrated into societal newstreams. Blogs provide an excellent forum, when used well, for informal writing and feedback from peers and faculty. Here blogs are essentially interactive, dynamic web pages.

Students can be encouraged to sign up to blogging web sites and create their own blogs (see part 3.5), while increasing numbers of professionals use blogs to share specialised news and test ideas. On the other hand, blogs can be little more than egotistical random musings. Most academic bloggers write fewer than 1000 words per post. Blogs might be attempts to explore ideas which may grow into a formal piece of writing or which, indeed, are intended to be formal pieces of research writing. Many scholars devote considerable time to writing entries, and some attract large readerships. What is called 'continual publishing' across journals, blogs and social media maximises visibility for academic authors and so increases the impact of the research. Some of the more useful ones are listed in List 11.12.

List 11.11   Mailing Lists

Academic Writing Discussion list for UK community. https://www.jiscmail. ac.uk/cgi-bin/webadmin?A0=ACADEMIC-WRITING-RIG

ACW-L (Alliance for Computers and Writing List) List committed to supporting teachers at all levels of computer-enhanced, computer-supported and computer-based instruction. List: listproc@listserv.ttu.edu Web site: http://www2.nau. edu/~acw-p/

Linguist List Information on language, books, jobs and language analysis. http:// linguistlist.org/

Mike's writing workshop Group that offers writers a place to post work, ask questions, and discuss ways to improve their writing. http://groups.yahoo. com/group/mikeswritingworkshop/?v=1&t=search&ch=web&pub=groups& sec=group&slk=6

Newsgroups and mailing lists for translators http://www.iol.ie/~mazzoldi/lang/ maillist.htm

Group on creative writing, including short stories, cross-genre, romance, detective stories, etc.

Second language writing List https://www.jiscmail.ac.uk/cgi-bin/webadmin? A0=SECOND-LANGUAGE-WRITING

Teaching Composition A listserv devoted to first-year composition teachers. http://www.mhhe.com/socscience/english/tc/

TechRhet A list that explores the intersections among teaching, learning, communication, community and the new literacies. www.interversity.org/lists/techrhet/ subscribe.html

WAC-L The leading list for discussion of writing across the curriculum. http:// www.lsoft.se/scripts/wl.exe?SL1=WAC-L&H=LISTSERV.UIUC.EDU

WPA-L: Writing Program Administration Sponsored by the Council of Writing Program Administrators. http://www.wpacouncil.org/wpa-l

Writing and criticism A group for creative writers to post and get feedback on their work. https://groups.yahoo.com/neo/groups/critical_writing/info?v=1& t=search&ch=web&pub=groups&sec=group&slk=2

Writing Development HE The teaching of expository and creative writing. https://www.jiscmail.ac.uk/cgi-bin/webadmin?A0=WRITING-DEV-HE

List 11.12   Writing Blogs

Academic Writing Librarian Blog that provides support for library staff who wish to write for publication. http://academicwritinglibrarian.blogspot.hk/

blogger.com Free weblog publishing tool from Google for sharing text, photos and video. https://www.blogger.com/

Business Writing Blog Talk and tips for professionals writing business genres http://www.businesswritingblog.com/

Copyblogger list of 10 best creative writing sites http://www.copyblogger.com/creative-writing-blogs-2011/

Doctoral Writing SIG Regular posts on thoughts on thesis writing. https://doctoral writing.wordpress.com/home/

edublogs.org Massively popular site which allows users to easily create and manage student and teacher blogs, customise designs and include videos, photos and podcasts. https://edublogs.org/

Explorations of style A blog on academic writing. http://explorationsofstyle.com/

I'd rather be writing Technical writing trends and innovations blog. http://idratherbewriting.com/

Linguist list blog http://blog.linguistlist.org/

Mindtouch Most influential technical bloggers list. http://www.mindtouch.com/blog/2010/07/29/the-most-influential-technical-communicator-bloggers

Patter Link to several blogs on academic writing. http://patthomson.net/academic-writing/

Positive Writer Top 25 Writing blogs Best creative writing sites for inspiration, encouragement and motivation. http://positivewriter.com/top-25-writing-blogs/

Text and Academic Authors Blog Various academic writing topics. http://blog.taaonline.net/

The art of business writing http://www.artofbusinesswriting.com/

The Creative Penn Resources for creative writers. http://www.thecreative penn.com/

The English Learners' blog https://theenglishlearnersblog.wordpress.com/

ThinkWrite Commercial site but interesting blog posts. http://www.thinkwrite.biz/blog/

This itch of writing Creative writing thoughts and responses. http://emmadarwin.typepad.com/thisitchofwriting/2007/08/welcome-to-my-b.html

Why the Writing Works Different essayists break down a short story, novel, book or poem, focusing on one particular aspect of writing that makes it work. www.WhyTheWritingWorks.com

Wikispace Allows teachers and students to set up shared online classroom spaces. https://www.wikispaces.com/

11.6   Online Corpora and Concordancers

A corpus is simply a collection of naturally occurring language samples (often consisting of millions of words) which represent a speaker's experience of language in some restricted domain, such as a discipline or genre, or a particular register, such as journalism or legal writing. Searching a corpora for its salient features can therefore provide a more adequate basis for descriptions than intuition of what written genres are like and how writers shape their meanings to be most effective in those genres. There are a number of corpora and concordance tools on the web which allow you to search a range of academic, student, newspaper and literary texts. Many, but not all, of these are free, and some allow you to either download a concordance tool to your computer or to upload your own texts for analysis.

The two lists which follow suggest those which I have found most useful. List 11.13 contains sites which offer access to written text corpora. These either allow users to search the corpus using their own concordancer, or, more usually, come with an interface which allows basic word and phrase searches and concordance displays. Some, such as *Check My Words* and VLE, offer student tools (see part 9.5) while the *Word and Phrase Info* site is based around the Academic Vocabulary List (part 9.3). List 11.14, on the other hand, comprises stand-alone corpus analysis tools such as *AntConc* (discussed in part 9.2) together with commercial concordancers such as *WordSmith Tools*.

List 11.13   Online Searchable Corpora

Amazon Search Inside Search in books by word or phrase, and then browse relevant books online. http://www.amazon.com/exec/obidos/tg/browse/-/1019 7021/104–1065722–9759142

British Academic Written English (BAWE) Some 3000 'good standard' student assignments produced across 35 disciplines from first-year undergraduate to masters level (6.5 million words). Users must register with the Oxford Text Archive (free). http://www.coventry.ac.uk/bawe

British National Corpus (BNC) Searchable corpus of the 100 million word collection of written and spoken language from a range of sources representing a cross-section of British English. http://www.natcorp.ox.ac.uk/index.xml

Byu-bnc http://corpus.byu.edu/bnc

Check My Words Free student writing aid with word processor accessed concordancer. http://www.compulang.com/cmw/

Cobuild corpus sampler http://www.collins.co.uk/Corpus/CorpusSearch.aspx

COCA (Corpus of Contemporary American English) 450 million words divided by register and year; allows users to search and compare two corpora simultaneously. A fantastic resource. http://corpus.byu.edu/coca/

Corpuseye Allows searches in different corpora, including Wikipedia plus morpho-syntactic analysis of concordance lines. http://corp.hum.ou.dk/index.html

Google Book Search Search in books by word or phrase, and then browse relevant books online. https://books.google.com/?hl=en

Lextutor Variety of corpora including sections of BNC and COCA, fiction, professional, journalism and academic. http://lextutor.ca/conc/eng/

N-gram Phrase Extractor This programme will pull out all its recurring word strings up to and including the length specified by the user. http://lextutor.ca/n_gram/ .

Oxford text archive Collection of electronic literary and linguistic resources with searchable corpus of British novels. http://ota.ahds.ac.uk/

The web concordances Searchable corpora of poems by Shelley, Keats, Blake, Milton, etc. http://www.dundee.ac.uk/english/wics/wics.htm

VLC Web concordancer At Polytechnic University of Hong Kong. http://vlc.polyu.edu.hk/concordance/

Web Vocabprofile Vocabulary profiler from lexical tutor site. http://www.lextutor.ca/vp/

WebCorp Lets users access the web as a corpus—a large collection of texts from which examples of real language use can be extracted. http://www.webcorp. org.uk/live/

Word and Phrase info This site uses the academic section of COCA to analyse user-inputted text, returning colour-coded results showing technical, specific and academic words and phrases. http://www.wordandphrase.info/academic/

Wordtree A graphical version of the traditional 'keyword-in-context' method which enables rapid querying and exploration of text. Uses the BAWE corpus. http://wordtree.coventry.ac.uk/?BAWE

List 11.14   Online Concordancers and Text Analysers

Antconc A free, fully functional downloadable concordancer. Very popular. http://www.antlab.sci.waseda.ac.jp/software.html

Concordance multi-functional text analysis software (commercial programme) http://www.concordancesoftware.co.uk/index.htm

Monolonc Pro A comprehensive concordance package by Michael Barlow (commercial programme). www.athel.com

Spaceless Allows users to upload and search texts. http://www.spaceless.com/ concordancer.php

TurboLingo Analyses a text or web page of your choice, including a KWIC concordance, frequency lists and other features. http://www.staff.amu.edu. pl/~sipkadan/lingo.htm

Wordle Generates word clouds from user-supplied text. The clouds give greater prominence to words that appear more frequently. http://www.wordle.net/

Wordsmith Tools 5 By Mike Scott. Most advanced text analysis software available (commercial programme). http://www.lexically.net/wordsmith/index.html

---

11.7   Websites for Writing Advice

The web is heaving with writing sites of all types and quality, and I am not aiming for a comprehensive overview here. Most sites are based in the U.S., but I have tried to include a variety of both source and focus. The lists below simply present some of the best sites that I am aware of and which seem to represent key sources and starting points for further reading and exploration. The lists are divided according to the main focus of each one. List 11.15 contains a variety of sites for writers and teachers of writing, providing advice and resources, while Lists 11.16 to 11.18 are largely resources of various kinds for students. List 11.16 refers to some of the many college and university hosted online writing labs (OWLs), some of which include instructional materials and quizzes that are suitable for writers of all ages and academic levels. List 11.17 contains various online guides and resources for grammar, writing and the processes of text creation. In List 11.18 you will find links to sites which are concerned more specifically with genres and specific types of writing.

List 11.15   Sites for Writers and Writing Teachers

Association of writers and writing programs (AWP) Provides guide to U.S. creative writing courses, conferences, retreats, workshops and other resources. http://www.awpwriter.org/

Daedalus Educational Software Tools for collaborative learning and encouraging the processes of writing (commercial programme). www.daedalus.com

Dave's ESL Café Lots of links and ideas for EFL teachers. http://www.eslcafe.com/

English Club Q&A forum on English language issues. https://www.englishclub.com/esl-forums/index.php

Google Docs Allows teachers and students to share their written texts. https://docs.google.com/document/u/0/?showDriveBanner=true#

Inkspot Allows users to create an online portfolio to showcase their talents. http://inkspot.com/

Lancaster Literacy Research Centre www.literacy.lancs.ac.uk

Literacy matters Teaching materials and shop for school literacy. http://www.literacymatters.com/

Resources for Writers Citing styles, writing tips, genres and styles. http://www.ccp.rpi.edu/resources/

Rhetoric and composition A variety of resources useful to rhetoricians including links to works of classical rhetoric, articles on literacy and education, bibliographies, mailing lists and links to glossaries. http://eserver.org/rhetoric

UEAP A guide and resources for students in higher education in using English for academic purposes. http://www.uefap.com/index.htm

Writer's Web Designed and maintained by University of Richmond students and faculty with advice and information on academic writing. http://writing2.richmond.edu/writing/wweb.html

Writers workshop: Writer resources University of Illinois. Grammar handbook, citation styles and other resources. http://www.cws.illinois.edu/workshop/writers/

Writing Across the Curriculum Clearinghouse Publishes journals, books and other resources for teachers who use writing in their courses. http://wac.colostate.edu/index.cfm

List 11.16   Online Writing Centres

Academic writing course At Hong Kong PolyU Writing Centre. http://vlc.polyu.edu.hk/academicwriter/Questions/writemodeintro.htm

Aims Community College OWL http://www.aims.edu/student/online-writing-lab/

Coventry Academic writing resources http://www.coventry.ac.uk/study-at-coventry/student-support/academic-support/centre-for-academic-writing/support-for-students/academic-writing-resources/

Colorado State University Writing Studio http://writing.colostate.edu/

Excelsior College OWL http://owl.excelsior.edu/

Garbl's Fat-Free Writing Links An annotated directory of web sites that give advice on writing. http://garbl.home.comcast.net/~garbl/writing/concise.htm
LEO: Literacy Education Online http://leo.stcloudstate.edu/index.html
High School Writing Centres http://www.wcenters.com/
Hyper-grammar at Ottawa http://arts.uottawa.ca/writingcentre/en/hypergrammar
My Access Writing Commercial site for school children. https://www.myaccess.com/myaccess/do/log
Purdue OWL One of the best sites devoted to the teaching of academic writing. http://owl.english.purdue.edu/
The Writing Machine An Internet resource created at the Centre of Applied English Studies at the University of Hong Kong. It is designed to help students understand and master the process of writing academic essays. http://ec.hku.hk/writingmachine/
UVic Writers Guide http://web.uvic.ca/wguide/Pages/StartHere.html
Writing Den Designed to assist young learners to write creatively. http://www2.actden.com/writ_den/
Writing tutorials (Monash) http://www.monash.edu.au/lls/llonline/writing/index.xml

List 11.17   Style Guides, Mechanics and Process

ABCs of the writing process http://www.angelfire.com/wi/writingprocess/
APA style resources http://www.psychwww.com/resource/apacrib.htm
Economist magazine style guide http://www.economist.com/styleguide/introduction
Enhance my Writing.com More writing resources. http://www.enhancemywriting.com/
Plagiarism and how to avoid it http://www4.caes.hku.hk/plagiarism/introduction.htm
Quick and Dirty Tips http://www.quickanddirtytips.com/grammar-girl
Research and Writing Step by Step Research and writing for high school and college students. http://www.ipl.org/div/aplus/stepfirst.htm
The Writer style guide http://www.thewriter.com/what-we-think/style-guide/
Writers online https://www.writers-online.co.uk/

List 11.18   Genres and Specific Text Types

Blogs about genre (creative writing) http://wordpress.com/tag/genre-writing/
Business persuasion materials http://www.superwriter.com/persuasi.htm
Business writing center Catalogue of courses. http://www.businesswriting.com/
Essay writing University of Reading https://www.reading.ac.uk/internal/studyadvice/StudyResources/Essays/sta-developessay.aspx
Guide to writing an essay http://members.tripod.com/~lklivingston/essay/

> ***On-line technical writing*** List of free online technical writing courses. http://
> study.com/articles/List_of_Free_Online_Technical_Writing_Courses_and_
> Training_Programs.html
> ***PIZZAZ*** Creative writing with poetry fiction and creative ideas for writing
> teachers. http://darkwing.uoregon.edu/~leslieob/pizzaz.html
> ***Science Research paper*** http://www.ruf.rice.edu/~bioslabs/tools/report/report
> form.html
> ***Writing and presenting theses*** http://www.learnerassociates.net/dissthes/
> ***Writing and rhetoric Dartmouth site for writers*** http://www.dartmouth.edu/~
> writing/materials/student/humanities/write.shtml
> ***Writing humanities papers*** http://www.geneseo.edu/~easton/humanities/con
> vhumpap.html

11.8   Text Repositories and Network Sites

Finally, we come to sites for researchers seeking access to the vast literature related to writing. This section refers to sites where research articles, theses, conference papers and so on are archived and accessible. While many individual researchers provide access to their research via their own sites, institutional repositories are not restricted to individual authors but rely on writers uploading their work, thereby ensuring greater coverage. The list below also includes the main scholarly networking sites which have emerged in recent years. *ResearchGate.net, Academia.edu* and *Mendeley.com* collectively claim over 20 million followers, offering users a way to organise their research, create personal profiles, and search for people with similar scholarly interests. By serving as research repositories and platforms for connecting researchers, they encourage research sharing and support networks for scholars across the globe

> ## List 11.18   Repositories, Text Archives and Networking Sites
>
> ***Academia.edu*** A social networking website for academics with over 21 million registered users. The platform can be used to share papers, monitor their impact, and follow the research in a particular field. https://www.academia.edu/
> ***ERIC document reproduction service*** ERIC provides access to more than 1.2 million records of journal articles and other education-related materials, with hundreds of new records added twice weekly. Links to full text are included. http://www.eric.ed.gov/
> ***Google Scholar*** Search engine for scholarly papers, metrics and profiles of academics. http://scholar.google.co.uk/ http://journalseek.net/cgi-bin/journal seek/journalsearch.cgi?field=issn&query=0024–8215
> ***Linguist List publications*** 25,000 books, reviews, dissertation abstracts, etc. on language and linguistics. http://www.linguistlist.org/pubs/index.cfm
> ***Mendeley*** A free reference manager and academic social network site. Users can make their own searchable library, cite as they write, and read and annotate PDFs. https://www.mendeley.com/

MLA international bibliography of books and articles on modern languages and literature Database with limited access to 45,000 citations, indexed from over 3,000 periodicals, series, books, conference proceedings and dissertations on language, literature, linguistics and folklore.

Proquest linguistics and language behaviour abstracts Linguistics and language behavior abstracts covers all aspects of the study of language in the international literature. Subscription required. http://www.proquest.com/products-services/llba-set-c.html

Proquest Dissertation Abstracts Online A definitive subject, title and author guide to virtually every American dissertation accepted at an accredited institution since 1861. Archives more than 90,000 new works a year. Subscription required. http://library.dialog.com/bluesheets/html/bl0035.html

Proquest UK dissertations and theses A comprehensive listing of over 500,000 theses with abstracts accepted for higher degrees by universities in Great Britain and Ireland. Subscription required. http://www.proquest.com/products-services/pqdt_uk_ireland.html

ResearchGate A social networking site for scientists and researchers to share papers, ask and answer questions, and find collaborators. Claims 80 million publications and 6 million users. https://www.researchgate.net/home.Home.html

Science Direct Operated by the publisher Elsevier, this is the world's largest electronic collection of academic journals with free access to abstracts and subscription access to full text articles. http://www.sciencedirect.com/

Scopus The largest abstract and citation database of research literature and web sources with 55 million records of 20,000 journal titles by 5000 publishers. Includes tools to track, analyse and visualise research. Subscription required. http://www.elsevier.com/online-tools/scopus

Glossary

These definitions are to help you understand how I use the terms in this book and offer a general resource for reading and talking about writing more generally. They are, however, brief, and perhaps idiosyncratic, so readers interested in more precise and extensive definitions should refer to specialist language encyclopaedias such as:

> Long, M.H. and Doughty, C. (eds) (2009) *Handbook of language teaching*. Oxford: Blackwell.
> Malmkjær, K. (ed) (2009) *Routledge encyclopedia of linguistics*, 3rd edn. London: Routledge.
> Brown, K. (ed) (2006) *Encyclopedia of language and linguistics*, 2nd edn. Oxford: Elsevier.
> Cummins, A. and Davison, C. (eds) (2006) *The international handbook of English language education.* Norwell, MA: Springer.

Alternatively, you might consult a good grammar such as Biber at al. (1999) for grammatical terms or Wikipedia (https://en.wikipedia.org/wiki/Main_Page) for media and Internet terms.

action research   A method suited to practitioners involving a cycle which refines methods and understandings of a situation by action followed by reflection and further action.

affordance   A term for the way we see elements of the environment, such as a new technology, in terms of how we might use them.

audience   The writer's construction of his or her readers, whose imagined beliefs, understandings and values are anticipated and appealed to in the conventional features and structure of a text.

auto-ethnography   A research method which focuses on the writer's subjective experience and connects this to wider cultural, political and social meanings.

Automated Writing Evaluation (AWE)   Computer applications which evaluate and score written work, some of which also provide formative feedback to the writer.

British Academic Written English (BAWE)   A 6.5-million-word corpus of 3000 'good standard' student assignments, produced at British universities across 35 disciplines from first-year undergraduate to master's level. Available free of charge on registration.

blogs   A means for writers to publish their ideas quickly and easily to an audience beyond the teacher and to receive delayed responses to those ideas.

case study   A research method which examines a single person, group or situation to produce an in-depth account of events.

cognitivist view   A perspective which stresses the psychological aspects of writing and sees it as an exploratory and generative process where writers discover their ideas as they write.

coherence   The ways a text makes sense to readers through the relevance and accessibility of its concepts, ideas and theories.

cohesion   The grammatical and lexical relationships which tie a text together.

collocation   The regular occurrence of a word with one or more others in a text. The term can also refer to the meanings associated with a word as a result of this association.

community of practice   A term coined by Lave and Wenger (1991) to describe a group of people who share an interest, a craft or a profession. The term highlights the fact that it is through the process of sharing information and experiences with the group that the members learn from each other and develop communicative practices.

concordance   A list of unconnected lines of text called up by a concordance programme with the search word at the centre of each line. This list allows common patterns to be seen.

context   The relationship between linguistic and non-linguistic dimensions of communicative events. These dimensions are mutually influencing each other, with text and the interpretive work it creates helping to shape context, and context influencing the conventions, values and knowledge a text appeals to.

consciousness-raising tasks   Language learning activities that encourage learners to notice salient features of texts.

contrastive rhetoric (also intercultural rhetoric)   The view that the rhetorical features of L2 texts may reflect different writing conventions learned in the L1 culture, and the cross-cultural study of these differences.

control group   In experimental research, the control group is a group taught or given feedback in a traditional way so the effect of the experimental treatment of the other group can be observed.

controlled writing   Teaching exercises that involve students writing for accuracy using substitution tables, cloze passages or completion tasks.

corpus   A collection of texts, usually stored electronically, seen as representative of some subset of language and used for linguistic analysis.

course management system (CMS)   Online resources such as Blackboard and Moodle which allow teachers to create a single site for their course materials, readings, tasks and message posts.

Critical Discourse Analysis (CDA)   An approach which seeks to reveal the interests, values and power relations in any institutional and sociohistorical context through the ways that people use language.

culture   An historically transmitted and systematic network of meanings which allow us to understand, develop and communicate our knowledge and beliefs about the world.

deductive   (top down) Reasoning or way of writing where the thesis or main point is stated first—compared with inductive, where the main point is delayed in a text or reasoning where the support for an argument leads to the conclusion.

direct writing assessment   Testing methods based on a communicative purpose of writing, emphasising validity, particularly the psychological reality of the task, rather than just statistical reliability.

discourse   Language produced as an act of communication. This language use implies the constraints and choices which operate on writers in particular contexts and reflects their purposes, intentions, ideas and relationships with readers.

discourse community   A rather fuzzy concept used in genre studies to refer to a group of writers (or speakers) who share a communicative purpose and use commonly agreed texts to achieve these purposes. The term carries a core meaning of like-mindedness of membership which is widely used in research on writing to help explain discourse coherence.

discursive practices   A CDA term which refers to the acts of production, distribution and interpretation which surround a text and which must be taken into account in text analysis. These practices are themselves embedded in wider social practices of power and authority.

D-I-Y corpus (Do-It-Yourself)   A student-built corpus, either of their own or others' writing, which they then analyse, encouraging analysis and consciousness-raising while addressing students' specialist needs.

drafting   The recursive process of text creation, rewriting and polishing: it involves getting ideas on paper and responding to potential problems for readers.

editing   Typically the final stage in the writing process where the writer attends to surface-level corrections of grammar and spelling.

emic   A term used to describe an insider's view of events—how the situation is understood by the participants.

etic   An outsider's view of events—considered to be more neutral or objective.

ethnography   A research approach which seeks to gather a variety of naturally occurring data to provide a highly situated, minutely detailed and holistic account of writers' behaviours.

expertise   Knowledge in action, particularly the knowledge of community uses of language conventions.

experimental group   In experimental research, this is the group which receives the new treatment—a new teaching or feedback practice—which is studied to see how it will change behaviour.

Expressivist view   The belief that the free expression of ideas leads to self-discovery and that teachers should help students to find their own voices to produce fresh and spontaneous prose.

feedback   The response given to student writing. It can refer to either oral or written types provided by peers, teachers or computers. Widely regarded as central to writing development.

focus groups   Groups of people with some similar characteristics who are brought together to discuss an issue in depth for research purposes.

genre   Broadly, a set of texts that share the same socially recognised purpose and which, as a result, often share similar rhetorical and structural elements to achieve this purpose.

hedging   Linguistic devices used to indicate either the writer's lack of commitment to the truth of a statement or a desire not to express that commitment categorically for interpersonal reasons.

hypertext   In-text links to other parts of the same text or to other texts, either visual, audio or written.

identity   A controversial and unsettled term which is often used in the social sciences to mean the ways that people display who they are to each other through language by drawing on appropriate linguistic resources at particular times.

inductive   (bottom up) Reasoning or way of writing where the main point is delayed and conclusions are drawn from specific points.

interaction   Refers to the social routines and relationships which surround acts of writing or the ways that these are expressed in a text. The former have been studied to elaborate the influence of context on writing processes, and the latter to show how texts can reflect a writer's projection of the understandings, interests and needs of a potential audience.

intertextuality   An element of one text that takes its meaning from a reference to another text, for instance, by quoting, referring to or critiquing that other text.

interdiscursivity   The rhetorical and generic factors which make one text recognisably similar to another by borrowing conventions and forms to create new texts.

learner corpora   Collections of students' writing used to generate insights into how particular groups of students typically express certain meanings or approach rhetorical problems.

lexico-grammar   A term used in SFL to stress the close relationship between grammar and lexis. Meaning is conveyed by words working in grammatical parameters rather than separately from them.

Listserv   A trademark name for electronic mailing list software applications which allow a sender to send one email to the list which sends it on to the addresses of the subscribers to the list.

literacy practices   The general ways of using written language within a cultural context which people draw on in their lives.

longitudinal research   Research where data is collected from a particular site or participants over a period of time.

Mobile Assisted Language Learning (MALL)   Use of mobile technologies such as tablet computers, smart phones and MP3 players for writing and learning.

membership   An ability to display credibility and competence through familiarity or exploitation of discourse conventions typically used in a community. This can identify one as an 'insider', belonging to that community and possessing the legitimacy to address it.

narrative   Along with exposition, argumentation and description, narration is one of four Classical rhetorical modes of discourse. In SFL, it is an elemental genre which can contribute to macro-genres such as newspaper stories and novels. It is often described with a structure of Orientation—Complication—Evaluation—Resolution.

New Rhetoric perspective   An approach to text analysis that foregrounds the social and ideological realities that underlie the regularities of texts and which employs the use of ethnographic methods to unpack the relations between texts and contexts.

New Literacy Studies   (NLS) The view that written language is socially and historically situated and that literacy practices reflect broader social practices and political arrangements.

plagiarism   Using the words or ideas of another in writing without giving appropriate credit and often seen as deception or fraud.

portfolio   A collection of multiple writing samples selected either to showcase a student's most successful texts or to reveal a process of writing development. Used to structure writing courses, encourage reflection and provide more comprehensive and equitable assessment.

process approach   A teaching approach to writing which emphasises the development of good practices by stressing that writing is done in stages of planning, drafting, revising and editing, which are recursive, interactive and potentially simultaneous.

protocol research   A research technique widely employed in composition research as a means of getting at the processes which underlie writing by eliciting the verbalised thoughts of writers.

reader-oriented view   A perspective on writing research and teaching which focuses on the interpersonal aspects of writing and the purposes, goals and uses that the completed text may eventually fulfill.

register   A term from systemic linguistics which explains the relationship between texts and their contexts in terms of field (what), tenor (who) and mode (how). Registers refer to broad fields of activity such as legal papers, technical instructions, advertisements and service exchanges.

reliability   Concerns how consistently an assessment produces similar results across different repetitions of use.

research synthesis   A systematic review which provides a statistical and exhaustive summary of current literature relevant to a research question.

scaffolding   The role of interaction with experienced others to support learners towards a level of "potential performance" where they are able to work without help.

schema   A model of interpretation which suggests that readers make sense of a text by reference to a set of organised, culturally conventional understandings of similar prior experiences.

scripted talk   (i) A presentation memorised or read from a script; (ii) invented dialogue often found in language teaching textbooks which lack the repetition, redundancy, hesitation, back-channeling, etc., of authentic discourse.

situationist view   A perspective on writing which stresses the local context of the writer and the personal attitudes and beliefs the writer brings to that context.

social constructivism   The view that knowledge is created through the discourses of social communities.

social interactionism   The view that writing is interaction between a writer and reader and writing choices are based on the writer's projection of the interests, understandings and needs of a potential audience.

Systemic Functional Linguistics (SFL)   The theory of language developed by Michael Halliday based on the idea that language is a system of choices used to express meanings in context.

teaching learning cycle   A representation of genre teaching which shows the process as a cycle moving from modelling through joint construction to independent construction as the teacher support is gradually withdrawn to encourage learners to write unassisted.

text   A piece of spoken or written language.

textography   An ethnographic study which offers a rich description of a local context by focusing on texts and activities around texts.

think-aloud protocols   (TAPs) A research method which involves participants writing in their normal way while verbalising their thoughts at the same time, so that information can be recorded on their decisions, strategies and perceptions as they work.

Turnitin   Plagiarism detection software which can check student-written work and generate a report showing copied text.

validity   A measure which shows the extent to which an assessment is well-founded and corresponds accurately to what it seeks to assess, thus involving decisions about 'objectivity', rigour and generalisability.

Web 2.0   A shorthand term for the tools which allow the Internet to be used as a social platform for collaboration, knowledge-sharing, interaction and networking rather than a one-way information source.

wiki   A collaborative web space where pages can be created and edited by multiple users easily without any knowledge of web design.

writing frames   Outlines which can be used to scaffold the learner's writing by setting out a sequence of cohesive ties to which the writer supplies the content.

zone of proximal development   A term proposed by Soviet psychologist Lev Vygotsky to describe the difference between what a learner can do alone and what a learner can do through cooperation with capable peers.

References

Ädel, A. and Erman, B. (2012) Recurrent word combinations in academic writing by native and non-native speakers of English: a lexical bundles approach. *English for Specific Purposes*, 31(2): 81–92.

Afflerbach, P. and Johnson, P. (1984) On the use of verbal reports in reading research. *Journal of Reading Behaviour*, 16(4): 307–22.

Alderson, J.C., Clapham, C.M. and Wall, D. (1995) *Language test construction and evaluation.* Cambridge: Cambridge University Press.

Allison, D. (1996) Pragmatist discourse and English for academic purposes. *English for Specific Purposes*, 15(2): 85–103.

Ammon, U. (ed) (2001) *The dominance of English as a language of science.* Berlin: Mouton de Gruyter.

Anthony, L. (2014) AntConc 3.4.3. http://www.laurenceanthony.net/software.html

Arneil, S. and Holmes, M. (1998–2009) *Hot potatoes.* Victoria, BC: University of Victoria and Half-Baked Software Inc.

Aston, G. (1997) Involving learners in developing learning methods: exploiting text corpora in self-access. In P. Benson and P. Voller (eds), *Autonomy and independence in language learning* (pp. 204–14). Harlow: Longman.

Atkinson, D. (1999) *Scientific discourse in sociohistorical context.* Mahwah, NJ: Lawrence Erlbaum Associates.

Atkinson, D. (2004) Contrasting rhetorics/contrasting cultures: why contrastive rhetoric needs a better conceptualization of culture. *Journal of English for Academic Purposes*, 3(4): 277–89.

Attali, Y. (2004) Exploring the feedback and revision features of criterion. Paper presented at the National Council on Measurement in Education, San Diego, CA.

Australian Curriculum Assessment and Reporting Authority (ACARA) (2015) *Australian Curriculum: English. Version 7.4.* Sydney: Australian Curriculum Assessment and Reporting Authority. http://www.australiancurriculum.edu.au/english/curriculum/f-10

Bailey, K.M. (1990) The use of diary studies in teacher education programs. In J.C. Richards and D. Nunan (eds), *Second language teacher education* (pp. 215–26). Cambridge: Cambridge University Press.

Bakhtin, M. (1986) *Speech genres and other late essays.* Austin, TX: University of Texas Press.

Barlow, M. (2005) Computer based analyses of learner language. In R. Ellis and G. Barkhuizen (eds), *Analysing learner language* (pp. 335–58). Oxford: Oxford University Press.

Bartholomae, D. (1986) Inventing the university. *Journal of Basic Writing*, 5: 4–23.

Barton, D. (2000) Researching literacy practices: learning from activities with teachers and students. In D. Barton, M. Hamilton and R. Ivanic (eds), *Situated literacies: reading and writing in context* (pp. 167–79). London: Routledge.

Barton, D. (2007) *Literacy: an introduction to the ecology of written language*, 2nd edn. Oxford: Blackwell.

Barton, D. and Hall, N. (1999) *Letter-writing as a social practice*. Amsterdam: John Benjamins.

Barton, D. and Hamilton, M. (1998) *Local literacies*. London: Routledge.

Barton, D., Ivanic, R., Appleby, Y., Hodge, R. and Tusting, K. (2007) *Literacy, lives and learning*. London: Routledge.

Bauer, L. and Nation, P. (1993) Word families. *International Journal of Lexicography*, 6(4): 253–79.

Bawarshi, A. and Reiff, M.-J. (2010) *Genre: an introduction to history, research and pedagogy*. West Lafayette, IN: Parlour Press.

Baynham, M. (1995) *Literacy practices*. Harlow: Longman.

Bazerman, C. (1988) *Shaping written knowledge*. Madison, WI: University of Wisconsin Press.

Bazerman, C. (1994) *Constructing experience*. Carbondale, IL: Southern Illinois University Press.

Bazerman, C. (2004) Speech acts, genres, and activity systems: how texts organize activity and people. In C. Bazerman and P. Prior (eds), *What writing does and how it does it: an introduction to analyzing texts and textual practices* (pp. 83–96). Hillsdale, NJ: Lawrence Erlbaum Associates.

BBC (1983) *Bid for power*. London: BBC English by Television.

Beach, R., Anson, C., Kastman Breuch, L.-A. and Reynolds, T. (2014) *Understanding and creating digital texts.* Washington D.C.: Rowman and Littlefield.

Beatty, K. (2010) *Teaching and researching computer-assisted language learning*. Harlow: Pearson.

Becher, T. and Trowler, P. (2001) *Academic tribes and territories: intellectual inquiry and the cultures of disciplines*, 2nd edn. Milton Keynes: SRHE and Open University Press.

Benesch, S. (1996) Needs analysis and curriculum development in EAP: an example of a critical approach. *TESOL Quarterly*, 30(4): 723–38.

Benesch, S. (2001) Critical English for academic purposes. Mahwah, NJ: Lawrence Erlbaum Associates.

Benson, P. (2013) *Teaching and researching autonomy in language learning*, 2nd edn. London: Routledge.

Benwell, B. and Stokoe, E. (2006) *Discourse and identity*. Edinburgh: Edinburgh University Press.

Bereiter, C. and Scardamalia, M. (1987) *The psychology of written composition*. Hillsdale, NJ: Lawrence Erlbaum Associates.

Berkenkotter, C. and Huckin, T. (1995) *Genre knowledge in disciplinary communication*. Hillsdale, NJ: Lawrence Erlbaum Associates.

Bestgen, Y. and Granger, S. (2014) Quantifying the development of phraseological competence in L2 English writing: an automated approach. *Journal of Second Language Writing*, 26: 28–41.

Bhatia, V.K. (1993) *Analysing genre: language use in professional settings*. Harlow: Longman.

Bhatia, V.K. (2004) *Worlds of written discourse.* London: Continuum.

Bhatia, V., Candlin, C. and Engberg, J. (2008) Legal discourse across cultures and systems. Hong Kong: Hong Kong University Press.

Biber, D., Johansson, S., Leech, G., Conrad, S. and Finegan, E. (1999) *Longman grammar of spoken and written English.* London: Longman.

Bitchener, J. (2008) Evidence in support of written corrective feedback. *Journal of Second Language Writing,* 17: 102–18.

Bitchener, J. and Knoch, U. (2010) The contribution of written corrective feedback to language development: a ten month investigation. *Applied Linguistics,* 31: 193–214.

Bleich, D. (2001) The materiality of language and the pedagogy of exchange. *Pedagogy: Critical Approaches to Teaching Literature, Language, Composition, and Culture,* 1: 117–41.

Bloch, J. (2001) Plagiarism and the ESL student: from printed to electronic texts. In D. Belcher and A. Hirvella (eds), *Linking literacies: perspectives on L2 reading-writing connections* (pp. 209–28). Ann Arbor, MI: University of Michigan Press.

Bloch, J. (2008) *Technology in the second language composition classroom.* Ann Arbor, MI: University of Michigan Press.

Bloch, J. (2012) *Plagiarism, intellectual property and the teaching of L2 composition.* Bristol: Multilingual Matters.

Bloch, J. and Crosby, C. (2006) Creating a space for virtual democracy. *The Essential Teacher,* 3: 38–41.

Blommaert, J. (2005) *Discourse.* Cambridge: CUP.

Bosher, S. (1998) The composing processes of three southeast Asian writers at the postsecondary level: an exploratory study. *Journal of Second Language Writing,* 7(2): 205–33.

Braine, G. (1995) Writing in the natural sciences and engineering. In D. Belcher and G. Braine (eds), *Academic writing in a second language: essays on research and pedagogy* (pp. 113–34). Norwood, NJ: Ablex.

Brandt, D. (1986) Text and context: how writers come to mean. In B. Couture (ed), *Functional approaches to writing: research perspectives* (pp. 93–107). Norwood, NJ: Ablex.

Breen, M. (2001) The social context for language learning: a neglected situation? In C. Candlin and N. Mercer (eds), *English language teaching in its social context* (pp. 122–44). London: Routledge.

Breen, M. and Littlejohn, A. (eds) (2000) *Classroom decision-making: negotiation and process syllabuses in practice.* Cambridge: Cambridge University Press.

Bridgeman, B., Trapani, C. and Yigal, A. (2012) Comparison of human and machine scoring of essays: differences by gender, ethnicity, and country. *Applied Measurement in Education,* 25(1): 27–40.

Brown, J.D. and Hudson, T. (1998) The alternatives in language assessment. *TESOL Quarterly,* 32(4): 653–75.

Brown, J.S., Collins, A. and Duguid, P. (1989) Situated cognition and the culture of learning. *Educational Researcher,* 18(1): 32–42.

Brown, K. (ed) (2006) *Encyclopedia of language and linguistics,* 2nd edn. Oxford: Elsevier.

Bruffee, K. (1984) Collaborative learning and the 'conversation of mankind'. *College English,* 46: 635–52.

Bruffee, K. (1986) Social construction: language and the authority of knowledge. A bibliographical essay. *College English,* 48: 773–9.

Bruner, J.S. (1978) The role of dialogue in language acquisition. In A. Sinclair, R. Jarvelle and W. Levelt (eds), *The child's concept of language* (pp. 241–56). New York: Springer.

Bruner, J.S. (1990) *Acts of meaning*. Cambridge, MA: Harvard University Press.

Bruton, S. and Childers, D. (2015) The ethics and politics of policing plagiarism: a qualitative study of faculty views on student plagiarism and Turnitin. *Assessment & Evaluation in Higher Education*. doi: 10.1080/02602938.2015.1008981

Bull, J. and McKenna, C. (2004) *A blueprint for computer-assisted assessment*. London: Routledge.

Burns, A. (2010) *Doing action research in English language teaching: a guide for practitioners*. New York: Routledge.

Burns, A. (2013) Innovation through action research and teacher-initiated change. In K. Hyland, and L.C.L. Wong (eds), *Innovation and Change in English Language Education* (pp. 90–105). Oxon: Routledge.

Burstein, J. (2003) The *e-rater* scoring engine: automated essay scoring with natural language processing. In M. Shermis and J. Burstein (eds), *Automated essay scoring: a cross-disciplinary perspective* (pp. 113–22). Hillsdale, NJ: Lawrence Erlbaum Associates.

Byrne, R., Tang, M., Truduc, J. and Tang, M. (2010) eGrader, a software application that automatically scores student essays: with a postscript on the ethical complexities. *Journal of Systemics, Cybernetics & Informatics*, 8(6): 30–5.

Canagarajah, A.S. (1996) 'Nondiscursive' requirements in academic publishing, material resources of periphery scholars, and the politics of knowledge production. *Written Communication*, 13(4): 435–72.

Canagarajah, A.S. (1999) *Resisting linguistic imperialism in English teaching*. Oxford: Oxford University Press.

Canagarajah, A.S. (2002) *Critical academic writing and multilingual students*. Ann Arbor, MI: University of Michigan Press.

Candlin, C.N. (1999) How can discourse be a measure of expertise? Paper presented at the International Association for Dialogue Analysis. Birmingham: University of Birmingham.

Carter, M. (1990) The idea of expertise: an exploration of cognitive and social dimensions of writing. *College Composition and Communication*, 41(3): 265–86.

Carter, R.A. and McCarthy, M.J. (2006) *Cambridge grammar of English*. Cambridge: Cambridge University Press.

Casanave, C. (2004) *Controversies in second language writing*. Ann Arbor, MI: University of Michigan Press.

Chamcharatsri, P. (2009) Negotiating identity from auto-ethnography: second language writers' perspectives. *Asian EFL Journal. Professional Teaching Articles*, 38: 3–19.

Chandler, J. (2003) The efficacy of various kinds of error correction for improvement of the accuracy and fluency of L2 student writing. *Journal of Second Language Writing* 12(3): 267–96.

Chapelle, C. and Jamieson, J. (2008) *Tips for teaching with CALL: practical approaches to computer-assisted language learning*. New York: Pearson-Longman.

Chapelle, C.A. and Douglas, D. (2006) *Assessing language through computer technology*. Cambridge: Cambridge University Press.

Charles, M. (2012) 'Proper vocabulary and juicy collocations': EAP students evaluate do-it-yourself corpus-building. *English for Specific Purposes*, 31: 93–102.

Charles, M. (2015) After EAP courses, what next? Students' independent use of corpora. Paper presented at BALEAP, Leicester University, April 2015.

Chen, B. and Bryer, T. (2012) Investigating instructional strategies for using social media in formal and informal learning. *The International Review of Research in Open and Distance Learning*, 13(1). http://www.irrodl.org/index.php/irrodl/article/view/1027/2073

Chen, C.-F. and Cheng, W.-Y. (2006) The use of a computer-based writing program: facilitation or frustration? Paper presented at the 23 International Conference on English Teaching and Learning, Wenzao Ursuline College of Languages, Kaohsiung.

Cherry, R. (1988) Ethos versus persona: self-representation in written discourse. *Written Communication*, 5: 251–76.

Cheville, J. (2004) Automated scoring technologies and the rising influence of error. *English Journal*, 93(4): 47–52.

Chin, E. (1994) Redefining 'context' in research on writing. *Written Communication*, 11: 445–82.

Christie, F. (2005) *Language education in the primary school*. Sydney: UNSW Press.

Clark, R. and Ivanic, R. (1997) *The politics of writing*. London: Routledge.

Coe, R.M. (2002) The new rhetoric of genre: writing political briefs. In A.M. Johns (ed), *Genre in the classroom* (pp. 195–205). Mahwah, NJ: Lawrence Erlbaum Associates.

Cohen, A., Glasman, H., Rosenbaum-Cohen, P.R., Ferrara, J. and Fine, J. (1988) Reading English for specialized purposes: discourse analysis and the use of standard informants. In P. Carrell, J. Devine and D. Eskey (eds), *Interactive approaches to second language reading* (pp. 152–67). Cambridge: Cambridge University Press.

Cohen, J. (1992) A power primer. *Psychological Bulletin*, 112: 155–59.

Cohen, L., Manion, L. and Morrison, K. (2013) *Research methods in education*, 7th edn. London: Routledge.

Condon, W. (2013) Large-scale assessment, locally-developed measures, and automated scoring of essays: fishing for red herrings? *Assessing Writing* 18(1): 100–8.

Coniam, D. (2009) Experimenting with a computer essay-scoring program based on ESL student writing scripts. *ReCALL*, 21: 259–79.

Connor, U. (1994) Text analysis. *TESOL Quarterly*, 28(4): 673–703.

Connor, U. (1996) *Contrastive rhetoric*. Cambridge: Cambridge University Press.

Connor, U. (2011) *Intercultural rhetoric in the writing classroom*. Ann Arbor, MI: University of Michigan Press.

Connor-Greene, P.A. (2000) Making connections: evaluating the effectiveness of journal writing in enhancing student learning. *Teaching of Psychology*, 27: 44–6.

Cooke-Plagwitz, J. (2008) New directions in CALL: an objective introduction to Second Life. *CALICO Journal*, 25(3): 547–57.

Coxhead, A. (2000) A new academic word list. *TESOL Quarterly*, 34(2): 213–38.

Coxhead, A. and Nation, I.S.P. (2001) The specialized vocabulary of English for academic purposes. In J. Flowerdew and M. Peacock (eds), *Research perspectives on English for academic purposes* (pp. 252–67). Cambridge: Cambridge University Press.

Crème, P. and Lea, M. (2008) *Writing at university*, 3rd edn. Maidenhead: McGraw-Hill.

Crookes, G. (1986) Towards a validated analysis of scientific text structure. *Applied Linguistics*, 7: 57–70.

Crystal, D. (2012a) *English as a global language*. Cambridge: Cambridge University Press.

Crystal, D. (2012b) An interview with David Crystal with Rakesh Bhanot. *Language Issues*, 23(1): 29–37.

Cummins, A. and Davison, C. (eds) (2006) *The international handbook of English language education.* Norwell, MA: Springer.

Cummins, J. and Sayers, D. (1995) *Brave new schools: challenging cultural illiteracy through global learning networks.* New York: St. Martin's Press.

Cutting, J. (2002) *Pragmatics and discourse: a resource book for students.* London: Routledge.

Davies, M. (2012) Corpus of contemporary American English (1990–2012). Available at http://corpus.byu.edu/coca/. Accessed June 2015.

De Cock, S. (2011) Preferred patterns of use of positive and negative evaluative adjectives in native and learner speech: an ELT perspective. In A. Frankenberg-Garcia, L. Flowerdew and G. Aston (eds), *New trends in corpora and language learning* (pp. 198–212). London: Continuum.

De Guerrero, M.C. and Villamil, O.S. (2000) Activating the ZPD: mutual scaffolding in L2 peer revision. *The Modern Language Journal*, 84: 51–68.

de Larios, J., Murphy, L. and Manchon, R. (1999) The use of restructuring strategies in EFL writing: a study of Spanish learners of English as a foreign language. *Journal of Second Language Writing*, 8(1): 13–44.

Denzin, N. and Lincoln, Y. (2011) *The Sage handbook of qualitative research*, 4th edn. Thousand Oaks, CA: Sage Publications.

Department of Education and Children's Development (DECD) (2013) *Professional learning module: genres in secondary school.* Government of South Australia: Department of Education and Children's Development.

Department of Education and Children's Services (DECS) (2004) *R-10 English teaching resource.* Government of South Australia: Department of Education and Children's Services.

Derewianka, B. (1990) *Exploring how texts work.* Newtown, NSW: Primary English Teaching Association.

Derewianka, B.M. (2012a) Knowledge about language in the Australian curriculum: English. *Australian Journal of Language and Literacy*, 35(2): 127–46.

Derewianka, B.M. (2012b) Change and innovation in the primary curriculum. In K. Hyland and L. Wong (eds), *Innovation and change in English language education* (pp. 155–71). London: Routledge.

Devitt, A., Reiff, M.J. and Bawarshi, A. (2004) *Scenes of writing: strategies for composing with genres.* New York: Longman.

Dias, P., Freedman, A., Medway, P. and Paré, A. (1999) *Worlds apart: acting and writing in academic and workplace contexts.* Mahwah, NJ: Lawrence Erlbaum Associates.

Dooly, M. (2008) Constructing knowledge together. In M. Dooly (ed), *Telecollaborative language learning: a guidebook to moderating intercultural collaboration online* (pp. 21–45). Bern: Peter Lang.

Doughty, C. and Long, M. (2003) *The handbook of second language acquisition.* Oxford: Blackwell.

Douglas, J.Y. (1998) Will the most reflexive relativist please stand up: hypertext, argument and relativism. In I. Snyder (ed), *Page to screen: taking literacy into the electronic era* (pp. 144–62). London: Routledge.

Dudeney, G. and Hockly, N. (2012) ICT in ELT: how did we get here and where are we going? *English Language Teaching Journal*, 66(4): 533–42.

Duranti, A. and Goodwin, C. (eds) (1992) *Rethinking context: language as an interactive phenomenon.* Cambridge: Cambridge University Press.

Ebyary, K. and Windeatt, S. (2010) The impact of computer-based feedback on students' written work. *International Journal of English Studies*, 10(2): 121–42.

Ede, L. and Lunsford, A. (1984) Audience addressed/audience invoked: the role of audience in composition theory and pedagogy. *College Composition and Communication*, 35: 155–71.

Elbow, P. (1994) *Voice and writing.* Davis, CA: Hermagoras Press.

Elbow, P. (1998) *Writing with power: techniques for mastering the writing process.* New York and Oxford: Oxford University Press.

Elbow, P. and Belanoff, P. (1991) SUNY Stony Brook portfolio-based evaluation program. In P. Belanoff and M. Dickson (eds), *Portfolios: process and product* (pp. 3–16). Portsmouth, NH: Boynton/Cook.

Ellis, R. (2006) Current issues in the teaching of grammar: an SLA perspective. *TESOL Quarterly*, 40(1): 83–107.

Ellis, R., Sheen, Y., Murakami, M. and Takashima, H. (2008) The effects of focused and unfocused written corrective feedback in an English as a foreign language context. *System*, 36: 353–71.

Emig, J. (1983) *The web of meaning.* Upper Montclair, NJ: Boynton/Cook.

Evans, S. and Green, C. (2007) Why EAP is necessary: a survey of Hong Kong tertiary students. *Journal of English for Academic Purposes*, 6(1): 3–17.

Faigley, L. (1986) Competing theories of process: a critique and a proposal. *College English*, 48: 527–42.

Faigley, L., Daly, J. and Witte, S. (1981) The role of writing apprehension in writing performance and competence. *Journal of Educational Research*, 75: 16–20.

Fairclough, N. (1992) *Discourse and social change.* Cambridge: Polity Press.

Fairclough, N. (1995) *Critical discourse analysis.* Harlow: Longman.

Fairclough, N. (2003) *Analysing discourse: textual analysis for social research.* London: Routledge.

Fairclough, N. and Wodak, R. (1997) Critical discourse analysis. In T. van Dijk (ed), *Discourse as social interaction* (pp. 258–84). London: Sage Publications.

Fang, Y. (2010) Perceptions of the computer-assisted writing program among EFL college learners. *Educational Technology and Society*, 13(3): 246–56.

Farrell, P. (1990) *Vocabulary in ESP: a lexical analysis of the English of electronics and a study of semi-technical vocabulary.* CLCS Occasional Paper No. 25. Dublin: Trinity College.

Fazio, L. (2001) The effect of corrections and commentaries on the journal writing accuracy of minority- and majority-language students. *Journal of Second Language Writing*, 10(4): 235–49.

Feak, C. and Swales, J.M. (2009) Telling a research story: writing a literature review. Ann Arbor, MI: University of Michigan Press.

Feak, C. and Swales, J.M. (2011) Creating contexts: writing introductions across genres. Ann Arbor, MI: University of Michigan Press.

Feez, S. (1998) *Text-based syllabus design.* Sydney: McQuarie University/AMES.

Feez, S. (2001) Heritage and innovation in second language education. In A.M. Johns (ed), *Genre in the classroom* (pp. 47–68). Mahwah, NJ: Lawrence Erlbaum Associates.

Ferris, D. (1999) The case for grammar correction in L2 writing classes: a response to Truscott (1996). *Journal of Second Language Writing*, 8(1): 1–10.

Ferris, D. (2003) Response to student writing. Mahwah, NJ: Lawrence Erlbaum Associates.

Ferris, D.R. (2004) The "grammar correction" debate in L2 writing: where are we, and where do we go from here? (and what do we do in the meantime . . .?) *Journal of Second Language Writing*, 13: 49–62.

Ferris, D.R. (2006) Does error feedback help student writers? New evidence on the short- and long-term effects of written error correction. In K. Hyland and F. Hyland (eds), *Feedback in second language writing: contexts and issues* (pp. 81–104). Cambridge: Cambridge University Press.

Ferris, D.R. and Roberts, B.J. (2001) Error feedback in L2 writing classes: how explicit does it need to be? *Journal of Second Language Writing*, 10: 161–84.

Ferris, D., Liu, H., Sinha, A. and Senna, M. (2013) Written corrective feedback for individual L2 writers. *Journal of Second Language Writing*, 22: 307–29.

Firbas, J. (1986) On the dynamics of written communication in light of the theory of functional sentence perspective. In C. Cooper and S. Greenbaum (eds), *Studying writing: linguistic approaches* (pp. 40–71). London: Sage Publications.

Flick, U. (2007) *An introduction to qualitative research*, 4th edn. Thousand Oaks, CA: Sage Publications.

Flower, L. (1989) Cognition, context and theory building. *College Composition and Communication*, 40: 282–311.

Flower, L. (2003) Talking across difference: intercultural rhetoric and the search for situated knowledge. *College Composition and Communication*, 55(1): 38–68.

Flower, L. and Hayes, J. (1981) A cognitive process theory of writing. *College Composition and Communication*, 32: 365–87.

Flower, L., Stein, V., Ackerman, J., Kantz, M., McCormick, K. and Peck, W. (1990) *Reading-to-write: exploring a social and cognitive process*. Oxford: Oxford University Press.

Flowerdew, L. (2012) *Corpora and language education*. London: Palgrave.

Freedman, A. (1994) "Do as I say?": the relationship between teaching and learning new genres. In A. Freedman, and P. Medway (eds), *Genre and the new rhetoric* (pp. 191–210). London: Taylor and Francis.

Freedman, A. and Adam, C. (2000) Write where you are: situating learning to write in university and workplace settings. P. Dias, and A. Pare (eds), *Transitions: writing in academic and workplace settings* (pp. 31–60). Creskill, NJ: Hampton Press.

Freedman, A. and Medway, P. (1994) *Genre and the new rhetoric*. London: Taylor & Francis.

Freire, P. (1994) *Pedagogy of hope: reliving the pedagogy of the oppressed*. New York: Continuum.

Freire, P. (2007) *Pedagogy of the oppressed*. New York: Continuum.

Furneaux, C. (1998) Process writing. In K. Johnson and H. Johnson (eds), *Encyclopedic dictionary of applied linguistics* (pp. 257–60). Oxford: Blackwell.

Gardner, D. and Davies, M. (2014) A new academic vocabulary list. *Applied Linguistics*, 35(3): 305–327.

Gass, S. (2015) Experimental research. In B. Paltridge and A. Phakiti (eds), *Research methods in applied linguistics: A practical resource* (pp. 101–18). London: Bloomsbury.

Geertz, C. (1973) Thick description: toward an interpretive theory of culture. In *The interpretation of cultures: selected essays* (pp 3–30). New York: Basic Books.

Gibbons, P. (2009) *English learners, academic literacy and thinking*. Portsmouth, NH: Heinemann.

Gibbons, P. (2002) *Scaffolding language; scaffolding learning*. Portsmouth, NH: Heinemann.

Gilquin, G., Granger, S. and Paquot, M. (2007) Learner corpora: the missing link in EAP pedagogy. *Journal of English for Academic Purposes*, 6: 319–35.

Goldstein, L. (2005) *Teacher written commentary in second language writing classrooms*. Ann Arbor, MI: University of Michigan Press.

Gosden, H. (1996) Verbal reports of Japanese novices' research writing practices in English. *Journal of Second Language Writing*, 5: 109–28.

Government of South Australia (2014) *Genres in primary school facilitator notes*. http://www.decd.sa.gov.au/literacy/pages/esl/genre/?reFlag=1.

Graddol, D. (2006) *English next*. London: The British Council.

Grande, S.M. (2004) *Red pedagogy: Native American social and political thought*. Lanham, MD: Rowman & Littlefield Publishers.

Granger, S. (2003) The international corpus of learner english: a new resource for foreign language learning and teaching and second language acquisition research. *TESOL Quarterly*, 37(3): 538–46.

Granger, S. (2009) The contribution of learner corpora to second language acquisition and foreign language teaching: a critical evaluation. In K. Aijmer (ed), *Corpora and language teaching* (pp 13–32). Amsterdam: John Benjamins.

Grice, H.P. (1975) Logic and conversation. In P. Cole and J. Morgan (eds), *Syntax and semantics, Vol. 3, speech acts* (pp. 41–58). New York: Academic Press.

Ha, Y.-H. (2015) Technical vocabulary in finance: a corpus-based study of annual reports and earnings calls. Unpublished Ph.D. thesis. University of Hong Kong.

Halliday, M.A.K. and Mathieson, C. (2013) *Halliday's introduction to functional grammar*, 4th edn. London: Routledge.

Hamilton, M. (2000) Expanding the new literacy studies: using photographs to explore literacy as social practice. In D. Barton, M. Hamilton and R. Ivanic (eds), *Situated literacies: reading and writing in context* (pp. 16–34). London: Routledge.

Hammond, J. and Macken-Horarik, M. (1999) Critical literacy: challenges and questions for ESL classrooms. *TESOL Quarterly*, 33(3): 528–44.

Hamp-Lyons, L. and Condon, W. (1993) Questioning assumptions about portfolio-based assessment. *College Composition and Communication*, 44(2): 176–90.

Hamp-Lyons, L. and Condon, W. (2000) *Assessing the portfolio: principles for practice, theory and research*. Cresskill, NJ: Hampton Press.

Harklau, L. (2005) Ethnography and ethnographic research on second language teaching and learning. In E. Hinkel (ed), *Handbook of research in second language teaching and learning* (pp. 179–94). Mahwah, NJ: Erlbaum.

Hatch, E. and Lazaraton, A. (1991) *The research manual*. Boston, MA: Heinle & Heinle.

Hattie, J. and Timperley, H. (2007) The power of feedback. *Review of Educational Research*, 77(1): 81–112.

Heath, S. (1983) *Ways with words: language life and work in communities and classrooms*. Cambridge: Cambridge University Press.

Hedge, P. (2005) *Writing*, 2nd edn. Oxford: Oxford University Press.

Helms-Park, R. and Stapleton, P. (2003) Questioning the importance of individualized voice in undergraduate L2 argumentative writing: an empirical study with pedagogical implications. *Journal of Second Language Writing*, 12(3): 245–65.

Hesse-Biber, S. and Leavy, P. (2006) *The practice of qualitative research*. Thousand Oaks: Sage Publications.

Higgins, J.P.T. and Green, S. (eds) (2011) Cochrane handbook for systematic reviews of interventions, version 5.1.0. The Cochrane Collaboration. http://handbook.cochrane.org/

Hinds, J. (1990) Inductive, deductive, quasi-inductive: expository writing in Japanese, Korean, Chinese, and Thai. In U. Connor and A. Johns (eds), *Coherence in writing: research and pedagogical perspectives* (pp. 87–110). Alexandria, VA: TESOL.

Hinkel, E. (1994) Native and nonnative speakers' pragmatic interpretations of English texts. *TESOL Quarterly*, 28(2): 353–76.

Hoey, M. (1983) *On the surface of discourse*. London: Allen & Unwin.

Hoey, M. (2001) *Textual interaction: an introduction to written text analysis*. London: Routledge.

Hopkins, D. (2008) *A teacher's guide to classroom observation*. Maidenhead: McGraw-Hill.

Horrowitz, D. (1986) What professors actually require: academic tasks for the ESL classroom. *TESOL Quarterly*, 20(3): 445–62.

Howard, R.M. (1993) A plagiarism pentimento. *Journal of Teaching Writing*, 11(3): 233–45.

Hunston, S. (2002) *Corpora in applied linguistics*. Cambridge: Cambridge University Press.

Hyland, F. (1998) The impact of teacher written feedback on individual writers. *Journal of Second Language Writing*, 7: 255–86.

Hyland, F. (2003) Focusing on form: student engagement with teacher feedback. *System*, 31: 217–30.

Hyland, F. and Hyland, K. (2001) Sugaring the pill: praise and criticism in written feedback. *Journal of Second Language Writing*, 10: 185–212.

Hyland, K. (2002) Options of identity in academic writing. *ELT Journal*, 56(4): 351–8.

Hyland, K. (2003) *Second language writing*. New York: CUP.

Hyland, K. (2004a) *Disciplinary discourses: social interactions in academic writing*. Ann Arbor, MI: University of Michigan Press.

Hyland, K. (2004b) 'Graduates' gratitude: the generic structure of dissertation acknowledgements. *English for Specific Purposes*, 23(3): 303–24.

Hyland, K. (2004c) *Genre and second language writing*. Ann Arbor, MI: University of Michigan Press.

Hyland, K. (2005) *Metadiscourse*. London: Continuum.

Hyland, K. (2008a) As can be seen: lexical bundles and disciplinary variation. *English for Specific Purposes*, 27(1): 4–21.

Hyland, K. (2008b) Genre and academic writing in the disciplines. *Language Teaching*, 41(4): 543–62.

Hyland, K. (2013a) Student perceptions of hidden messages in teacher written feedback. *Studies in Educational Evaluation*, 39(3): 180–7.

Hyland, K. (2013b) Corpora, innovation and English language education. In K. Hyland and L. Wong (eds), *Innovation and change in English language education* (pp. 218–32). London: Routledge.

Hyland, K. (2013c) Faculty feedback: perceptions and practices in L2 disciplinary writing. *Journal of Second Language Writing*, 22: 240–53.

Hyland, K. (2015a) *Academic publishing: issues and challenges in the construction of knowledge*. Oxford: Oxford University Press.

Hyland, K. (2015b) Corpora and written academic English. In D. Biber and R. Reppen (eds), *The Cambridge handbook of corpus linguistics* (pp. 292–308). Cambridge: CUP.

Hyland, K. and Hyland, F. (1992) Go for gold: integrating process and product in ESP. *English for Specific Purposes*, 11: 225–42.

Hyland, K. and Hyland, F. (2006) Interpersonal aspects of response: constructing and interpreting teacher written feedback. In K. Hyland and F. Hyland (eds), *Feedback in second language writing* (pp. 206–24). Cambridge: Cambridge University Press.

Hyland, K. and Milton, J. (1997) Qualification and certainty in L1 and L2 students' writing. *Journal of Second Language Writing*, 6(2): 183–205.

Hyland, K. and Tse, P. (2005) Hooking the reader: a corpus study of *evaluative that* in abstracts. *English for Specific Purposes*, 24(2): 123–39.

Hyland, K. and Tse, P. (2007) Is there an "academic vocabulary"? *TESOL Quarterly*, 41(2): 235–54.

Hyon, S. (1996) Genre in three traditions: implications for ESL. *TESOL Quarterly*, 30(4): 693–722.

Ivanic, R. (1998) *Writing and identity: the discoursal construction of identity in academic writing*. Amsterdam: John Benjamins.

Ivanic, R. and Weldon, S. (1999) Researching the writer–reader relationship. In C.N. Candlin and K. Hyland (eds), *Writing: texts, processes and practices* (pp. 168–92). Harlow: Longman.

Jarratt, S., Losh, E. and Puente, D. (2006) Transnational identifications: biliterate writers in a first-year humanities course. *Journal of Second Language Writing*, 15(1): 24–48.

Jenkins, S., Jordan, M. and Weiland, P. (1993) *English for Specific Purposes*, 12: 51–67.

JISC (2008) *Effective Practice with e-portfolios: supporting 21st century learning*. Bristol: JISC Innovation Group.

Johns, A.M. (1997) *Text, role and context: developing academic literacies*. Cambridge: Cambridge University Press.

Johns, A.M. (ed) (2002) *Genre in the classroom: multiple perspectives*. Mahwah, NJ: Lawrence Earlbaum Associates.

Johns, A., Bawashi, A., Coe, R., Hyland, K., Paltridge, B., Reiff, M. and Tardy, C. (2006) Crossing the boundaries of genres studies: commentaries by experts. *Journal of Second Language Writing*, 15(3): 234–49.

Johns, T. (1991) Should you be persuaded: two examples of data-driven learning. *English Language Research Journal*, 4: 1–16.

Johnson, R. (2011) *A study of the impact of professional development on teacher attitude toward writing and implementation of writing strategies*. Thesis (Ed.D.), Texas A&M University.

Jones, K. (2000) Becoming just another alphanumeric code: farmers' encounters with the literacy and discourse practices of agricultural bureaucracy at the livestock auction. In D. Barton, M. Hamilton and R. Ivanic (eds), *Situated literacies* (pp. 70–90). London: Routledge.

Jones, R.H., Garralda, A., Li, D.C.S. and Lock, G. (2006) Interactional dynamics in on-line and face-to-face peer-tutoring sessions for second language writers. *Journal of Second Language Writing*, 15: 1–23.

Jordan, S. (2012) Student engagement with assessment and feedback: some lessons from short-answer free-text e-assessment questions. *Computers & Education*, 58(2): 818–34.

Kaufer, D. and Young, R. (1993) Writing in the content areas: some theoretical complexities. In L. Odell (ed), *Theory and practice in the teaching of writing: rethinking the discipline* (pp. 71–104). Carbondale, IL: Southern Illinois University Press.

Kellogg, R.T. (1994) *The psychology of writing.* Oxford: Oxford University Press.

Killingsworth, M.J. and Gilbertson, M.K. (1992) *Signs, genres, and communication in technical communication.* Amityville, NY: Baywood.

Kirszner, L.G. and Mandell, S.R. (2012) *The brief Wadsworth handbook,* 7th edn. Boston, MA: Wadsworth.

Kitzhaber, A.R. (1960) Death—or transfiguration? *College English,* 21: 367–73.

Knapp, P. and Watkins, M. (2005) *Genre, text, grammar.* Sydney: University of NSW Press.

Kostouli, T. (ed) (2005) *Writing in context(s): textual practices and learning processes in sociocultural settings.* New York: Springer.

Kramsch, C. (1997) Rhetorical models of understanding. In T. Miller (ed), *Functional approaches to written text: classroom applications* (pp. 50–63). Washington, DC: USIA.

Kress, G. (2003) *Literacy in the new media age.* London: Routledge.

Kress, G. and van Leeuwen, T. (2006) *Reading images: the grammar of visual design,* 2nd edn. London: Routledge.

Krishnamurthy, R. and Kosem, I. (2007) Issues in creating a corpus for EAP pedagogy and research. *Journal of English for Academic Purposes,* 6(4): 356–73.

Krishnamurthy, S. (2005) A demonstration of the futility of using Microsoft Word's spelling and grammar check. http://faculty.washington.edu/sandeep/check/. Accessed Feb. 12, 2008.

Kubota, R. and Lin, A. (eds) (2009) *Race, culture, and identity in second language education: exploring critically engaged practice.* New York: Routledge.

Kuiken, F. and Vedder, I. (2008) Cognitive task complexity and written output in Italian and French as a foreign language. *Journal of Second Language Writing,* 17(1): 48–60.

Kuteeva, M. and Airey, J. (2013) Disciplinary differences in the use of English in higher education: reflections on recent language policy. *Higher Education.* doi: 10.1007/s10734-013-9660-6

Lantolf, J.P. (1999) Second culture acquisition: cognitive considerations. In E. Hinkel (ed), *Culture in second language teaching and learning* (pp. 28–46). Cambridge: CUP.

Latif, M.M.A. (2009) A state-of-the-art review of the real-time computer-aided study of the writing process. *International Journal of English Studies,* 8(1): 29–50.

Lave, J. and Wenger, E. (1991) *Situated learning: legitimate peripheral participation.* Cambridge: Cambridge University Press.

Lecercle, J.-J. (2000) *Interpretation as pragmatics.* London: Palgrave.

Lee, D. and Swales, J. (2006) A corpus-based EAP Course for NNS doctoral students: moving from available specialized corpora to self-compiled corpora. *English for Specific Purposes,* 25(1): 56–75.

Lee, G. and Schallert, D. (2008) Meeting in the margins: effects of the teacher–student relationship on revision processes of EFL college students taking a composition course. *Journal of Second Language Writing,* 17(3): 165–82.

Lee, I. (2004) Error correction in L2 secondary writing classrooms: the case of Hong Kong. *Journal of Second Language Writing,* 13(4): 285–312.

Leech, G. (1997) Teaching and language corpora: a convergence. In A. Wichmann and S. Fligelstone (eds), *Teaching and language corpora* (pp. 1–24). Harlow: Longman.

Leech, G. (1998) Preface. In S. Granger (ed), *Learner English on computer* (pp. xiv–xx). Harlow: Longman.

Lei, X. (2008) Exploring a sociocultural approach to writing strategy research: mediated actions in writing activities. *Journal of Second Language Writing.* 17(4): 217–36.

Leighton, J. and Gierl, M. (eds) (2007) *Cognitive diagnostic assessment for education: theory and applications.* Cambridge: Cambridge University Press.

Leijten, M. and van Waes, L. (2013) Keystroke logging in writing research using Inputlog to analyze and visualize writing processes. *Written Communication,* 30(3): 358–92.

Leki, I., Cumming, A. and Silva, T. (2008) *A synthesis of research on second language writing in English.* London: Routledge.

Lewis, M. and Wray, D. (1997) *Writing frames.* Reading: NCLL.

Li, J. (2006) The mediation of technology in ESL writing and its implications for writing assessment. *Assessing Writing,* 11(1): 5–21.

Li, J., Link, S. and Hegelheimer, V. (2015) Rethinking the role of automated writing evaluation (AWE) feedback in ESL writing instruction. *Journal of Second Language Writing,* 27: 1–18.

Li, Y.-Y. and Casanave, C. (2012) Two first-year students' strategies for writing from sources: patchwriting or plagiarism? *Journal of Second Language Writing,* 21(2): 165–80.

Li, Y.-Y. and Flowerdew, J. (2009) English or Chinese? The trade-off between local and international publication among Chinese academics in the humanities and social sciences. *Journal of Second Language Writing,* 18(1): 17–29.

Litosseliti, L. (ed) (2010) *Research methods in linguistics.* London: Bloomsbury.

Little, M., Jordens, C. and Sayers, E.-J. (2003) Discourse communities and the discourse of experience. *Health,* 7: 73–86.

Lo, J. and Hyland, F. (2007) Enhancing students' engagement and motivation in writing: the case of primary students in Hong Kong. *Journal of Second language Writing,* 16(4): 219–37.

Lomax, R. and Hahs-Vaughn, D.L. (2012) *An introduction to statistical concepts,* 3rd edn. London: Routledge.

Long, M.H. and Doughty, C. (eds) (2009) *Handbook of language teaching.* Oxford: Blackwell.

Louhiala-Salminen, L. (2002) The fly's perspective: discourse in the daily routine of a business manager. *English for Specific Purposes,* 21(3): 211–31.

Lundstrom, K. and Baker, W. (2009) To give is better than to receive: the benefits of peer review to the reviewer's own writing. *Journal of Second language Writing,* 18: 30–43.

MacCallister, C. (2016). Critical perspectives. In K. Hyland and P. Shaw (eds), *The Routledge handbook of English for academic purposes.* London: Routledge.

Malmkjær, K. (ed) (2009) *Routledge encyclopedia of linguistics,* 3rd edn. London: Routledge.

Malinowski, W. (1949) The problem of meaning in primitive languages. In A. Ogden and C. Richards (eds), *The meaning of meaning: a study of influence of language upon thought and of the science of symbolism* (pp. 296–336). London: Routledge and Kegan Paul.

Manchón, R.M. (ed) (2011) *Learning-to-write and writing-to-learn in an additional language.* Amsterdam: John Benjamins.

Manchon, R.M., Murphy, L. and Roca de Larios, J. (2005) Using concurrent protocols to explore L2 writing processes: methodological issues in the collection and analysis of data. In P.K. Matsuda and T. Silva (eds), *Second language writing research:*

perspectives on the process of knowledge construction (pp. 191–205). Mahwah, NJ: Lawrence Erlbaum Associates.

Maréchal, G. (2010) Autoethnography. In A.J. Mills, G. Durepos and E. Wiebe (eds), *Encyclopedia of case study research*, Vol. 2 (pp. 43–5). Thousand Oaks, CA: Sage Publications.

Marefat, F. (2002) The impact of diary analysis on teaching/learning writing. *RELC Journal*, 33(1): 101–21.

Markoff, J. (2013) Essay-grading software offers professors a break. *New York Times*. http://www.nytimes.com/2013/04/05/science/new-test-for-computers-grading-essays-at-college-level.html?pagewanted=all&_r=3&

Martin, J.R. (1992) *English text: system and structure*. Amsterdam: John Benjamins.

Martin, J.R. (1993) Genre and literacy—modeling context in educational linguistics. In W. Grabe (ed), *Annual review of applied linguistics*, Vol. 13 (pp. 141–72). Cambridge: Cambridge University Press.

Martin, J.R., Christie, F. and Rothery, J. (1987) Social processes in education: a reply to Sawyer and Watson (and others). In I. Reid (ed), *The place of genre in learning: current debates* (pp. 58–82). Deakin, Australia: Deakin University Press.

Martinez, I., Beck, S. and Panza, C. (2009) Academic vocabulary in agriculture research articles. *English for Specific Purposes*, 28: 183–98.

McCarthey, S.J., Guo, Yi-H. and Cummins, S. (2005). Understanding changes in elementary Mandarin students' L1 and L2 writing. *Journal of Second Language Writing*, 14(2): 71–104.

McCarthy, M. and McCarten, J. (2012) Corpora and materials design. In K. Hyland, M-H Chau, and M. Handford. (eds), *Corpus applications in applied linguistics* (pp. 225–41). London: Continuum.

McCarthy, M.J., McCarten, J. and Sandiford, H. (2006) *Touchstone*. Cambridge: Cambridge University Press.

McLeod, S. (1987) Some thoughts about feelings: the affective domain and the writing process. *College Composition and Communication*, 38(4): 426–35.

McKay, S.L. (2002) Reflections on being a gatekeeper. In C. Casanave and S. Vandrick (eds), *Writing for scholarly publication* (pp. 91–102). Mahwah, NJ: Lawrence Earlbaum Associates.

Meneghini, R. and Packer, A.L. (2007) Is there science beyond English? Initiatives to increase the quality and visibility of non-English publications might help to break down language barriers in scientific communication. *EMBO Reports*, 8(2): 112–16.

Miller, L., Hafner, C.A. and Ng Kwai Fun, C. (2012) Project-based learning in a technologically enhanced learning environment for second language learners: students' perceptions. *E-Learning and Digital Media*, 9(2): 183–95.

Milton, J. (2006) Resource-rich web-based feedback: helping learners become independent writers. In K. Hyland and F. Hyland (eds), *Feedback in second language writing* (pp. 123–39). Cambridge: Cambridge University Press.

Milton, J. (2010) *My Words* 1.9.7. Software programme. http://mws.ust.hk/cmw/index.php?

Min, H.-T. (2006) The effects of trained peer review on EFL students' revision types and writing quality. *Journal of Second Language Writing*, 15(2): 118–41.

Mittan, R. (1989) The peer review process: harnessing students' communicative power. In D. Johnson and D. Roen (eds), *Richness in writing: empowering ESL students* (pp. 207–19). New York: Longman.

Moffett, J. (1982) Writing, inner speech and mediation. *College English*, 44: 231–44.

Motteram, G. (ed) (2013) *Innovations in learning technologies for English language teaching.* London: British Council.

Murray, D. (1985) *A writer teaches writing,* 2nd edn. Boston, MA: Houghton Mifflin.

Myers, G. (2010) *The discourse of blogs and wikis.* London: Bloomsbury.

Nagy, W. and Townsend, D. (2012) Words as tools: learning academic vocabulary as language acquisition. *Reading Research Quarterly,* 47: 91–108.

Nation, I.S.P. and Webb, S. (2011) *Researching and analyzing vocabulary.* Boston, MA: Heinle.

Nesi, H. and Gardner, S. (2011) *Genres across the disciplines: student writing in higher education.* Cambridge: Cambridge University Press.

Nesselhauf, N. (2005) *Collocations in a learner corpus.* Amsterdam: John Benjamins.

Noblit, G.W. and Hare, R.D. (1988) *Meta-ethnography: synthesizing qualitative studies.* Newbury Park: Sage Publications.

Norris, J. and Ortega, L. (2006) Effectiveness of L2 instruction: a research synthesis and quantitative meta-analysis. *Language Learning,* 50: 417–528.

North, S. (1987) *The making of knowledge in composition.* London: Heinemann.

Nunan, D. and Bailey, K. (2009) *Exploring second language classroom research.* Boston, MA: Heinle.

Nystrand, M. (1987) The role of context in written communication. In R. Horowitz and S.J. Samuels (eds), *Comprehending oral and written language* (pp. 197–214). San Diego, CA: Academic Press.

Nystrand, M. (1989) A social interactive model of writing. *Written Communication,* 6: 66–85.

Nystrand, M., Doyle, A. and Himley, M. (1986) A critical examination of the doctrine of autonomous texts. In M. Nystrand (ed), *The structure of written communication* (pp. 81–107). Orlando, FL: Academic Press.

Nystrand, M., Greene, S. and Wiemelt, J. (1993) Where did composition studies come from? *Written Communication,* 18(3): 267–333.

Okamura, A. (2006) Two types of strategies used by Japanese scientists when writing research articles in English. *System,* 34(1): 68–79.

O'Keefe, J. (2000) *Invitation to reading and writing.* Upper Saddle River, NJ: Prentice Hall.

O'Regan, D. (2003) *Vocabulary.* http://www.bilkent.edu.tr/%7Eodavid/Vocabulary/vocabularyhome.html

Ortega, L. (2015) Research synthesis. In B. Paltridge and A. Phakiti (eds), *Research methods in applied linguistics: A practical resource* (pp. 225–44). London: Bloomsbury.

Paltridge, B. & Phakiti, A. (eds) (2015) *Research methods in applied linguistics: A practical resource.* London: Bloomsbury.

Paré, A. (2000) Writing as a way into social work: genre sets, genre systems, and distributed cognition. In P. Dias, and A. Paré (eds), *Transitions: writing in academic and workplace settings* (pp. 145–66). Kresskill, NJ: Hampton Press.

Park, D. (1982) The meanings of 'audience'. *College English,* 44(3): 247–57.

Pecorari, D. (2006) Visible and occluded citation features in postgraduate second-language writing. *English for Specific Purposes,* 25: 4–29.

Pecorari, D. (2013) *Teaching to avoid plagiarism: how to promote good source use.* Maidenhead: Open University Press.

Pecorari, D. (2016) Intertextuality and plagiarism in EAP. In K. Hyland and P. Shaw (eds) *Handbook of EAP.* London: Routledge.

Pecorari, D. and Shaw, P. (2012) Types of student intertextuality and faculty attitudes. *Journal of Second Language Writing*, 21(2): 149–64.

Pegrum, M. (2009) *From blogs to bombs*. Crawley: UWA Publishing.

Pegrum, M. (2014) *Mobile learning: languages, literacies and cultures*. London: Palgrave.

Pennycook, A. (1996) Borrowing others' words: texts, ownership, memory, and plagiarism. *TESOL Quarterly*, 30: 201–30.

Pennycook, A. (2010) *Language as local practice*. London: Routledge.

Perelman, L. (2012) Mass-market writing assessments as bullshit. In N. Elliot and L. Perelman (eds), *Writing assessment in the 21st century: essays in honor of Edward M. White* (pp. 425–38). New York: Hampton Press.

Perelman, L. (2013) Critique of Mark D. Shermis & Ben Hamner, "Contrasting state-of-the-art automated scoring of essays: analysis". *The Journal of Writing Assessment*, 6(1). http://www.journalofwritingassessment.org/article.php?article=69

Petticrew, M. and Roberts, H. (2006) *Systematic reviews in the social sciences*. Oxford: Blackwell.

Phillipson, R. (1992) *Linguistic imperialism*. Oxford: Oxford University Press.

Phillipson, R. (2008) Lingua franca or lingua frankensteinia? English in European integration and globalisation. *World Englishes*, 27(2): 250–67.

Pierce, B.N. (1995) Social identity, investment, and language learning. *TESOL Quarterly*, 29(1): 9–31.

Pogner, K.-H. (2003) Writing in the discourse community of engineering. *Journal of Pragmatics*, 35: 855–67.

Pole, C., and Morrison, M. (2003) *Ethnography for education.* Maidenhead: Open University/McGraw Hill.

Polio, C., Fleck, C. and Leder, N. (1998) "If I only had more time": ESL learners' changes in linguistic accuracy on essay revisions. *Journal of Second Language Writing*, 7(1): 43–68.

Polio, C. and Glew, M. (1996) ESL writing assessment prompts: how students choose. *Journal of Second Language Writing*, 5(1): 35–49.

Polio, C. and Shea, M. (2014) An investigation into current measures of linguistic accuracy in second language writing research. *Journal of Second Language Writing*, 26: 10–27.

Porte, G. (2012) *Replication research in applied linguistics*. Cambridge: Cambridge University Press.

Prior, P. (1998) *Writing/disciplinarity: a sociohistoric account of literate activity in the academy*. Hillsdale, NJ: Lawrence Erlbaum Associates.

Purcell, K., Buchanan, J. and Friedrich, L. (2013) The impact of digital tools on student writing and how writing is taught in schools. National Writing Project. http://pewinternet.org/Reports/2013/Teachers-technology-and-writing

Purves, A.C.E., Quattrini, J. and Sullivan, C. (eds) (1995) *Creating the writing portfolio*. Lincolnwood, IL: NTC.

Raimes, A. (1987) Language proficiency, writing ability and composing strategies. *Language Learning*, 37: 439–68.

Ramanathan, V. and Atkinson, D. (1999a) Individualism, academic writing, and ESL writers. *Journal of Second Language Writing*, 8(1): 45–75.

Ramanathan, V. and Atkinson, D. (1999b) Ethnographic approaches and methods in L2 writing research: a critical guide and review. *Applied Linguistics*, 20(1): 44–70.

Richards, J. (2001) *Curriculum development in language teaching*. Cambridge: Cambridge University Press.

Roen, D. and Willey, R. (1988) The effects of audience awareness on drafting and revising. *Research in the Teaching of English*, 22(1): 75–88.

Rohman, D.G. (1965) Pre-writing: the stage of discovery in the writing process. *College Composition and Communication*, 16: 106–12.

Römer, U. (2010) Using general and specialized corpora in English language teaching: past, present and future. In M. Campoy-Cubillo, B. Bellés-Fortuño and M. Gea-Valor (eds), *Corpus-based approaches to English language teaching* (pp. 18–38). London: Continuum.

Rothery, J. (1986) Teaching genre in the primary school: a genre-based approach to the development of writing abilities. In *Writing project-report 1986* (pp. 3–62). Sydney: University of Sydney, Department of Linguistics.

Russell, D.R. (1997) Rethinking genre in school and society: an activity theory analysis. *Written Communication*, 14(4): 504–54.

Rutherford, W. (1987) The meaning of grammatical consciousness-raising. *World Englishes*, 6(3): 209–16.

Sa, J. (2001) Diary writing: a research method of teaching and learning. Education Line. http://www.leeds.ac.uk/educol/documents/00001698.htm. Accessed February 2015.

Sabbaghan, S. (2013) How noticing is affected by replay of writing process during stimulated recall. *Procedia—Social and Behavioral Sciences*, 83: 629–33.

Santos, T. (1992) Ideology in composition: L1 and ESL. *Journal of Second Language Writing*, 1: 1–15.

Scardamalia, M. and Bereiter, C. (1986) Research on written composition. In M. Wittrock (ed), *Handbook of research on teaching* (pp. 778–803). New York: Macmillan.

Schank, R. and Abelson, R. (1977) *Scripts, plans, goals and understanding*. Hillsdale, NJ: Lawrence Erlbaum Associates.

Schmitt, D. and Schmitt, N. (2005) *Focus on vocabulary: mastering the academic word list*. London: Longman.

Schmitt, N. and Schmitt, D. (2014) A reassessment of frequency and vocabulary size in L2 vocabulary teaching. *Language Teaching*, 47(4): 484–503.

Schriver, K. (1992) Teaching writers to anticipate readers' needs. *Written Communication*, 9(2): 179–208.

Scollon, R. and Scollon, S. (1981) *Narrative, literacy and face in interethnic communication*. Norwood, NJ: Ablex.

Scott, M. and Tribble, C. (2006) *Textual patterns: keywords and corpus analysis in language education*. Amsterdam: Benjamins.

Scribner, S. and Cole, M. (1981) *The psychology of literacy*. London: Harvard University Press.

Seidlhofer, B. (2005) English as a lingua franca. *ELF Journal*, 59(4): 339–40.

Selwyn, N. (2008) 'Not necessarily a bad thing . . .': A study of online plagiarism amongst undergraduate students. *Assessment & Evaluation in Higher Education*, 33(5): 465–79.

Shannon, C. and Weaver, W. (1963) *Mathematical theory of communication*. Champaign, IL: University of Illinois Press.

Shaw, P. (1991) Science research students' composing process. *English for Specific Purposes*, 10: 189–206.

Shermis, M.D. and Hammer, B. (2012) *Contrasting state-of-the-art automated scoring of essays: analysis*. Retrieved Dec. 3, 2014, from http://www.scoreright.org/NCME_2012_Paper3_29_12.pdf

Shi, L. (2010) Textual appropriation and citing behaviors of university undergraduates. *Applied Linguistics*, 31(1): 1–24.

Shuman, A. (1993) Collaborative writing: appropriating power or reproducing authority? In B. Street (ed), *Cross-cultural approaches to literacy* (pp. 247–71). Cambridge: Cambridge University Press.

Silva, T. (1993) Toward an understanding of the distinct nature of L2 writing: the ESL research and its implications. *TESOL Quarterly*, 27: 665–77.

Sinclair, J. (1991) *Corpus, concordance, collocation*. Oxford: OUP.

Smagorinsky, P. (ed) (1994) *Speaking about writing: reflections on research methodology*. London: Sage Publications.

Song, M. and Suh, B. (2008) The effects of output task types on noticing and learning of the English past counter factual conditional. *System*, 36: 295–312.

Spelman Miller, K., and Sullivan, K.P.H. (2006) Keystroke logging: an introduction. In K.P.H. Sullivan and E. Lindgren (eds), *Computer key-stroke logging: methods and applications* (pp. 1–9). Oxford: Elsevier.

Spelman Miller, S., Lindgren, E. and Sullivan, K. (2008) The psycholinguistic dimension in second language writing: opportunities for research and pedagogy using computer keystroke logging. *TESOL Quarterly*, 42(3): 433–54.

Sperber, D. and Wilson, D. (1986) *Relevance: communication and cognition*. Oxford: Basil Blackwell.

Stake, R. (1995) *The art of case study research*. Thousand Oaks, CA: Sage Publications.

Stapleton, P. (2003) Assessing the quality and bias of web-based sources: implications for academic writing. *Journal of English for Academic Purposes*, 2(3): 229–45.

Starfield, S. (2004) "Why does this feel empowering?" Thesis writing, concordancing and the corporatizing university. In B. Norton and K. Toohey (eds), *Critical pedagogies and language learning* (pp. 138–57). Cambridge: Cambridge University Press.

Starfield, S. (2015) Ethnographies. In B. Paltridge and A. Phakiti (eds), *Research methods in applied linguistics: A practical resource* (pp. 137–55). London: Bloomsbury.

Starfield, S., Paltridge, B. and Ravelli, L. (2014) Researching academic writing: what textography affords. In J. Huisman and M. Tight (eds), *Theory and method in higher education research II* (pp. 103–20). Oxford: Emerald.

Stern, L. (1883) *The life and opinions of Tristram Shandy, gentleman*. https://archive.org/details/lifeopinionstri01stergoog

Stockwell, G. (2013) Mobile assisted language learning. In M. Thomas, H. Reinders and M. Warschauer (eds), *Contemporary studies in linguistics: contemporary computer-assisted language learning* (pp. 201–16). Continuum: London.

Storch, N. (2005) Collaborative writing: product, process, and students' reflections. *Journal of Second Language Writing*, 14(3): 153–73.

Street, B. (1995) *Social literacies*. Harlow: Longman.

Street, B. and Lefstein, A. (2008) *Literacy: an advanced resource book*. London: Routledge.

Sullivan, K.P.H. and Lindgren, E. (2002) Self-assessment in autonomous computer-aided L2 writing. *ELT Journal*, 56: 258–66.

Sullivan, K. and Lindgren, E. (eds) (2006) *Computer keystroke logging and writing*. London: Elsevier.

Suvorov, R. (2010) Using Moodle in ESOL writing classes. *TESOL-EJ*, 14(2). http://www.tesl-ej.org/wordpress/issues/volume14/ej54/ej54m1/

Swales, J. (1990) *Genre analysis: English in academic and research settings*. Cambridge: Cambridge University Press.

Swales, J. (1998) *Other floors, other voices: a textography of a small university building*. Hillsdale, NJ: Lawrence Erlbaum Associates.

Swales, J. (1999) How to be brave in EAP: teaching writing in today's research world. In D. Novotna (ed), *Proceedings of "LSP Forum 99"* (pp. 61–88). Prague: Charles University Press.

Swales, J.M. and Feak, C. (2009) *Abstracts and the writing of abstracts*. Ann Arbor, MI: University of Michigan Press.

Swales, J.M. and Feak, C. (2011) *Navigating academia: writing supporting genres*. Ann Arbor, MI: University of Michigan Press.

Swales, J. and Feak, C. (2013) *Academic writing for graduate students: essential tasks and skills*, 3rd edn. Ann Arbor, MI: University of Michigan Press.

Tardy, C. (2004) The role of English in scientific communication: lingua franca or tyrannosaurus rex? *Journal of English for Academic Purposes*, 3: 247–69.

Teo, A.K. (2006) Social-interactive writing for English language learners. *The CATESOL Journal*, 18: 160–78.

Teo, P. (2000) Racism in the news: a critical discourse analysis of news reporting in two Australian newspapers. *Discourse and Society*, 11: 7–49.

Thomas, M. (ed) (2009) *Handbook of research on Web 2.0 and second language learning*. Hershey, PA., New York and London: Information Science Reference.

Thomas, M., Reinders, H. and Warschauer, M. (eds) (2013) *Contemporary computer assisted language learning*. London: Bloomsbury.

Tribble, C. (1997) *Writing*. Oxford: OUP.

Tribble, C. and Jones, C. (1990) *Concordances in the classroom*. London: Longman.

Truscott, J. (1996). The case against grammar correction in L2 writing classes. *Language Learning*, 46: 327–69.

Truscott, J. (2007) The effect of error correction on learners' ability to write accurately. *Journal of Second Language Writing*, 16: 255–72.

Truscott, J. and Hsu, A. (2008) Error correction, revision, and learning. *Journal of Second Language Writing*, 17: 292–305.

Turkle, S. (1995) *Life on the screen: identity in the age of the internet*. New York: Simon and Shuster.

Turnitin (2012) *The plagiarism spectrum*. White paper. Oakland, CA. http://turnitin.com/assets/en_us/media/plagiarism_spectrum.php

University College London (2014) Plagiarism. http://www.ucl.ac.uk/current-students/guidelines/plagiarism

University of Oslo (2006) *In the next hundred years: the University of Oslo and language in that age of internationalization*. Recommendation of the Committee on Language Policy at the University of Oslo. http://www.uio.no/om_uio/innstillinger/

Usher, R. and Edwards, R. (1994) *Postmodernism and education*. London: Routledge.

van Beuningen, C., de Jong, N.H. and Kuiken, F. (2012) Evidence on the effectiveness of comprehensive error correction in second language writing. *Language Learning*, 62(1): 1–41.

van Dijk, T.A. (2008) *Discourse and context: a sociocognitive approach*. Cambridge: Cambridge University Press.

van Waes, L., Leijten, M. and van Weijen, D. (2009) Keystroke logging in writing research: observing writing processes with Inputlog. *GFL-German as a Foreign Language*, 2(3): 41–64.

Vygotsky, L. (1962) *Thought and language*. Cambridge, MA: MIT Press.

Vygotsky, L. (1978) Mind in society: the development of higher psychological processes. M. Cole, V. John-Steiner, S. Scribner and E. Souberman (eds). Harvard, MA: Harvard University Press.

Walker, R. (1985) *Doing research.* London: Methuen.

Wallace, D. (2015) *Writ 101: becoming an effective writer.* Wellington: University of Victoria.

Wang, J., Liang, S. and Ge, G. (2008) Establishment of a medical academic word list. *English for Specific Purposes,* 27: 442–58.

Ward, J. (2009) A basic engineering English word list for less proficient foundation engineering undergraduate. *English for Specific Purposes,* 28(3): 170–82.

Wardlaw, J.M. (2010) Advice on how to write a systematic review. http://www.sbirc. ed.ac.uk/documents/advice%20on%20how%20to%20write%20a%20systematic%20 review.pdf

Ware, P. and Kessler, G. (2013) CALL and digital feedback. In M. Thomas, H. Reinders and M. Warschauer (eds), *Contemporary studies in linguistics: contemporary computer-assisted language learning* (pp. 323–39). London: Continuum.

Ware, P. and Warshauer, M. (2006) Electronic feedback. In K. Hyland, and F. Hyland (eds), *Feedback in second language writing* (pp. 105–22). Cambridge: Cambridge University Press.

Warschauer, M. (2000). Online learning in second language classrooms: an ethnographic study. In M. Warschauer and R. Kern (eds), *Network-based language teaching: concepts and practice* (pp. 41–58). New York: Cambridge University Press.

Warschauer, M. (2007) Technology and writing. In C. Davison and J. Cummins (eds), *The international handbook of English language teaching* (pp. 907–12). Norwell, MA: Springer.

Warschauer, M. and Ware, P. (2006) Automated writing evaluation: defining the classroom research agenda. *Language Teaching Research,* 10(2): 1–24.

Warwick, P., Stephenson, P., Webster, J. and Bourne, J. (2003) Developing pupils' written expression of procedural understanding through the use of writing frames in science: findings from a case study approach. *International Journal of Science Education,* 25(2): 173–92.

Watson-Gegeo, K. (1988) Ethnography in ESL: defining the essentials. *TESOL Quarterly,* 22: 575–92.

Webb, P., Williams, Y. and Meiring, L. (2008) Concept cartoons and writing frames: developing argumentation in South African science classrooms? *African Journal of Research in Mathematics, Science and Technology Education,* 12(1): 5–17.

Weigle, S. (1999) Investigating rater/prompt interactions in writing assessment: quantitative and qualitative approaches. *Assessing Writing,* 6(2): 145–78.

Weissberg, R. (2006) *Connecting speaking and writing.* Ann Arbor, MI: University of Michigan Press.

Wertsch, J. (1991) *Voices of the mind.* Cambridge, MA: Harvard University Press.

Whalen, K. and Ménard, N. (1995) L1 and L2 writers' strategic and linguistic knowledge: a model of multiple-level discourse processing. *Language Learning,* 44: 381–418.

Wheeler, G. (2009) Plagiarism in the Japanese universities: truly a cultural matter? *Journal of Second Language Writing,* 18(1): 17–29.

White, A. (2007) A tool for monitoring the development of written English: T-unit analysis using the SAWL. *American Annals of the Deaf,* 152(1): 29–41.

White, R. and Arndt, V. (1991) *Process writing.* Harlow, UK: Longman.

Widdowson, H. (2000) The theory and practice of critical discourse analysis. *Applied Linguistics,* 19: 136–51.

Willey, I. and Tanimoto, K. (2013) "Convenience editors" as legitimate participants in the practice of scientific editing: an interview study. *Journal of English for Academic Purposes,* 12(1): 23–32.

Williams, R. (1962) *Communications*. Harmondsworth: Penguin.

Willis, D. (1990) *The lexical syllabus: a new approach to language teaching*. London: Harper Collins.

Wilson, D. (2002) *The Englishization of academe: a Finnish perspective*. Jyvaskyla, Finland: University of Jyvaskyla Language Centre.

Winter, E.O. (1977) A clause relational approach to English texts: a study of some predictive lexical items in written discourse. *Instructional Science*, 6(1): 1–92.

Wodak, R. (1996) *Disorders of discourse*. Harlow: Longman.

Wodak, R. and Chilton, P. (eds) (2007) *A new agenda in (critical) discourse analysis*, 2nd edn. Amsterdam: John Benjamins.

Wong, A.T.Y. (2005) Writers' mental representations of the intended audience and of the rhetorical purpose for writing and the strategies that they employed when they composed. *System*, 33(1): 29–47.

Wong, L. (2013) Technological innovation and teacher change: IT in teacher professional development. In K. Hyland and L. Wong (eds), *Innovation and change in English language education* (pp. 248–62). London: Routledge.

Wray, D. and Lewis, M. (1997) *Extending literacy: children reading and writing nonfiction*. London: Routledge.

Xue, G. and Nation, I.S.P. (1984) A university word list. *Language Learning and Communication*, 3(2): 215–99.

Yancey, K.B. (1999) Looking back as we look forward: historicizing writing assessment. *College Composition and Communication*, 50(3): 483–503.

Yang, H. (1986) A new technique for identifying scientific/technical terms and describing science texts. *Literacy and Linguistic Computing*, 1: 93–103.

Yang, M.-N. (2015) A nursing academic word list. *English for Specific Purposes*, 37: 27–38.

Yi, Y. (2007) Engaging literacy: a biliterate student's composing practices beyond school. *Journal of Second Language Writing*, 16(1): 23–39.

Yoon, H. (2008) More than a linguistic reference: the influence of corpus technology on L2 academic writing. *Language Learning and Technology*, 12(2): 31–48.

Yoon, H. and Hirvela, A. (2004) ESL student attitudes toward corpus use in L2 writing. *Journal of Second Language Writing*, 13: 257–83.

Young, L. and Harrison, C. (2004) Introduction. In L. Young and C. Harrison (eds), *Systemic functional linguistics and critical discourse analysis* (pp. 1–11). London: Continuum.

Zamel, V. (1983) The composing processes of advanced ESL students: six case-studies. *TESOL Quarterly*, 17: 165–87.

Zamel, V. (1985) Responding to student writing. *TESOL Quarterly*, 19(1): 79–101.

Zhu, W. and Flaitz, J. (2005) Using focus group methodology to understand international students' academic language needs: a comparison of perspectives. *TESOL-EJ*, 8(4): A-3.

Zimmerman, E. (2012) Showcasing your work in an online portfolio. *The New York Times*, June 30, 2012. http://www.nytimes.com/2012/07/01/jobs/an-online-portfolio-can-showcase-your-work-career-couch.html

Index